# NEW PEOPLE IN OLD NEIGHBORHOODS

# NEW PEOPLE
# IN OLD
# NEIGHBORHOODS

The Role of New Immigrants in
Rejuvenating New York's Communities

Louis Winnick

Russell Sage Foundation                    New York

# The Russell Sage Foundation

The Russell Sage Foundation, one of the oldest of America's general purpose foundations, was established in 1907 by Mrs. Margaret Olivia Sage for "the improvement of social and living conditions in the United States." The Foundation seeks to fulfill the mandate by fostering the development and dissemination of knowledge about the political, social, and economic problems of America. It conducts research in the social sciences and public policy and publishes books and pamphlets that derive from the research.

The Board of Trustees is responsible for oversight and the general policies of the Foundation, while administrative direction of the program and staff is vested in the President, assisted by the officers and staff. The President bears final responsibility for the decision to publish a manuscript as a Russell Sage Foundation book. In reaching a judgment on the competence, accuracy, and objectivity of each study, the President is advised by the staff and selected expert readers. The conclusions and interpretations in Russell Sage Foundation publications are those of the authors and not of the Foundation, its Trustees, or its staff. Publication by the Foundation, therefore, does not imply endorsement of the contents of the study.

**Library of Congress Cataloging-in-Publication Data**

Winnick, Louis, 1921–
   New people in old neighborhoods : the role of new immigrants in
rejuvenating New York's communities / Louis Winnick.
       p.      cm.
   Includes bibliographical references and index.
   ISBN 0-87154-952-2
   1. Sunset Park (New York, N.Y.)—Emigration and immigration—
History—20th century.   2. Sunset Park (New York, N.Y.)—Economic
conditions.   3. New York (N.Y.)—Emigration and immigration—
History—20th century.   4. New York (N.Y.)—Economic conditions.
5. Immigrants—New York (N.Y.)—History—20th century.    I. Title.
F128.68.S94W56     1990      90-38765
974.7'1—dc20

*#21676383*

10 9 8 7 6 5 4 3 2 1

*107/55*

# Contents

# List of Tables

# List of Maps

# Prologue and Acknowledgments

It is virtually certain that the immigration reforms of 1965 will enter the national annals bearing this epigraph: A modest enactment that mushroomed, unplanned, into a towering monument to unpremeditated policy. Though no one so intended, the renewed flows of the foreign-born are, and for some years have been, the dominant component of U.S. population growth. The full dimensions of that Congressional stroke were slow to seep into public consciousness. But by now there is keen and cumulating awareness that the 1965 law, together with its legislative progeny, are radically reshaping the social and economic contours of American society. Historians may one day place immigration reform alongside the Great Society's statutory roll-call as among the most transforming bodies of domestic legislation in our time.

Some policy analysts are already prone to do so. By inadvertence and over uncharted pathways, mass immigration has advanced any number of goals congruent with the social agenda of the sixties. Included are urban renewal, richer ethnic and racial diversification of schools and neighborhoods, and a productive labor force better matched, albeit far from perfectly, to the productive capacities of the American economy. Multitudes of new people arrived, all with an indefatigable zeal for work, and very large numbers with eminently marketable skills, advanced education, and unbounded career ambitions. In short, they brought with them the precise qualities that a myriad of Great Society's compensatory and manpower training programs tried to instill—with (to put it gently) indifferent success. Any urban society afflicted with an intractable underclass is entitled to a balancing uplift, even, if in this case, the serendipitous source happens to be external.

In truth, no aspect of American life has been left untouched by the inflow of millions upon millions of mainly hardworking, mainly striving immigrants. The nation's demographics, the size and quality of its labor force, its communities, its public schools and universities, its cultural affinities are not now what they were and, since the inflow continues without abatement, will not be what they are. Soon enough, even the nation's politics and voting patterns will be affected, as they were, with due lag, after the great migrations before the first World War. Hawaii, Florida, and California are tell-tales.

The public is split between a majority who view the changes with apprehension and a substantial minority who are heartened by an America refreshed. The split within the ranks of the social scientists and policy analysts who most closely monitor and measure the New Immigration is more lopsidedly reverse. The overwhelming consensus is that benefits have far outweighed costs.

One of the more beneficial of the New Immigration's social reshapings is the restoration of life to the decaying and depopulating neighborhoods in many of America's ebbing industrial cities. As with the labor supply, demographic renewal achieved much of what the official urban renewal programs tried to do, but so often failed. What inspired this book was an urge to fill in the account of how, in one city and in one community, that reinvigoration has taken place. The 2 million new foreign faces in New York's neighborhoods and the 20,000 new foreign faces in Sunset Park are deposits of the new wave of immigration, ever-widening ripples directly traceable to a legislative deed performed 25 years ago.

The annals of legislation are rife with ironies. When the reforms were enacted Congress had small inkling that it was engaged in anything monumental or that its handiwork would have so many dramatic and lasting consequences. Because the book's introduction is also its prologue, it is fitting to say a few more words about that unwitting Congressional action, which colors everything salient in the eight chapters that follow.

The Hart-Celler Immigration and Nationality Act of 1965 was, first of all, a collective and colossal failure in demographic forecasting, of perhaps unprecedented magnitude. Yet as an exercise in national legislation it was no casual affair. On the contrary. The debates between immigration reformers and immigration standpatters stretched across the regimes of four presidents and eight sessions of the Congress. The committee and floor deliberations immediately preceding the Act's passage were extensive, fiery, and well-attended. So equally determined and mobilized were the embattled sides that the legislation seemed headed for impasse.

In the finale, the reformers prevailed. But it was not by brandishing what nowadays is called the vision thing, some grand mosaic of a demographically recharged and pluralistically enriched America. The pro-immigrationists carried the day by stressing precisely the opposite. The ensuing flow of new immigrants, they assured, would be so incremental and absorbable it would go virtually unnoticed. That avowal would not have sufficed had the reformers not simultaneously appealed to Congress's latent sense of guilt and contrition regarding the racial transgressions of the past, sensitized by the fevers of a convulsive civil rights revolution. Even so, a pro-reform majority might have proved elusive but for Lyndon Johnson's 1964 landslide: it swept a contingent of younger and more racially tolerant members into both Houses.

The decisive votes for the bill were assembled from those in the Congress with a gnawing obligation to redress two flagrant offenses perpetrated during a cramped era of America's past—blatant insults to the principles of a free and compassionate democracy over which, not so long ago, a global war had been waged. One offense was a sequence of statutes promulgated between 1882 and 1924 which brutally slammed the gates on further Asian immigration. Worse, any Asians already admitted were declared by a 1922 Supreme Court decision to be ineligible for citizenship. The second offense was the National Origins Act of 1924, demagogic demography magnified to a high power. It imposed discriminatory quotas upon the peoples of Eastern and Southern Europe and accorded favorable quotas to the peoples of North Europe and the British Isles. As the then-Attorney General Robert Kennedy sermonized the Congress a year before Hart-Celler:

> [The national-origins system] is a standing affront to many Americans and to many countries. It implies what we . . . know from our own experience is false: that regardless of individual qualifications, a man or woman born in Italy, or Greece, or Poland, or Czechoslovakia, or the Ukraine, is not as good as someone born in Ireland, or England, or Germany, or Sweden. Everywhere else in our national life, we have eliminated discrimination based on national origins. Yet, this system is still the foundation of our immigration law.

The 1924 National Origins statute was an unfeigned contrivance to congeal forever in its pre-1890 complexion the predominantly Anglo-

Saxon and Nordic physiognomy of America, which is to say America's ethnographic structure before its cities had been inundated by masses of Slavs and Jews, Italians and Greeks, and other inferiors of their ilk. That inferiority had been affirmed by the then-flourishing science of eugenics and reaffirmed by the newer science of intelligence testing, administered en masse to the hapless Army draftees of World War I; for the Jews, Slavs, and Mediterraneans of recent immigrant origin, the results bordered on the calumnious.

The Hart-Celler Act was less a manifesto than an atonement. It rectified the shamelessly skewed quotas of 1924 by establishing equal national quotas, subject to a global ceiling of 290,000, 170,000 for the Eastern Hemisphere and 120,000 for the Western Hemisphere. Thus Congress rotated the torch on the Statue of Liberty back again to Southern and Eastern Europe and reopened doorways to Asia. The bill was a belated genuflection to domestic ethnic and racial immigrant stocks whose sons had served by the millions in every U.S. combat branch in World War II. It was also an expiation to the even greater millions of Slavic and Asian people who had been America's valiant allies on the Eastern and Pacific fronts.

Thus, the 1965 law was conceived more as a ritual of national purification than as a major redirection of substantive policy. That distinction was made unmistakably clear by President Johnson upon signing the legislation:

> This is not a revolutionary bill. It does not affect the lives of millions. It will not reshape the structure of our daily lives, or add importantly to our wealth and power. Yet, it is still one of the most important acts of this Congress and this Administration. For it repairs a deep and painful flaw in the fabric of American justice. . . . The days of unlimited immigration are past. But those who come will come because of what they are—not because of the land from which they sprung.

The president was wrong. It was in fact a revolutionary bill. And in fact it profoundly affected the lives of millions, and not alone the 12 million who have entered the U.S. since Hart-Celler or the millions more waiting patiently on line poised to follow or the impatient millions who risked a jump from that line. Hart-Celler and a tag-on series of refugee laws have likewise affected the lives of the immigrants' host nation and especially the hundreds of millions who share the regions of concentrated immigrant settlement, a gigantic arc that envelops the eastern and western seaboards and a broad swath of the southern perimeter between Florida and California.

Johnson's misreading of Hart-Celler's import was exceeded only by the miscalculations of Congress and its advisers. A legion of professionals had confidentially projected an incremental flow no more than a few ten thousands above the pre-1965 levels, previously raised to admit refugees, displaced people, and war brides. None, in their candid moments, actually expected the 290,000 bi-hemispheric total to be reached.

As Congress only too quickly discovered, the numerical forecasts went startlingly awry. Expanded by the special provisions for refugees, the level of legal immigrants mounted steadily. By 1974 the number crossed the 400,000 mark, and by the early eighties approached 600,000. In 1988 the volume of legal admissions surpassed 640,000 and is currently within the 650,000–680,000 range. Add in an average of perhaps 300,000 illegal entries and the total exceeds four times the Congressional working assumption of 20 years earlier. The total is also not very far from the peak tides of the years before the first world war.

Congress's second miscalculation was more breathtaking. It placed the world's sending countries on equal footing in full belief that the great preponderance of new people would come from Europe rather than Asia or Latin America. There was good reason for that belief. That had been preeminently the experience during the long era of free immigration since Colonial times. And that had been the case after World War II, when the immigration barriers were lowered a crack to admit small numbers of the displaced and the political asylees. To convert its presumption into a self-fulfilling prophecy, Congress built a family-reunification structure into the legislation. Within the liberalized national quotas, four of the six preferences were assigned to "the family circle," the relatives of U.S. citizens or permanent residents. Moreover, petitions for the nuclear family—spouses, parents, children—were exempted from the various categorical ceilings. Since the overwhelming majority of Americans were of European ancestry, the bulk of the requests for admission, it was safely assumed, would also be European. Q.E.D.

In the event, the great mass of new people—varying between 80 and 85 percent—streamed not from Europe but from the Third World, a mirror-like reversal of American immigrant experience. The Law of Unintended Consequences had once again triumphed, this time in favor of the public weal, as testified to by a preponderance of the immigration research community. The post-1965 inflow of some 12 million people has palpably enlarged our economic, intellectual, and cultural capital. And, in benefiting ourselves, we have simultaneously benefited the poorer places of the world, possibly in a measure that rivals foreign aid.

If my book reads like a paean to immigration, it is because there is so much to celebrate. But celebrations tend also to be shadowed by unwelcome guests, not all of them invited. Immigration policies, like all public policies, must be weighed by double-entry bookkeeping; the debit accounts on the social ledger are by no means minuscule. No one can ignore the immense coping problems of the unassimilated, many, no doubt, unassimilatable. Nor should one peremptorily resist the oft-times justifiable resentments and tensions of heavily impacted areas, the threatened job markets, the specter of cultural inundation and adulterated language. There are severe remedial burdens on the schools and mounting welfare burdens on public agencies. Immigration has also a dark underside, plainly observable in the drug-trafficking haunts of the gateway cities and in the multihued, polyglot felons who crush the criminal justice system. Yet when the full accounts are cast up, the credits demonstrably exceed the debits, yielding an impressive return. There are some who are impervious to accounting metaphors, noting rightly that data of less than dead-eye accuracy are weighed on scales of uncertain calibration. To these skeptics one may offer an alternative calculus—the political litmus test. Our national electoral system is so exquisitely attuned to the mainstream's will that it is rare for a popular groundswell to go unattended in the Congress; the abrupt repeal of the Catastrophic Healthcare Act is a recent case in point. Were it true that the New Immigration was inflicting insupportable pain upon the majority, evidenced not merely in attitudinal polls but by voter retribution, lawmakers, whose dominating political ethos is pain aversion, would soon close or narrow the immigrant gateways. One sees the contrary. Despite murmurings in the Congress, more resonant in the Senate than in the House, current legislative initiatives are more likely to expand rather than to contract admissions.

My book adumbrates in narrative and statistics the processes by which the New Immigration has revitalized America's leading gateway city—New York—viewing those processes through the lens of one of its typical neighborhoods—Sunset Park. Without its new foreigners New York would be an emptied-out city of no more than six million, a doleful fate toward which the demographic trends of the last generation were inexorably dragging it. And Sunset Park's bustling Eighth Avenue, without its burgeoning new Chinatown (New York's third), would have remained the deserted corridor of bricked-over stores it had fallen to by 1970.

It has been personally rewarding to an unapologetic pro-immigrationist to study and to record the New Immigration's rescue of a neighborhood that had been built by the old immigrations. It has also been a demanding labor of research, impossible to start or to finish without the cooperation and kindnesses of many helping hands. The individuals and organizations who furnished me with base data, their reflections and their experiences, are listed at the end of the book in Appendix D. Here I wish to pay thanks to a complement of professional colleagues who assisted in other ways.

Heading that list is Mitchell Sviridoff—urbanologist supreme and research broker extraordinaire—who arranged the players and pieces that brought me to the New School for Social Research as a Senior Fellow, swaddled in a generous grant from the Ford Foundation for a 15-month project that inevitably stretched to two years. Mike was much more than an expediter. He was and is a good friend and an astute advisor, possessed of that quality which beguiles a beleaguered author into believing that his product will be a boon to the ages. And the Ford Foundation was more than a financier. A large measure of thanks belongs both to Susan Berresford, vice-president and overseer of urban issues plus an ensemble of other themes and to Barry Gaberman, her deputy, who was the program officer for the grant. They offered not just liberal access to Ford's fine library, office facilities, and secretarial staff—comforts not in abundant supply at a crowded university—but kindness and encouragement as well. Nor can I end these tributes to the Ford Foundation without expressing my obligations to Frank Thomas, its president. My gratitude for the many intellectual spaces he allowed me freely to occupy has been acknowledged on prior occasions and I hope again to do so. Here I register a debt he probably does not know I owe him. It was by plunging at his behest into a brief assignment involving New York's new immigrants that my curiosities about that subject were first aroused, curiosities which have since become an abiding attachment.

The New School, unable to provide much of a physical habitat, substituted a stimulating intellectual climate, a fair-enough tradeoff. Professor Avis Vidal, Director of the Community Development Research Center to which I was attached, combed my early drafts with a sharp eye for the distinction between mere reportorial exposition and the analytic rigor expected of university-sponsored research, a distinction, I fear, I have never successfully mastered, neither here nor in other of my confections. President Jonathan Fanton, too, was a loyal ally. He evinced an early and continuing appreciation for the principal thesis of the book. It was at a dinner meeting of the School's Trustees in his home that I delivered the study's first results and gained much from the lively discussion that ensued. Later, he became an energetic distributor of its prepublication draft copies. Former Dean Robert Curvin and his successor, Richard Schaffer, were likewise and supportive readers and cheerleaders.

The most practical gift the New School conferred upon me was a quartet of graduate students as research assistants. Fittingly enough for a study of the flow of new immigrants into New York to which Asia contributes a steadily increasing stream, all four were recent arrivals from that continent. Yuan-Ho Hsu, Sanjeetha Purushothomam, Xu Xiao, and Sunil Verma did most of the heavy lifting involved in data assembly, classification, and computation. They carried out what were always burdensome and oft-times tedious tasks with enthusiasm and ingenuity; they retired from the project as perhaps Asia's foremost experts on the socioeconomic characteristics of Sunset Park, an accomplishment, I suspect, that will have only peripheral value for their subsequent professional careers.

I drew upon, also to my profit, two academic stalwarts at City University's Graduate Center, Professors John Mollenkopf and William Kornblum. Mollenkopf allowed our little band to tap into CUNY's mainframe database to retrieve historical census tabulations. Kornblum, a leading authority on New York's changing social structure, gave me the notes and comments of an attentive reading of the near-finished draft, which warded off a number of errors and pointed me toward pertinent overlooked sources.

Dan McCarthy, a watchful monitor of Brooklyn's housing, people, and employment, was a consultant to the project, a dependable guide to the community leaders of Sunset Park and to the administrative gatekeepers of the base data. Of the many residents who shared with me their observations and memories of Sunset Park, and so acknowledged in Appendix D, I must single out Kathy Wylde and Alice and Robert Walsh. Kathy, once the factotum of Sunset Park's community development programs and a character in the book's dramatis personae, scrutinized the entire manuscript. She corrected the fallibilities of dates, names, and circumstances that only an insider can detect and inserted important pieces of information not available in documentary files. Alice Walsh is a former head of the Sunset Park Restoration Committee, and Bob handles community relations for the Lutheran Medical Center, an institution that figures prominently throughout the book. It was this couple, longtime residents and boosters of Sunset Park, who graciously permitted me to publish a precious trove of old photographs of Sunset Park's past. Other photographs in that historical display were furnished by Elizabeth White, the Brooklyn Public Library's archivist, who makes no secret of her love for all things Brooklyn and who took extra steps to retrieve, from a scatter of files, glimpses of Sunset Park's waterfront during its prime. The photographs of contemporary Sunset Park, only a small fraction of which, for limitations of space, are shown here, are entirely the handiwork of Laslo Szekely, a graphic artist employed by my publisher, the Russell Sage Foundation. Laslo's pictorial prowess extends beyond the camera; he is also largely responsible for the many meticuously constructed charts and maps contained in the volume. Supervising and contributing to the graphics was John Johnston, Russell Sage's layout wizard. It was fun to watch a master craftsman at work. I cannot exit the precincts of Russell Sage without wafting a huge dollop of appreciation to Priscilla Lewis, the head of its book department who has since left to write a new career chapter elsewhere. Every author should be blessed with a Priscilla Lewis. With a Charlotte Shelby, my book editor, too. Charlotte's marginal inscriptions seemed seldom more than hesitant suggestions. Yet so perspicacious were they that only a fool could read them as anything save a rescue from folly.

Marian Sameth, that indispensable mainstay of the Citizens Housing and Planning Council, gave me free rein to her organization's splendid library, a priceless repository of those fugitive unpublished plans and reports that tend to be lodged in wayward corners of institutional libraries or else escape them altogether.

I've saved repayment to my most prodigal creditor for last. If there is one person who more than any other deserves the status of coauthor, it is my secretary, Mona C. Clark. Over the full two years, and through uncounted drafts, Mona collaborated with me line by line, page by page, table by table. Along the way, she too was seized by the immigrant saga still unfolding before our eyes. On a typical morning Mona would lay upon my desk not just yesterday's manuscript, but also a newspaper clipping or two relating some Dominican or Chinese or Russian immigrant episode or, more likely, some vignette about her neighborhood, Jackson Heights, which is, arguably, the most polyglot immigrant enclave on the continent. Without her nimble mind and fingers, her cool demeanor during the inevitable periods of vexation and stress, it is improbable that the work would have come to fruition.

# CHAPTER 1
## Introduction

This study focuses upon a modest neighborhood in Brooklyn that became a time capsule of America's immigrant experience. It was born out of the massive tides of migration from European lands in the second half of the nineteenth century and nurtured by those that followed in the first decades of the twentieth. In more recent decades, it has been transformed by migrations from a far broader cross section of the globe, conspicuously from the Caribbean Basin and Asia. That transformation is still going on. The latest wave of immigration has no determinate end nor are its consequences wholly foreseeable. What is already seen is that the new immigrants, like the old, have strengthened the neighborhood where they live, the city where they work, and the nation that welcomed them.

The earlier European immigrants went to work in the burgeoning waterfront industries, the shipyards, piers, and factories sprawled along Brooklyn's western littoral, an outpost of the maritime economy that girdled the nation's premier seaport. The newcomers and their offspring created a community on the slopes ascending from that waterfront. They subdivided farms and pastures into homesteads, cut and paved streets, dug canals and deepened channels, laid down trolley and rail lines, built wharves and warehouses, houses and churches. It was a lunch-bucket community, sustained by men who worked with their hands and who were paid by the day, and by women who worked longer hours with no pay at all. It was known by various names or none at all, sometimes merely as "the place next to" (e.g., Bush Terminal). Much later, it called itself Sunset Park, an appellation now official.

By 1930, Sunset Park had attained full maturity, its economic growth stimulated by World War I and postwar prosperity, its population growth by new public transit. Most of the housing and shops that now line its streets and avenues, its schools and subway lines were by then in place, and virtually all its vacant land was gone. Though not then—or ever—an affluent neighborhood, substantial numbers of its first settlers, Irish and Scandinavian, rose to comfortable working-class, even middle-class, status, and later-arriving Italians, Poles, and Greeks were not far behind. It was for them that the area's extensive stock of small homes was built, typically with two apartments, one for the owner's family, another for the renter who helped pay the costs.

The Great Depression of the thirties visited upon Sunset Park the tribulations that the Depression brought everywhere. In 1939, however, the dormant waterfront was awakened by the distant thunder of World War II. Factories and shipyards hung out hiring signs and soon went on second and third shifts. The dockside heaved, convulsed by the comings and goings of endless convoys laden with armies of men and masses of matériel to liberate the continent from which the shipyard and dockside workers had sprung. Not all of Sunset Park's labor force was on the shore; on the outgoing troopships were thousands of the immigrants' sons and grandsons.

After the war, things went badly for Sunset Park. In the fifties, it entered a long twilight that edged toward darkness. It was sundered by a cruel highway that cut across its heart, built without its consent and to none of its benefit. Its waterfront and industry atrophied and their workers went elsewhere. By the tens of thousands, the descendants of the first immigrants left for leafier abodes in the suburbs.

The dwellings of the departed were reoccupied by yet another wave of settlers, this time from Puerto Rico. The arriving Hispanics brought an unfamiliar life-style into a community that, over the century between its Genesis and Exodus, had evolved a culture unrelievedly Euro-American. For many of the remaining residents of Sunset Park, that life-style was not merely unfamiliar but jarring. Those in the community who proffered welcoming hands were matched by others who vented resentments, even raw hostility. The latter summoned airbrushed memories of a Camelot in overalls, of a proud legacy now brought to ruin by a mass of uncaring, some of them predacious, intruders.

The Puerto Rican entrants demonstrated, neither for the first time in the annals of human migrations nor surely for the last, that not all settlers are alike in their readiness to climb the immigrant's ladder, and that not all economic eras are alike in providing the requisite opportunities. The era of arrival was unpropitious with respect to the last. By then the structure of New York's economy had been profoundly recast; manual and factory jobs—historically the urban immigrants' starting rung—had drastically receded in favor of occupations inaccessible to those without education and English proficiency. And, unlike most of the older European migrants who, after a long sea voyage, came as permanent settlers bent on rapid Americanization, the Puerto Ricans, a short plane ride away from native culture and village, were ambivalent over the choice of sojourner or settler. That ambivalence turned many into circular migrants, a condition, ethnic scholars say, that retards the acquisition of language and job skills and, more generally, the processes of rooting and assimilating.

The time of arrival was unpropitious in another respect: By the sixties, not only had the economic order changed but the social order as well. A deep urban rot had set in. Traditional social mores, a decent respect for authority and for the discipline of communal sanctions, had withered. So, too, even among the middle class, had the lifetime marriage, two-parent homes, and stay-at-home mothers.

For Puerto Ricans the social erosion was as costly as the job erosion. Crime, drugs, and teenage pregnancy became rampant. Succor for the distressed, in earlier migrations provided principally by relatives, friends, and church, was now the province of an elephantine welfare system, a necessary but grievously flawed substitute. For many it would turn into a trap. Large numbers of Puerto Ricans were fated to remain indefinitely on the bottom rungs of the immigrant ladder, a status too often transmitted to a second generation and sometimes a third. For all these reasons and others, the initial impact of the Puerto Rican migration on Sunset Park was to aggravate its decline. Not all the ripples of that impact have subsided. Though large numbers of the Hispanic community have progressed from their bleakest years and many are manifestly middle-class, to this day Sunset Park has more than a due share of poverty and dependency.

The neighborhood has now turned another cycle. It is in the midst of an unmistakable comeback. The revival has multiple causes. Among them is the powerful resurgence of New York's economy that generated jobs by the hundreds of thousands and purchasing power by the scores of billions. Another decisive factor was a chronic housing shortage that elevated older housing and, by extension, older neighborhoods to higher standing in a desperate consumer's favor. Bolstering the competitive attraction of old housing and neighborhoods were public policies and subsidies tilted heavily in their favor. The market for such neighborhoods was further strengthened by community organizations that pressed tenaciously to enact those policies and subsidies, toiling unstintingly to improve the quality of their habitats.

Transcending all these factors were pivotal shifts in the City's demography. Population exodus began to abate, followed by a repopulation of older neighborhoods, albeit in modest numbers and with uneven impact. Sunset Park has been among the gainers, revivified by the entry of thousands of new people. Many of the new arrivals are young professionals, giving some basis to the perception of Sunset Park as an emergent yuppieville. But much the larger number are New Immigrants. In recent years there have poured into Sunset Park from everywhere more than 20,000 foreigners, counting aliens whose whereabouts are known to the Immigration and Naturalization Service and allowing for others who are not. The New Immigrants constitute one-fifth, possibly more, of Sunset Park's present population. They come from 60 different countries and have created in Sunset Park an ethnic diversity immeasurably richer than anything in its immigrant past. The new people have rescued a fallen housing market and have uplifted a once-sagging retail sector. They heighten the prospects for Sunset Park's long-term future.

Sunset Park is thus replaying its historic role as a catchment area for intercontinental flows of human beings. The community is indeed a three-dimensional exhibit of those migrations. It displays their accretions of more than a century, layer by layer like the strata in an archaeologist's dig. Every wave of newcomers left distinctive imprints, and the latest wave is leaving its own. The marks of immigrant yesteryears have, however, grown faint. The fading sign that proclaims "Scandinaviske Varer" is affixed to a superette once owned by a Scandinavian and now by an Italian immigrant. There is still Halvorsen's funeral home and Scandinavian bread at Olsen's bakery. And a Finnish newspaper is still locally published, though not as frequently and not in its pristine format. There are also periodic ceremonial ingatherings of progeny to keep memory alive. But, by and large, the chapters written by past migrants are imperfectly recoverable, primarily from a scatter of local histories and public records and the reminiscences of its oldest residents. The local schools and churches are filled by the people who have come in later times and from very different places, not by the descendants of those who built them.

The marks of the latest migrations are, by contrast, fresh, strikingly observable in the Hispanicization of Sunset Park's schools, churches, retail stores, and street life. They are likewise observable in the rapid (and unexpected) settlement of Chinese in a community in which their prior representation was a handful of laundrymen. The New Immigration is also evidenced by the (inevitable) Korean greengroceries, the Moslem mosque, the Indian spice shop, a new Polish restaurant, and the polyethnic, polyglot staff of Lutheran Medical Center. The foreigners' names are on the doorbells, in the latest telephone books and deed recordings. Who and what they are may be ascertained in part from current statistical and administrative records of a dozen public agencies. They constitute history in the present tense. They also constitute the major theme of this study, as is enlarged upon in the next chapter.

# CHAPTER 2
# The Study's Perspective

Although the book's emphasis is on the shifting fortunes of one neighborhood in one city, it derives from two ideas of broader moment. The first is the proposition that the demographic renewal of an urban area is a more dependable guarantor of its viability than is almost any amount of physical renewal. Some will see this proposition as a mere rephrase of the maxim that prevailed in the federal urban-redevelopment era, namely, "people programs" are more important than "bricks and mortar programs." A rephrase it is, but also more than that. The term demographic renewal herein denotes beneficial changes in the mix of a community's population and not just the betterment of people already there.

The second proposition is that concurrent research is superior to retrospective research. The impact of the New Immigrants on urban life can be more efficaciously (and accurately) grasped by continuous monitoring of events as they unfold rather than by retrievals from the past. In other words, watch things as they happen, arrange to watch a fixed set of observation points, and keep watching that set in the years ahead. That proposition, too, may seem a truism. Yet it is remarkable how infrequent in social science are the uses of what is a routine mode in medical or biological research, where organic development or the course of a drug or treatment is tracked forward for decades. In social research, among the best known examples are the University of Michigan's Panel Study of Income Dynamics, a continual resurvey of the changing status of low-income families, and the National Longitudinal Study of Youth that focuses on the passage of young people from school into the labor market. Such watch-as-it-happens surveys are as important as they are rare. They produce indispensable and unduplicated findings on crucial aspects of public policy and serve as correctives to incomplete or faulty notions based on historical, cross-sectional, or short-term data. They nourish the intellectual roots of social science and enlighten the makers of social policy.

## THE STRUCTURE OF COMMUNITY VALUES

To return to the first proposition, a cumulation of evidence indicates that the character of an urban area is largely the product of the character and behavioral propensities of the people who live there. The degree of a community's organization or disorganization is determined primarily by individual values and collective systems of belief. Their nature needs no extended elaboration. Among them are commitment to family and education, willingness to defer present gratifications, regard for authority and for the good opinion of neighbors. This code cuts across race and income. It is possessed by minorities as well as by the mainstream and need not be undermined by deprivation. Urban poverty in the thirties was inordinately worse than in the seventies. But it was not accompanied by the sequelae of neighborhood disorganization so prevalent in our morally disheveled era of violent street crime, drug trafficking, padlocked doors, and steel-shuttered shops. That was as true of black Harlem as of white Sunset Park. Jobs and income shriveled but the social order held.

Many of the urban dilemmas of our time stem from the fact that an insufficiency of income has ceased to be the sole definer of poverty; deficits in income may or may not be accompanied by other kinds of deficits. It has become necessary to distinguish money poverty from behavioral poverty. Indeed, the very idea of poverty has become disfigured. The youth who earns $500 a day by dealing drugs will spend most or all of it on his own merchandise and wake up each morning penniless. By the official census definition of poverty he would, if the income were reported, be counted as exceptionally affluent. By community standards he is among the most abject of the poor.

The distinction between economic and behavioral poverty is fundamental. In its most distilled form, that distinction is manifested by the widening incidence of failure in public housing, once a laudable social innovation and, during its first two or three decades, a superior habitat for millions of the working poor. Now, in city after city, thousands of public housing units have been, or soon will be, reduced to rubble. Pruitt-Igoe, the St. Louis project leveled by dynamite, was the precursor of a tragic trend. At a time of a severe shortage of low-income housing, it is bewildering to behold more public housing being demolished than is being built. Bewildering or not, such demolition is not irrational: The structures had deteriorated beyond the hope of effective salvage. There are all kinds of explanations for that wrenching turn of events, but the critical one involves the behavioral deficits of successive groups of occupants.

The two faces of poverty—one defined by income, the other by behavior—have generated a large literature concerning the emergence of an urban underclass. It has been accompanied by fiery controversies about causes and cures and, not least, about the concept's validity. In a recent book, W. Julius Wilson admirably summarizes that literature. After weighing conflicting evidence and arguments, he has this to say:

> By 1980, . . . the problems of inner-city social dislocations had reached such catastrophic proportions that liberals were forced to readdress the question of the ghetto underclass, but this time their reactions were confused and defensive. The extraordinary rise in inner-city social dislocations following the passage of the most sweeping antidiscrimination and antipoverty legislation in the nation's history could not be explained by the 1960 explanations of ghetto-specific behavior. Moreover, because liberals had ignored these problems throughout most of the 1970s, they had no alternative explanations to advance and were therefore ill prepared to confront a new and forceful challenge from conservative thinkers.[1]

Professor Wilson goes on:

> . . . Liberals will have to change the way they have tended to approach this subject in recent years. They can no longer afford to be timid in addressing these problems, to debate whether or not concepts such as the *underclass* should even be used, to look for data to deny the very

---

1. W. Julius Wilson, *The Truly Disadvantaged: The Inner City, the Underclass, and Public Policy* (Chicago: The University of Chicago Press, 1987), p. 15.

existence of an underclass, or, finally, to rely heavily on the easy explanation of racism.[2]

A corollary of our first proposition—the saliency of communal value codes—is that any policy adversely affecting a neighborhood's social structure will adversely affect its destiny, whether or not it was so intended. It is by now a commonplace that the interstate highway system and the federal mortgage programs of the post–World War II era served to empty America's large cities of millions of people who adhered to generally approved values. It is likewise a commonplace that this exodus yielded decent housing opportunities for poorer people, thus draining inner-city neighborhoods of their striving families and reducing much of what was left to urban sinkholes.

What is not a commonplace—at least, not yet—is that the radically reformulated immigration law of 1965 is slowly and steadily replenishing deficits in the value structure of urban areas. It has led to the refilling of urban communities by masses of new people of every color and ethnicity, most of them ambitious, and many exhibiting an ethic of work and family that shrinks the hallowed Protestant ethic to apathy.

## THE NEW IMMIGRATION

Conjectural history, the might-have-beens of an immutable past, is rightly scorned as an idle indulgence. Still, those might-have-beens have a lingering fascination. Consider this one: How different might have been the predicament of American cities during the bleak decades that began in the fifties had we not reversed in the twenties a centuries-old policy of relatively free immigration? An answer to this query of make-believe history is the restored vitality of neighborhoods like Brighton Beach and Flushing and Sunset Park, not so long ago poised for a perhaps irreversible slide. What one sees now in so many neighborhoods in New York can also be seen in scores of other cities. Transposed in time, would not what is happening now have happened earlier?

In the array of causes of urban decline after World War II, little, if indeed any, weight is assigned to the consequences of those xenophobic walls raised against the foreigner after World War I. Congress did not foresee when it then lowered the gates on Europe, as it had

---

2. *Ibid.*, p. 19.

slammed them earlier on Asia, that, by creating a demographic hollow, it was imposing a penalty on the future of America's older cities. Inadvertently, it abruptly excluded a flow of community builders who for successive generations had nourished the growth and strengthened the quality of urban areas. As so frequently and dismayingly happens, a major public policy fell victim to the Law of Unintended Consequences.

It is a reasonable supposition that the course of urban events during the fifties and sixties would have been much less troubled had that demographic discontinuity not occurred, had our doors remained opened throughout the preceding years to the hapless millions sacrificed to Nazi death camps, and to the additional millions of uprooted in occupied Europe and Asia. Had there been sustained entry of the world's people in the decades preceding 1965, equal to the flow of the post-1965 decades, people acknowledged to be among humankind's more productive, might it not have balanced the population drains and filled the economic voids that in later years desolated American cities? Demographic renewal could have achieved much of what urban renewal programs tried and so often failed to do.

By the same token, Congress did not foresee when it lifted America's immigration gates in 1965 that it was legislating, de facto, a far-reaching urban program. The 1965 action, reinforced by subsequent immigrant and refugee legislation, is proving to be as determinative of the progress of catchment areas like Los Angeles, Miami, Seattle, Washington, D.C., and New York as was the cascade of consciously enacted urban grants-in-aid. On occasion, the Law of Unintended Consequences shows its benign side.

It would be folly to assert that the consequences of immigration are invariably positive. America's immigrant experience is too venerated a sacrament to be thus profaned or trivialized. Each group of newcomers brings with it distinguishable abilities and values, and each undergoes distinguishable processes of adjustment and acculturation. And all, without distinction, are prey to the blind fortune of time, place, and circumstance. The history of American migration is strewn with the sequelae of failed migrants who cursed their luck and died as unfulfilled as when they came, who added to the travails of the host society. Many declared defeat and returned to their origins. Notwithstanding the multitudes for whom the Golden Door proved dross and whose presence was a burden, America's experience with centuries of foreign migration has proved, by every significant measure, to have been of surpassing benefit to host and settler and to settler-turned-host.

Most of today's new immigrants are strivers with a higher partici-pation rate in the labor force than native-born Americans. Others, like their predecessors, climb a crooked ladder to achievement—the Chi-nese teenage extortion gangs, the Colombian hidalgos of cocaine, and, yes, the Odessa mafia of Brighton Beach. Many burden the schools with formidable teaching problems while others carry away, with astronomic regularity, all the glittering scholastic prizes.

The latest wave likewise promises to yield a wide margin of pluses over minuses. The post-1965 settlers are writing a chapter that might have been written by their excluded progenitors for whom only blank pages exist in the chronicles of America's immigrant experience. It is a chapter whose plot has different strands and will have different end-ings, neither simple nor wholly predictable. But this much is sure: How that chapter writes itself will have profound consequences for the future economic performance of the nation and for the quality of its life. It will probably make a good story, though not in every part. But it is a chapter best scrutinized while its pages are being inscribed.

## RESEARCH: CONCURRENT AND LONGITUDINAL

Which brings us to our second proposition: the urgency of "real time" research. The New Immigration cries out for synchronous and lon-gitudinal studies. The immigrant experience—settlement, accultur-ation, the reciprocal effects on newcomers and hosts—should be seized in every possible way as it is occurring. Contemporary immi-grant scholarship need not be condemned to its reconstructive skills. It may pluck the immigrant experience from living events and not solely from the graveyard of an interred past. Unlike earlier eras of immigration, modern social science has both the opportunity and capacity to catch the current immigrant wave in the course of its roll, to observe in all its immediacy the effort of millions—those here and those yet to come—to reorder their existence, to ascend to a better life, and to prepare a foundation from which their children might rise still higher.

A "New Immigration" research community has come into being. It is studying selected groups, in selected places, of those who came into the country during the past two decades. That research commu-nity grows larger each year and its agenda broader. It is compiling an illuminating literature on various aspects of the new people. A major challenge will be to shape self-initiated research into additive endeavors so that the results are more than an ensemble of disparate findings.

A good way of doing that is to evolve a paradigm of longitudinal research. One might call it Pilgrims' Progress—the continuous monitoring of fixed and representative sets of immigrants. Any number of research curiosities and public interests can be satisfied by the planned tracking of immigrants as they are now and, over the years, into what they are becoming or, for that matter, not becoming. Immigrants impose burdens as well as benefits, a harsh reality to which their ardent celebrants are at times oblivious. George Gilder-type parables about the superstars of immigration just will not do. Such stories can be a distorting mirror rather than a window to truth.

So numerous by now are New York's New Immigrants, so diverse their heritages and traits, that any serious effort to trace their passage through its economy, educational institutions, and communities (its welfare agencies and prisons, too) is a formidable task. It requires a panoptic scan, in the aggregate and in ethnic- and site-specific detail, of the trajectories along which New Immigrants adapt to the resident society, how their children proceed through the schools, how adults advance through the labor force, how families settle and resettle in the City's neighborhoods, how they participate (or fail to) in electoral politics and how, inevitably, many fall into crime and dependency.

That scan requires a marriage of the sensitive observational skills of urban anthropologists and participant observers to the measuring instruments and statistical skills of social scientists. The first set of disciplines is needed to retrieve the nuanced interactions between old and new residents, of how resources and neighborhoods and institutions are shared or fought over. The second set is needed to design and conduct the technical surveys and statistical indicators for monitoring immigrant groups as they spread across the social and economic landscape and as they mature with time.

Pilgrims' Progress is best ascertained through panel research. It is essential to pursue over long intervals not just census-derived cohorts of putatively comparable people but representative groups of the same people. Ideally, researchers would periodically revisit several such panels. Some would consist of adults to discern social and economic adaptations, particularly changing status in the labor force. Other panels would comprise younger children to measure their problems and performance in the schools, thus guiding educational and employment policies. If ethnic-specific data are to be obtained, these panels must be of sufficient size to assure statistically reliable subsets. To gather neighborhood-specific detail, the number of survey instruments would have to be further multiplied. Moreover, social scientists will be further challenged to devise survey techniques that elicit tolerably accurate answers from a population not always inclined to share private information with strangers whom they may distrust and who have no entitlement to ask. That is why participant observers are an indispensable supplement to panel surveys. They are curious about who people actually are and what they actually do and are not content with perfunctory responses. As often as not, they will sufficiently earn the confidence of the untrusting to pry out the actualities.

The research ideal—a comprehensive series of longitudinal surveys—is perhaps an unattainable goal. It is surely an exceedingly costly enterprise. As a matter of research economics, it becomes feasible only when conducted by a network of universities (including community colleges) from geographically dispersed campuses with the assistance of large numbers of students and faculty motivated as much by academic requirements and interests as by earnings.

There is no doubt of the superior rewards it would yield to both scholarship and public policy. There is genuine intellectual excitement in grasping history as it is made, in watching the reenactment of a centuries-old drama. Universities have every reason to be in the front rank of the research watch. That would be especially the case in a city like New York, which is to the immigrant saga what Jerusalem is to the established religions. New York owes an incalculable debt for its ascendancy to world-class status to the sacrifices and talents of aspiring foreigners who brought with them a fierce commitment to work, family, and education. Similarly, it owes much of its difficulties to those entrants who possessed or absorbed too little of those values. How the New Immigrants sort themselves by income, education, and social behavior will determine what New York will be in the twenty-first century, more so than the oscillations of its economy. Booms and busts come and go. It is a foregone conclusion that the exuberant prosperity of the eighties will be followed by a downturn and almost as certain that the economic curve will again turn up. But the social character of New York's people, the productivity of its labor force, and the nature of its civic order are structural and change only by imperceptible degrees.

This study's purpose was to discover what can be learned about the impact of new immigrants on old neighborhoods, without benefit of panel research or resident observers. Its scope is confined to the boundaries of a single affected community, though much is herein reported about the New Immigrants generally and about their impact on New York City. Measured against the ideal research design limned above, the findings set forth in the next six chapters are limited in depth and coverage—no more than a helpful prelude.

Brooklyn's Sunset Park was elected as a place to probe the nature of available information, to assemble those data sets within relatively easy reach, and to identify others that are accessible only by heavier expenditures of time and resources. The neighborhood is no more or less eligible to serve as a pilot than are a score of other candidates. Most of New York's neighborhoods have been shaped by immigrations of the past, and few are untouched by the latest one.

Sunset Park was picked for two reasons. First, though every neighborhood has its own history, social makeup, and physical environment, the community's experience seemed typical of how New York's immigrant-settled, working-class neighborhoods attained their peak growth and of the course of events thereafter. Sunset Park was typical, too, in that it suffered most of the pains of urban decline that emerged in the fifties and deepened in the sixties and seventies. The neighborhood's descent, however, as gauged by net population losses or housing destruction, was not as appalling as was, say, the South Bronx's or Brownsville's. Likewise, though it has enjoyed a pronounced revival, its uplift has not been as exuberant as that of such other city neighborhoods as the Upper West Side, Flushing, or Park Slope. In short, the amplitude of Sunset Park's fall and rise is somewhere about the middle of the cyclical experience.

A second, more practical, reason for the choice of Sunset Park was the forthcomingness of the community's leaders and institutions. The neighborhood is proud of its recuperative powers and its accomplishments, of the fact that it has once again become the habitat of a diversity of residents, indeed more diverse than anything in its past. But working-class neighborhoods are overshadowed by the media's preoccupation with Manhattan and other hot spots deemed more newsworthy. Sunset Park has not been smothered by a surfeit of attention, at least not until the recent funeral ceremony for two slain police officers at its largest Catholic church, which brought in masses of reporters, TV cameras, and 12,000 mourning fellow officers. In a book recently published by the *New York Times* that describes New York's neighborhoods, Sunset Park was not included among the dozen profiles devoted to Brooklyn.[3] In the computerized files of the

---

3. Michael Sterne (ed.), *The New York Times Guide to Where to Live In and Around New York* (New York: Times Books, 1985).

*New York Times* referring to Sunset Park, more space was accorded to the ups and downs of its Industrial Zone than to its ups and downs as a community. A complimentary citation in a national magazine a few years ago is enthusiastically recirculated by local community boosters; a videotape of achievements is of their own commissioning. Happily, journalism's interest in places like Sunset Park with its new life and new people has of late grown stronger, evidenced by regular features in the press and on television. The comeback of even the city's more workaday neighborhoods and the contributory role of New Immigrants to that comeback have become too eventful for the media to ignore.

## THE STUDY'S SETTING

Sunset Park is a very small component of New York City and its surrounding region and a mere flyspeck in the national and international cosmos. That fact looms over every study of the community's past, present, and future. The particulars of change in the community are therefore intelligible only when viewed against larger events. In analyzing Sunset Park one is compelled to look through both ends of a telescope, one focused upon the broad horizon and the other on the level of subneighborhoods, census tracts, streets, and avenues.

What follows, therefore, comprises two levels of discourse. The early chapters are given over to background events, among them the radical reform in national immigration policies that opened the sluices to a flood of New Immigrants into New York. Chapter 3 summarizes the highlights of the New Immigration. Another event is the post-1977 surge in New York's economic and cultural vitality that attracted multitudes of young adults with a keen appetite for central-city residence. Chapter 4 discusses the powerful expansion in the City's economy and employment. A third factor is the near-collapse in residential construction that generated an insatiable demand for old housing, reinforced by the emergence of a grass-roots community development and neighborhood preservation movement. Chapter 5 is given over to ethnogeography, the settlement patterns of New York's newcomers.

The volume's second half examines Sunset Park through a high-resolution lens. Chapter 6 is a long account of its growth and decline that concludes with a profile of its fallen status as disclosed in the 1980 census. Chapter 7 deals with Sunset Park's post-1980 revival, with a close look at the part played by new residents. The final chapter, 8, is a blend of projections, speculations, and musings about where Sunset Park seems headed as it approaches the turn of a new century.

The research impedimenta are relegated to a set of five appendices. Two are noteworthy. Appendix A—Data Sources and Data Gaps—is an extended discussion of a fertile new data source for ethnic research, *Cole's Directory*, a reverse telephone book. A second original data contribution is presented in Appendix E, wherein are summarized the results of Professor Roger Waldinger's survey of the ethnic traits of Sunset Park's retail proprietors. Waldinger sets these new data against comparable studies of other communities.

# CHAPTER 3
## The New Immigration: Nation and City

In 1968 a mammoth wave of foreign immigration began to roll over America. It followed congressional enactment in 1965 of landmark legislation that abolished the restrictive and discriminatory immigration quotas of 1924 and reaffirmed in 1952. The 1965 statute was a climactic event in U.S. social history, more momentous than any of its sponsors had imagined. Together with subsequent laws and amendments, it touched off a flow of people, far greater in volume and vastly wider in geographic origin than had then been projected by any lawmaker or demographer. Nationally, the estimated total—legal and illegal immigrants plus refugees—is nearing 12 million. Annual levels have risen steadily; they were substantially higher in the 1980s than in the 1970s and there is nothing in sight to indicate any reversal in the 1990s (Table 3–1). By 1986, the annual number of legal admissions topped 600,000, twice that of the early years, and that figure was matched in 1987. Adding a conservative estimate of illegal migrants, the level of current migration may be close to 900,000, a figure only marginally lower than the yearly averages of the pre–World War I peaks. The New Immigration constitutes a major demographic watershed. It accounts for nearly one-quarter of the nation's current population growth and for all of a new order of diversity.

That diversity is a consequence of seismic intercontinental shifts in migratory flows, with many more nations sending people and many more nations receiving people than ever before. America's New Im-

**TABLE 3–1**
**Immigrants Admitted to the United States, 1965–1988**

| Year | Number | Year | Number |
|------|--------|------|--------|
| 1988 | 643,025 | 1976 | 398,613 |
| 1987 | 601,506 | 1975 | 386,194 |
| 1986 | 601,708 | 1974 | 394,861 |
| 1985 | 570,009 | 1973 | 400,063 |
| 1984 | 543,903 | 1972 | 384,685 |
| 1983 | 559,763 | 1971 | 370,478 |
| 1982 | 594,131 | 1970 | 373,326 |
| 1981 | 596,600 | 1969 | 358,579 |
| 1980 | 530,639 | 1968 | 454,448 |
| 1979 | 460,348 | 1967 | 361,972 |
| 1978 | 601,442 | 1966 | 323,040 |
| 1977 | 462,315 | 1965 | 296,697 |
| TQ1976* | 103,676 | | |

Sources: 1970–1986 from W. Brian Arthur and Thomas J. Espenshade, "U.S. Immigration Policy, Immigrants' Ages, and U.S. Population Size," *Impacts of Immigration in California* (Washington, D.C.: The Urban Institute, June 1987); other years from the Annual Reports of the Immigration and Naturalization Service.
* Refers to the transition quarter, July 1, 1976 to September 30, 1976.

migrants come from more than 160 countries. Before 1914, 80 percent or more of the newcomers were European; since 1965, 80 percent or more are from the Third World (Latin America, Asia, the Caribbean, and Africa) and that proportion is rising. Amid such extraordinary diversity, two groups stand high above the others. First and long the foremost are the Hispanics; second and now leading are the Asians. Once when America's immigrants spoke of the Old World they meant Italy or Poland. Today, their Old World is more likely to be Mexico or China.

The immigrants' imprint on America's urban demographics, already broad and deep, is destined to become still broader and deeper. As did Honolulu before them, Miami and Los Angeles, Seattle and New York manifest in concentrated doses a polyethnicity that now appears in dilute versions in every metropolitan area.

## IMMIGRATION WITHOUT END

What has been slow to seep into the consciousness of national and urban planners is the sheer power of demographic cumulations that have no cutoff. The pace of the New Immigration is not likely to slacken, barring a severe U.S. depression (and perhaps not even then). That reality has immense significance for the future of most neighborhoods in most big cities, not least, as we shall see, Sunset Park. The backup of applicants for entry permits at U.S. consulates around the world is counted by the million. The hungry and politically vulnerable of the Third World, the suppressed of the Second, and the ambitious or unemployed of the First passionately yearn for America as lifeline or second chance. Haitian and Vietnamese boat people, the pre-Gorbachev refuseniks, and Iranian or Irish overstayers were very different kinds of people, driven by different urgencies. But all were made kindred by their zeal to venture a new life in America and by exposing themselves to grave legal and physical risks to do so.

A sustained volume of future immigration is assured by the preferments accorded to family reunions, provisions that now account for more than 80 percent of the inflow. Pending legislation, as discussed in the concluding chapter, would augment the flow of those not benefited by such preferences. Global strife and civil wars, suppression and tyranny, also bring sporadic waves of refugees. America has by now given asylum to over 1.2 million. Its role as host may increase as other countries become less receptive (as seems to be their wont) and as new political trouble spots appear; Hong Kong, South Korea, the Philippines, North India, Sri Lanka, parts of the Caribbean and Latin America (Haiti and Central America, among them) are all candidates. And lax or generous American attitudes—sporadic enforcement, a vigilant legal-aid network, a sympathetic judiciary—have held to a minimum the deportation of those with challengeable claims to asylum.

Because the New Immigration has neither a plausible ending nor is likely to diminish in volume, metropolitan America and most of its neighborhoods will be altered in every conceivable manner. The most obvious change will be in the size and composition of population, already discernible in all the immigrant-catchment areas.[4] Cities like New York and San Francisco, once depopulating, are now experiencing net growth, primarily attributable to the New Immigration. And

---

4. See, among others, Leon F. Bouvier, *The Impact of Immigration on U.S. Population Size* (Population Reference Bureau, January 1981); W. Brian Arthur and Thomas J. Espenshade, "U.S. Immigration Policy, Immigrants' Ages, and U.S. Population Size" (Washington, D.C.: The Urban Institute, June 1987).

in cities that are still shrinking, like Detroit and Newark, the rate of decline has decreased.

The high and sustained inflow, combined with the relatively high fertility rates of the newcomers, will make America's ethnic contours in the next century inestimably different from America's ethnic contours in 1965. Outmarriage, whose incidence varies considerably among different immigrant groups and which rises in successive generations, will add further to the ethnic medley.[5] Though neither the birthrates nor intermarriage rates of the various cohorts of New Immigrants can be confidently projected, those changes will permeate all of society.[6] Indeed, cities of major immigrant settlement—and not just in California, Texas, and Florida—were noticeably different in 1988 from what they were in 1965, several strikingly so.

As in past eras of immigration, the demographic unknowns have bred anxieties and fears of a threat to America's socioeconomic future. They have spawned restrictionist organizations and laws and referenda to assure the primacy of English as America's "official" language. Even pro-immigrationists are concerned about too much of a good thing and few are in favor of unlimited immigration. And no one, for or against a wide-open front door, is reconciled to a wide-open back door, to the perpetuation of a submerged class of millions of illegals whose ranks are endlessly enlarged by substantial flows across a porous southern border and by clandestine entry through a multitude of loosely fastened gates. Contrary to common perception, the illegals are not just Mexican "pollos" trailing their "coyotes." Nearly half of them are from other parts of the world, often those who violate their tourist, student, and worker visas.

When, in the seventies, it was perceived that the volume of new entrants was greatly overrunning expectations, a clamor arose to suppress illegal flows. An unusual coalition of environmentalists, trade unions, and nativist elements launched a strenuous campaign to "regain control of America's borders." Unable or unwilling to peel back the statutory quotas and preferences, the exclusionists campaigned for a system of sanctions to narrow the labor market for those without proper documents: If the supply of illegals could not be directly halted at the border, it could be indirectly constrained by reduc-

---

5. The outmarriage rates of women range from 88 percent for those reporting Hispanic ancestry to 35 percent for some categories of Asians to 24 percent for Mexicans. Cf. Stanley Lieberson and Mary C. Waters, *From Many Strands: Ethnic and Racial Groups in Contemporary America* (New York: Russell Sage Foundation, 1988), p. 207.

6. *Ibid.*, Chapter 6.

ing the pulling power of the job magnet (though with solicitous regard for the prosperity of agricultural employers). But year after year the campaign foundered in a hopelessly divided Congress. Success came at last in 1986 with the passage of the Immigration Reform and Control Act (IRCA), the requisite majority achieved by a balance of stiff penalties on employers who knowingly hire the undocumented, and by liberal amnesty rules for those with five years or more of proven residence.

The long-term effectiveness of IRCA in thinning out the population of old and new illegals is in dispute. Experience to date with implementation and enforcement indicates that it is likely to fall short of the hopes of its most optimistic sponsors. There was less than a rush, except in the West and Southwest, to petition for amnesty. In New York and the Northeast the queue was surprisingly short. By the end of the amnesty period approximately 1.7 million applications were filed, plus a million more from farm workers subject to less stringent rules. Measured by the most commonly accepted estimate of illegals, 3.5 to 4 million, a fair success rate is indicated. Less assessable is the ultimate effect of IRCA on the future volume of illegal entry; owing to administrative incapacities and political sensitivities, the sanction provisions have thus far been only spasmodically enforced. The deterrent power of employer sanctions in other nations where they have been in place since the seventies has not been impressive.

However the status of millions of illegals is eventually resolved, there is no overwhelming political consensus for a substantial curtailment of legal entries. As appears later, legislation reintroduced in the 1989 Congress would tinker with the existing rules only at the margins and is more likely to increase than to decrease future admissions. That is why the best guess is an indefinitely protracted inflow, a little above or a little below recent levels, but more likely the former.

Except to environmentalists and social or cultural purists, the quandary for America is not so much the magnitude of today's and tomorrow's arrivals. It is how well the next generations of the more disadvantaged newcomers will advance into the mainstream. Pessimists, while acknowledging the virtues of the Asians, fear that a predominantly Third World migration is not likely to duplicate the successes of the pre–World War I European migrations. Among the reasons are the poor school performances and high dropout rates of Hispanics, the largest group of entrants; a generous welfare system that dulls the urge to work; and the easy lures of a flourishing subeconomy of drugs and crime.

There is no room here to rehearse the vast scholarly literature on the various outcomes of the principal ethnic groups involved in the pre-1914 migrations, the differing lags in adjustment, and why performance so often confounded prediction. One recalls, though, that there was no dearth of pessimists in earlier times. Contempt for the "lazy and hard-drinking" Irish of the potato-famine years ran wide and deep, provoking a counterreaction of "Know Nothings." History showed that those phobics came rightly by their name and that their a priori judgments proved notoriously fallible. The Irish have, of course, conquered every peak in the nation's establishment, though, in recent years, not New York's political aeries in which they were once the unchallenged inhabitants. (It is easier these days, some wag quipped, for an Irishman to attain a seat in the rabbinical council than a borough presidency.)

East European Jews of the late nineteenth century were similarly adjudged to be pollutants of urban society, even by an otherwise enlightened elite, even by some of their assimilated coreligionists. Yet it took little more than a single generation for their leap into business, the professions, and the arts, surely one of the most mutually productive transplants in immigrant history. Southern Italians were likewise held in scorn. Their breakout took an additional generation. The vast majority are now well into the mainstream, and increased numbers have joined Irish and Jews at the highest echelons; in Sunset Park, to anticipate a later finding, they have displaced the Irish from a long-held political throne and now dominate the community's leadership. The Chinese, once the objects of naked racism, are, by every indicator, on an even faster track than yesteryear's Europeans; and even faster are the Koreans, who entered with relatively high educational qualifications. For other Asians the adjustment process is more variable, with East Indians, Pakistani, and urban Vietnamese refugees on the higher side of the progress scale and rural Indochinese on the lower.

The most frequent worries are about the outcomes of succeeding generations of America's largest and least-prepared body of newcomers: Mexicans, Central Americans, and Caribbeans. The first generation of Latin newcomers tends to regard a modestly paid factory or service job as a gratifying step forward from where they had been. The second and third generations may be of a different mind. Only time will tell how many will groom themselves for higher occupations and how many will be dropouts and lapse into the margins of the legal and illegal economy. It is true that school dropout rates among Hispanics are alarmingly high, higher than for any other ethnic group including native-born blacks. Yet in California and the Southwest where Mexican-American residence has been longest, substantial long-term progress is reported by the third generation. Though their ranks are slender, a growing Hispanic middle class has emerged in New York (whose presence will be noted later in Sunset Park). New York's experience with earlier West Indian immigrants had, on the whole, been favorable; from what can now be observed, the same holds true of the recent ones. The reverse seems true of the more recent arrivals of rural Indochinese. The first generation is substantially less capacitated than other Asians, more on welfare and more lodged in the low end of the job market. But experience thus far indicates that their children are performing tolerably well.

The past, however, is no guarantor of the future. As was noted, value codes are not immutable. The authority of the family, the church, and the school has waned. And the incubus of drugs casts a shadow on every social class and neighborhood from which even some of the much-lauded Asian youth are not spared. It is conceivable that the range of outcomes within and across ethnic groups may be more variable than in the past. Within particular ethnic groups, there may be a higher incidence of opposing results, that is, relatively more at the top and relatively more at the bottom. That has been the tendency for blacks over the past generation: As many more have progressed into the professional and middle class, many more, simultaneously, have fallen into the sediment of the underclass. Compared to a generation ago, America's colleges and prisons are both blacker. One can already observe that dualism among Hispanic immigrants.

Thus, the distributional patterns of New Immigrants will be as significant as the averages, and accurate generalizations will require a platoon of qualifiers. That is all the more reason for a program of synchronous, longitudinal research. Understanding can come only from a detailed analysis of disparate outcomes and all of them subject to revision as each cohort of immigrants ages and is replaced by a younger one.

## GEOGRAPHIC DISTRIBUTION

The geography of immigrant settlement has been selective, by region and city. Perimeter areas, especially metropolises on the eastern and western seaboards, account for an overwhelming majority of the New Immigrants.[7] Today's Ellis Island is California, which has dislodged

---

7. *1985 Statistical Yearbook of the Immigration and Naturalization Service* (Washington, D.C.: U.S. Department of Justice, 1986), p. 57.

New York State from its historic primacy as the new foreigners' main turnstile; during the 1983–1986 period California's annual admissions averaged nearly 150,000, compared with 103,000 for New York.[8] Florida and Texas are also key entry states. The arrival ports, however, are not necessarily places of final settlement. As with past migrations, external migration sooner or later becomes an internal migration that fans out in widening streams. Though less strikingly than in principal gateway areas, the demographic composition of practically all sizable urban centers—and many smaller ones as well—is being significantly altered by people of variegated color, tongue, and culture.

The internal movements of recent immigrants are hard to track accurately in overall numbers and still harder in the details: Small-area data are susceptible to considerable margins of error. The Immigration and Naturalization Service (INS), the primary source of numbers of immigrants by locale, is chronically understaffed, conspicuously in its statistical and record-keeping functions.[9] There are flaws, too, in the base census tabulations, of which the most serious are high nonresponse rates, substantial errors and ambiguities in the ancestry tabulations, and a sizable underenumeration of illegals who hide in the shadows. The census staff has attempted to estimate the magnitude of the 1980 uncounted immigrants, and believes it smaller than is commonly alleged.[10] But neither the errors nor the adjustments can be reliably pinpointed by locale and ethnicity. Estimates of illegals who entered since the 1980 census are a veritable free-for-all.

Errors and omissions in census ethnic classifications are likewise significant.[11] Not infrequently, respondents confuse the questions on ancestry and country of birth. Thus, ethnic Chinese who are natives of Vietnam sometimes report themselves as Indochinese; Hispanics from Central America or the Dominican Republic who have first migrated to Puerto Rico may list themselves as Puerto Rican, sometimes, if undocumented, deliberately so. Adding to the complexities are inevitable ambiguities of ancestral affiliation, a trait, like race, self-

---

8. James P. Allen and Eugene J. Turner, "Where to Find the New Immigrants," *American Demographics*, September 1988, p. 26.
9. For a thorough analysis of that problem, see Daniel B. Levine, Kenneth Hill, and Robert Warren (eds.), *Immigration Statistics: A Story of Neglect* (Washington, D.C.: National Academy Press, 1985).
10. Jeffrey S. Passel, "Undocumented Immigration," *Annals of the American Academy of Political and Social Science*, 1986, pp. 181–200.
11. Lieberson and Waters, *op. cit.* The introductory chapter of this comprehensive study of America's ethnic makeup in 1980 is a first-rate explication of the mysteries of ancestral identification, centered upon, but going beyond, the census tabulations.

determined by the respondent. People with similar ancestral lines frequently report themselves differently.

If census figures undercount New Immigrants, some alternative sources of local data (e.g., ethnic associations and ethnic media and marketing firms) tend to the opposite fault. For political or commercial reasons, they are prone to exaggerate the size of client populations. Municipal agencies do their best to assemble an up-to-date statistical base by piecing together data from INS, school enrollments, birth and death registrations, and the like. But they will generally acknowledge considerable margins of error in the aggregates and wider ones in the subaggregates. These and other data problems that affect the research on Sunset Park come up again later.

## THE NEW IMMIGRANTS: NEW YORK

Though New York State has relinquished first place to California, INS data show the New York metropolitan area to be the preferred immigrant port of arrival, at least for registered aliens.[12] Between 1984 and 1986, there was an annual average of 92,000 recorded arrivals compared to second-place Los Angeles with 58,000. Between 1965 and 1980, nearly 1 million immigrants entered New York legally, accounting for nearly one out of five of all U.S. arrivals. New York's City Planning Department calculates that 750,000 additional foreigners reside here without credentials.[13] But other estimates of illegals run a good deal lower, perhaps rightly so.[14] New York, as noted, experienced an unexpectedly low rate of applications for amnesty. Not all the reasons for that are clear, but one reason may well be exaggerated notions of their numbers.

Errors aside, the census reported that in 1980 the City had 1.6 million foreign-born, counting the old and the new. Of that total, 608,000 had entered in the 10 years between 1965 and 1974, and 354,000 more between 1975 and April 1, 1980 (Table 3–2).

Since 1980, additional foreigners, about 85,000 per year, have come in (Table 3–3). Adding an allowance for the undocumented and subtracting an allowance for net losses of the native-born, it is likely that

---

12. For an excellent account of New York's new immigrants—numbers, geographic distribution, costs, and benefits—see Elizabeth Bogen, *Immigration in New York* (New York: Praeger Publishers, Inc., 1987).
13. Allen and Turner, *op. cit.*, p. 24. Their data are derived from INS yearbooks.
14. For a discussion of this point, see Bogen, *op. cit.*, pp. 53–54.

**TABLE 3–2**
**New York City's Post-1965 Foreign-Born Population, by Country of Origin and Period of Entry**

| | 1965–1974 | | 1975–1980 | | Total | |
|---|---|---|---|---|---|---|
| | Number | Percent | Number | Percent | Number | Percent |
| Caribbean Basin | 230,260 | 39.0% | 101,600 | 28.7% | 331,860 | 35.2% |
| Dominican Republic/Other Hispanic | 84,160 | 14.3 | 37,780 | 10.7 | 121,940 | 12.9 |
| West Indies/Other British | 104,160 | 17.7 | 45,060 | 12.7 | 149,220 | 15.8 |
| Haiti/Other French | 30,400 | 5.2 | 13,940 | 3.9 | 44,340 | 4.7 |
| Other Caribbean | 11,540 | 2.0 | 4,820 | 1.4 | 16,360 | 1.7 |
| Asia | 76,340 | 12.9 | 70,380 | 19.9 | 146,720 | 15.5 |
| China | 36,900 | 6.3 | 25,520 | 7.2 | 62,420 | 6.6 |
| Korea | 7,640 | 1.3 | 11,680 | 3.3 | 19,320 | 2.0 |
| India, Pakistan, Bangladesh | 12,480 | 2.1 | 13,700 | 3.9 | 26,180 | 2.8 |
| Other Asia | 19,320 | 3.3 | 19,480 | 5.5 | 38,800 | 4.1 |
| Europe | 117,560 | 19.9 | 70,580 | 19.9 | 188,140 | 19.9 |
| USSR | 6,160 | 1.0 | 29,020 | 8.2 | 35,180 | 3.7 |
| Italy | 35,440 | 6.0 | 6,560 | 1.9 | 42,000 | 4.4 |
| Greece | 19,320 | 3.3 | 6,680 | 1.9 | 26,000 | 2.8 |
| Other | 56,640 | 9.6 | 28,320 | 8.0 | 84,960 | 9.0 |
| Middle East | 17,120 | 2.9 | 14,800 | 4.2 | 31,920 | 3.4 |
| Africa | 7,020 | 1.2 | 5,660 | 1.6 | 12,680 | 1.3 |
| North America | 3,040 | 0.5 | 2,160 | 0.6 | 5,200 | 0.6 |
| South America | 78,480 | 13.3 | 48,400 | 13.7 | 126,880 | 13.4 |
| Central America | 30,220 | 5.1 | 16,880 | 4.8 | 47,100 | 5.0 |
| Oceania and Not Reported | 47,480 | 6.9 | 23,380 | 6.6 | 70,860 | 7.5 |
| TOTAL | 607,520 | 100.0 | 353,840 | 100.0 | 961,360 | 100.0 |

Source: Population Division, New York City Department of City Planning, 1980 Public Use Microdata File (Sample A).
Note: Details may not add to totals because of rounding.

TABLE 3–3
Immigrant Arrivals in New York City, by Country of Birth, 1983–1987[a]

|  | Total | Brooklyn | Bronx | Manhattan | Queens | Staten Island |
|---|---|---|---|---|---|---|
| Total | 429,405 | 141,714 | 54,655 | 97,597 | 129,511 | 5,928 |
| Asia | 106,976 | 22,283 | 7,070 | 29,469 | 44,938 | 3,216 |
| China[b] | 44,584 | 9,318 | 1,270 | 18,838 | 14,599 | 559 |
| Korea | 12,417 | 1,559 | 897 | 1,559 | 7,776 | 626 |
| India | 12,740 | 1,872 | 1,102 | 1,458 | 7,609 | 749 |
| Philippines | 7,998 | 1,148 | 517 | 1,990 | 3,741 | 602 |
| Vietnam | 3,021 | 1,116 | 891 | 242 | 672 | 100 |
| Other Asia | 16,579 | 3,681 | 2,053 | 3,363 | 7,148 | 334 |
| Caribbean Basin | 211,772 | 88,156 | 35,458 | 45,827 | 41,634 | 697 |
| Dominican Republic | 74,176 | 12,868 | 12,863 | 37,438 | 10,914 | 93 |
| Jamaica | 45,018 | 20,892 | 12,597 | 1,846 | 9,541 | 142 |
| Guyana | 33,518 | 15,578 | 4,962 | 1,320 | 11,530 | 128 |
| Haiti | 26,461 | 19,425 | 557 | 1,767 | 4,654 | 58 |
| Other Caribbean | 34,208 | 15,444 | 4,709 | 3,915 | 5,294 | 293 |
| Central America | 16,889 | 5,482 | 3,494 | 2,798 | 5,019 | 196 |
| South America | 38,165 | 7,000 | 3,774 | 6,601 | 20,364 | 426 |
| Colombia | 15,635 | 2,211 | 814 | 1,776 | 10,652 | 182 |
| Ecuador | 11,273 | 2,283 | 1,995 | 2,092 | 4,291 | 83 |
| Peru | 4,301 | 666 | 495 | 752 | 2,347 | 41 |
| Other South America | 6,956 | 1,300 | 470 | 1,981 | 3,074 | 120 |
| Europe | 39,088 | 13,561 | 2,860 | 8,620 | 13,242 | 815 |
| Middle East[c] | 15,046 | 5,763 | 562 | 2,941 | 5,230 | 550 |
| Africa | 5,719 | 1,549 | 1,243 | 1,508 | 1,212 | 207 |
| Other Countries or Unknown | 3,792 | 980 | 301 | 1,390 | 1,052 | 59 |

Source: Population Division, New York City Department of City Planning and Immigration, based on INS files.
[a] Fiscal years ending September 30.
[b] Mainland, Hong Kong, and Taiwan.
[c] Includes Egypt and Turkey.

close to one out of three New Yorkers is now foreign-born. (These computations exclude Puerto Ricans who are American-born whether of mainland or island nativity.) Were immigration and the shrinkage of native-born to proceed at present levels, the proportion of New York's foreign-born by the year 2000 would match or surpass the historic peak of 40 percent recorded in 1910. More will be said on this in the final chapter.

The extraordinary diversity of America's New Immigrants is mirrored in New York City. The summary tables for recent years presented here compress what is actually more than 150 countries of origin. New York's ethnic makeup, however, differs from the U.S. mix. New York has a far lower (though moderately increasing) proportion of Mexicans, a far higher proportion of Caribbeans, a lower (but sharply rising) proportion of Asians, and higher proportions of Europeans.

New York's nationality roster continuously lengthens, owing to international turmoil and internal migration. For example, as a result of protracted turmoil in the Middle East, New York has now several thousand Egyptians, an ethnic group not hitherto much evident. The war in Afghanistan brought thousands of Afghans. The revolutions in Cuba, Nicaragua, and Haiti and the turbulence in Central America have substantially augmented the comparatively small numbers of those nationals already here. And Cambodians and Vietnamese, for whom New York had not been a primary port of entry, are now also counted in the many thousands as small colonies swell through ethnic agglomeration and "chain migrations," that is, relatives admitted under various preference rules.

The widening diversity was soon reflected in Board of Education data concerning foreign pupils who require language aid (Chapter 6). Both the number of pupils and the number of birth countries have increased since 1983 when nationality data were first collected.

The City's new diversity is not only evident in statistical tables. It is reflected in a United Nations-like display of foreign-language newspapers on any large newsstand,[15] in a cornucopia of ethnic restaurants and specialty shops, and in the speech and faces on every subway in Brooklyn. In some cars on the Queens No. 7 line, half the advertisements are not in English. On weekends, when the yuppies flee to the Hamptons or the ski slopes and the more sedate middle class attends to its barbecues and backswings, those subways belong to the immigrants. Indeed, the system assumes the aspect of a Third World railway, ensembles of every complexion and tongue.

As the tables show, more of New York's New Immigrants come from the Caribbean Basin than from any other place: The Caribbean is to New York what Mexico is to Texas and California. More than one-third of the near-million 1965–1980 entrants came from that region, and the inflow has continued since 1980 at a rate of over 40,000 per

---

15. See Bogen, *op. cit.*, Chapter 17, for a catalogue of today's ethnic media.

year. The Caribbean newcomers comprise three language groups: English-speaking West Indians from Jamaica, Trinidad/Tobago, Barbados, plus a dozen other islands; French- and Creole-speaking Haitians; and Hispanics primarily from the Dominican Republic, Cuba, and Central America. Together with multiple streams from Central and South America, even a trickle from Spain, Hispanics by 1980 constituted by far the largest component of New York's New Immigrants, one-third of the total. Since 1980, however, the Hispanic inflow of registered aliens fell to just 25 percent of the total. But since the incidence of undocumented Hispanics is known to be not only high but volatile as well, it is not certain how much of the drop is real.

Next in importance are Asians, who are now settling in New York in record numbers. In 1980, nearly 150,000 were reported as post-1965 entrants, 15 percent of the total. Rates of entry, both absolutely and relatively, have been increasing. Asians accounted for 13 percent of the 1965–1974 foreign-born inflow and for 20 percent of the 1975–1980 entrants. Since 1980, their weight increased still more, to 26 percent. Chinese and Koreans are the principal subgroups, followed by East Asians, Filipinos, and Indochinese.

Over 40 percent of all Asians were Chinese, both in the 1980 cumulations and among new arrivals since. The Chinese mainland is the principal place of origin, followed by Hong Kong (commonly a way station from the mainland) and Taiwan. Owing to their global diaspora, the total of new Chinese by ancestry is doubtless greater than is recorded by country of birth. The regional origins of those from China are more diverse than those of earlier settlers in New York who were primarily from the Toysan (or Toishan) region. The new Chinese speak Mandarin, Cantonese, Shanghaiese, and other regional tongues.[16]

In 1980, the census counted fewer than 20,000 post-1965 Koreans, an enumeration sharply disputed by Korean ethnic associations, who put the figure several times higher. Since 1980, the inflow of registered Koreans to New York has been at the rate of 2,500 a year, likewise thought a substantial understatement.

There was also a steep rise in Asians from the subcontinent, who comprised several nationalities and cultural groups. More than half of the 26,000 reported in 1980 as 1975–1980 entrants came from India, Pakistan, and Bangladesh. These Asians are further subdivided by

---

16. Betty Lee Sung, *The Adjustment Experience of Chinese Immigrant Children in New York City* (New York: Center for Migration Studies, 1987), p. 51.

religion (chiefly Hindu, Moslem, Sikh, and Buddhist) and language (chiefly Hindi, Urdu, Gujarat, and Tamil). The Philippines are likewise a substantial source of Asian immigrants. Some 20,000 Filipinos were counted in the 1965–1980 cohorts, and 2,000 to 3,000 more per year since. Vietnamese began to show up only after 1975, following the harrowing "boat people" episode. Though the 1980 census reported fewer than 4,000, and INS 4,000 or 5,000 since, many ethnic watchers believe the number to be higher. No doubt some reported as from Thailand or Malaysia are actually Vietnamese.

The importance of Europe as a place of origin has diminished greatly, measured against both prewar levels and the tide of displacees and refugees after World War II. But New York still draws heavily from the smaller pool. More than 188,000 new Europeans were reported in 1980, 19 percent of the total. Since 1980, the proportion has decreased, accounting for less than 10 percent of INS-reported arrivals. In the 1965–1974 decade, Italy was the leading country of origin, followed by Greece, Poland, and the USSR. The years 1975–1980 were an era of Soviet Jewish entry; in 1980, 29,000 gave the USSR as their birthplace, more than 46 percent of all European entrants during the period. Their numbers dried up in subsequent years, owing to a tightening of Soviet immigration policy. Post-Gorbachev, that policy has been gradually relaxed, as is further discussed in the final chapter.

There is also sustained migration from the Middle East; some 32,000 from this region were counted in 1980. The rate of inflow has been accelerating. Middle Easterners were 4 percent of the 1975–1980 total compared to 2.9 percent in 1965–1974. Since 1980, an annual average of more than 3,000 new arrivals has been registered. The principal countries of origin are Israel, Lebanon and, since the overthrow of the Shah, Iran. Africa, too, is a small but continuous sender—blacks from Ghana, Nigeria, Senegal, and elsewhere. Here again, one should note the divergence of ethnicity from country of birth. Some of the African migration includes ethnic Asians escaping from strife-torn sub-Saharan nations, even some whites from southern Africa.

New York's minorities, as they are traditionally classified, now add up to a majority of the population, 54 percent. According to current projections,[17] by the year 2000 they will be a much larger majority,

---

17. Leon F. Bouvier and Vernon M. Boggs, Jr., "The Population and Labor Force of New York: 1990 to 2050" (Population Reference Bureau, 1988), p. 35.

66 percent, with an overwhelming majority in Brooklyn and the Bronx. But the terms "minority" and "majority" have diminished significance. The traditional classifications—whites, blacks, Hispanics, and Asians—comprise distinctive subgroups that prize their distinctiveness. The social distance between Jamaicans and Haitians, and of both from native blacks, is considerable, comparable to the distance between, say, Hasidic and Soviet Jews.[18] The same is true of the many subgroups of Hispanics who are differentiated not only by nationality but by culture, class, and political leanings. Judged by ancestry and skin color, substantial numbers of Hispanics could justifiably identify themselves in the census racial question as black; in fact, relatively few do so. Unlike the U.S., where white-black is a dichotomous classification, blackness in the Caribbean and Latin America is calibrated on a complex social and cultural scale.

The truth is that New York has become a polity without a clear-cut ethnic majority. Its population is an assemblage of racial, cultural, religious, and linguistic groupings that can be combined and recombined in alternate ways for alternate ends. The combinations relevant to advertisers and the foreign-language media are not necessarily those that matter to electoral politics or neighborhood coalitions. And the classifications relevant to marketers or politicians are not necessarily those that engage ethnographers and sociologists.

## A STRENGTHENED LABOR FORCE

The masses of New Immigrants have enriched New York's stock of human capital. There is simply no way that the City's productive machine could have performed at so high a level without immigrant workers. Despite that presence, New York was throughout the late eighties still a place where more jobs chased people than people chased jobs, suggesting that more, rather than fewer, newcomers would have been welcome.[19]

---

18. In her study of Jamaicans in New York City, Nancy Foner writes: "While to most white New Yorkers Jamaican migrants are largely invisible in a sea of anonymous black faces, Jamaicans themselves are highly sensitive to their differences from 'native' blacks. Indeed, the movement from a society where being Jamaican was taken for granted to one where they are a definite minority and where they find themselves lumped with American blacks has sharply heightened Jamaicans' consciousness of their ethnic identity." Nancy Foner (ed.), *New Immigrants in New York* (New York: Columbia University Press, 1987), p. 204.
19. The Port Authority of New York and New Jersey ["The New York–New Jersey Regional Labor Market: Challenges and Opportunities for the Coming Decade," Sep-

Immigrants have entered the City's economy in full force, filtering into virtually every sector, especially its less glamorous manual and service occupations. Because immigrants are concentrated in the working-age groups, their impact on New York's labor force has been even greater than on its population. Of the more than 400,000 jobs added in New York since the seventies, the major share was accounted for by Asians, Hispanics, and blacks.[20]

In the aggregate, New York's newly arrived have higher labor-force participation rates and lower rates of unemployment and welfare dependency than the native-born. That is also true of the new blacks and Hispanics compared with the native blacks and Puerto Ricans. The most recent Hispanic arrivals from Latin America have extraordinarily high employment rates, 93 percent for males and 89 percent for females who arrived between 1975 and 1980 (Table 3–4). They are foursquare in the tradition of America's immigrant past.

Non-Hispanic Caribbeans—West Indian and Haitian blacks—also display very high rates of employment, about 90 percent for both sexes of those who came after 1975. And according to 1980 census data, foreign-born male ethnics of prime working age experienced less unemployment than did their native-born counterparts (Table 3–5).

Among gainfully employed immigrants, two features stand out. One is entrepreneurial drive, the other, occupational specialization. The newcomers have a pronounced penchant for small business and self-employment. That choice has a singular appeal for those deficient in English or lacking proper documents. Self-employment is also preferred over wage employment by many educated immigrants— Asians and Soviet émigrés—who may be deterred from pursuing homeland professions by credentialing or licensing barriers.

In either case, self-employment is richly nurtured by the almost limitless opportunities in New York, given both its economic structure as a haven of small business and the aging of prior generations of proprietors. To a remarkable degree, as Waldinger and other students

---

tember 1988] has this to say about the immigrant contribution to the regional economy: "How the region's economy fares in the coming decade will depend largely on how well it addresses the challenges of a labor-short economy. As the nation enters an era of slow labor force growth and intense international competition, the regions which are most successful in improving labor availability and quality will have a distinct advantage. The region's large, diverse labor force has been a major asset underlying the region's resurgence."
20. Thomas Muller, *Immigration Reform from an Urban Perspective* (New York: Twentieth Century Fund, forthcoming).

TABLE 3–4
**Employment Status: Percentage of Native and Foreign Employed Labor Force
in Private Sector Wage Employment, New York SMSA, 1970–1980**

|  | New York State | Rest of U.S. | Puerto Rico | Latin America | Non-Hispanic Caribbean | Asia |
|---|---|---|---|---|---|---|
| **Males** | | | | | | |
| 1970 | 69.5 | 73.8 | 84.3 | 88.9 | 84.2 | 73.6 |
| 1980 | 70.4 | 69.7 | 78.4 | 87.2 | 83.1 | 79.9 |
| Arrival | | | | | | |
| Before 1970 | | | | 84.6 | 77.9 | 73.0 |
| 1970–1974 | | | | 88.4 | 82.9 | 79.1 |
| 1975–1980 | | | | 92.7 | 94.6 | 86.8 |
| **Females** | | | | | | |
| 1970 | 77.8 | 73.1 | 85.3 | 88.1 | 85.4 | 77.7 |
| 1980 | 77.1 | 77.5 | 71.8 | 86.8 | 82.5 | 82.7 |
| Arrival | | | | | | |
| Before 1970 | | | | 86.4 | 80.5 | 81.1 |
| 1970–1974 | | | | 86.3 | 84.5 | 83.3 |
| 1975–80 | | | | 89.1 | 84.1 | 84.2 |

*Place of Birth*

*Sources:* New York City Department of City Planning. Unpublished data from the Census of Population and Housing 1970, Public Use Sample, and from the Census of Population and Housing 1980, Public Use Microdata Sample.

of immigrant enterprise have shown, Asian, Hispanic, and Middle Eastern immigrants are replacing older Jewish, Italian, and Greek storekeepers and factory owners no longer willing to cope with the anxieties of crime-ridden neighborhoods, or whose descendants, with abundant gateways to the professions and higher corporate echelons, are disinclined to carry on the parental business.

Asians have a strikingly high rate of self-employment, 33 percent compared to 10 percent for the labor force as a whole. The phenomenon affirms an old Confucian saying that it is better to be the head of a chicken than the tail of an ox. The self-employment rates of new Hispanics, Haitians, and West Indians, though well behind the Asian, are higher than those of the Puerto Rican and native black population. Middle Easterners, emanating from a trading culture, also have exceptionally high rates of self-employment. Syrian immigrants, who have long dominated the City's linen and rug shops, have more recently taken over much of the electronics retail trade and the manufacture and distribution of blue jeans; many East European

**TABLE 3–5**
**Unemployment Rates, Native- and Foreign-born Males Aged 25–44,**
**New York City, 1980**

|  | Percent | |
|---|---|---|
|  | Native-born | Foreign-born |
| All males | 7.0 | 6.2 |
| White, non-Hispanic | 4.6 | 4.7 |
| Black, non-Hispanic | 12.2 | 9.0 |
| Hispanic | 9.9 | 7.6 |
| Asian | 4.7 | 3.3 |

*Source:* Elizabeth Bogen, *op. cit.,* p. 89, derived from 1980 Census, U.S. Public Use Microdata File.

Jews, including those of Israeli nationality, have gravitated toward the diamond and jewelry business and Soviet Jews toward fur and leather goods.

Korean immigrants are the epitome of the Asian small entrepreneur. According to one source, 41 percent of Korean families operate an estimated 9,000 businesses in the metropolitan area, most of them in New York City.[21] Though few Koreans are residents of Sunset Park, our retail survey shows them to be well represented on the shopping streets (Chapter 7).

A characteristic of Korean retailers is their ubiquity. They are not pinned down to co-ethnic neighborhoods, resembling in that respect the Chinese laundries and restaurants, the German delicatessens, and the Italian barber and shoe repair shops of earlier times. Greengroceries—the stereotypic specialty—have multiplied as far and as fast as sites and offerings allow. This specialty, once diffidently tested in poor neighborhoods, has penetrated almost every middle- and upper-class enclave and spread throughout the central business district as well. With cumulating experience and capital, Korean greengrocers have broadened their product range; to the traditional lines of fruits and vegetables many have now added salad bars and delicatessen counters. A close rival to the Korean greengrocery are the Korean fish store and the Korean dry-cleaning establishment; the latter seems destined to become as much a Korean near-monopoly as was the neighborhood hand laundry for the Chinese. Koreans are also edging into gift shops and the florist trade. Moreover, Korean entrepreneurial expansion is becoming vertical as well as horizontal:

21. Illsoo Kim, "The Koreans," in Foner, *op. cit.,* p. 226.

many are ascending the rungs of the economic chain to wholesaling, processing, and distribution.

The increased Korean presence, within and across business categories, indicates that actualities are running ahead of the stereotypes. Indeed, even before the greengrocer phase, Koreans were dominant in the import and retail sale of wigs made of human hair, a product eventually displaced by artificial hair.[22] These rapid turnings in economic specialization again suggest the value of a continual watch on the immigrant experience, not only to capture these shifts as they occur but to relate them to changing background factors. The anecdotal or biographical staples of Pilgrim's Progress in earlier eras—the Greek immigrant's journey from dishwasher to short-order cook to ownership of a diner, or the Jewish immigrant's journey from peddler to retailer to department store magnate—tend to come to us poorly documented, devoid of statistical context and validated accounts of the circumstances and characteristics that differentiate starters from nonstarters and the achievers from the failures.

Another staple of immigrant enterprise is that their establishments are predominantly or exclusively co-ethnic.[23] A diamond-cutting shop or electronics emporium is typically a hierarchy of co-ethnics, from proprietor to shipping clerk. The same is true of Chinese- and Dominican-owned garment factories.[24] Present owners serve as their kinsmen's employers and mentors, advancing them to higher skills and preparing the ambitious for ventures into businesses of their own. Much of the investment capital and trade credit for start-up enterprises are also obtained from ethnic pools and banks as well as from individual savings. Once established, however, and willing and able to furnish verifiable financial statements, few immigrants lack access to conventional banking institutions, though many, for reasons of comfort and convenience, cling to familiar associations.

Chinese, while better represented in the professions than are the Koreans, share the latter's extraordinary bent for entrepreneurship. To be sure, the fabled neighborhood laundries are a vanishing

---

22. Illsoo Kim, *New Urban Immigrants: The Korean Community in New York* (Princeton: Princeton University Press, 1980), p. 123 ff.
23. In a Los Angeles study, it was found that 80 percent of employed Koreans worked in Korean-owned establishments. Ivan Light, "Immigrant Entrepreneurs in America: Koreans in Los Angeles," in Nathan Glazer (ed.), *Clamor at the Gates: The New American Immigration* (San Francisco: ICS Press, 1965), p. 162.
24. Roger Waldinger, "Immigration and Industrial Change in the New York Apparel Industry," in Marta Tienda and George Borjas (eds.), *Hispanics in the U.S. Economy* (New York: Academic Press, 1985).

breed. But their other stereotypic specialty, neighborhood restaurants offering ever-more variegated regional cuisines, are still expanding (though not in Chinatown, where soaring rents and property prices have forced some to give way to commercial uses.) It is a rare locale without one or more Chinese eating places boasting voluminous menus, even where, a generation ago, chop suey was thought an exotic dish. Despite a competitive profusion of Japanese and Mexican eating places, the metropolitan growth of Chinese restaurants seems to be constrained only by a shortage of Chinese help, who often have to be transported to and from the suburbs by private van. Chinese, too, have entered small-scale manufacturing, notably apparel, where Chinese female immigrants provide a productive, low-cost labor pool.[25] As will be seen later, the emergence of a considerable number of small garment factories was the proximate cause of Chinese settlement in Sunset Park. According to one source, restaurants and garment factories together accounted in 1985 for 50,000 Chinese workers.[26]

Hong Kong's uncertain political future encourages a steady flow of affluent Chinese possessing the requisite investment capital and experience to venture into a widening range of entrepreneurship. Thus, Chinese are becoming a recognized presence in trade, banking, and real estate. Judging from outward appearances, New York's wholesaling and importing axis—Broadway between Union Square and Herald Square—has been transferred from largely Jewish to largely Chinese, Korean, and other Asian hands. In Chinatown and Flushing, Chinese bankers vie with Chase and Citibank in resourcefulness if not in resources, providing special accommodation to co-ethnics (it is a virtual certainty that Sunset Park's Chinese enclave will sooner or later have a branch). In real estate, many have graduated from a speculator's role into that of developer and builder, at first in Chinatown and Flushing but now everywhere. In Sunset Park, where Chinese speculators ply a busy trade (Chapter 7), the successful bidder for the reconstruction of City-owned apartment property is a Chinese developer, a first in that area's housing program. Poorer entrepreneurially inclined Chinese immigrants, lacking money for an establishment of their own, hawk food and wares on the sidewalks, sometimes before or after a shift as waiter or busboy. Chinatown's

25. Roger Waldinger, *Through the Eye of the Needle: Immigrants and Enterprise in New York's Garment Trade* (New York: New York University Press, 1986).
26. Bernard Wong, "The Chinese," in Foner, *op. cit.*, p. 225.

streets in the daytime or early evening resemble more an Asian city than a tourist haunt.

Like Chinese, large numbers of Indians and Pakistani, who arrive with above-average educational preparation, are drawn toward the professions. They are also prominent in small business and retailing. Indian and Pakistani groceries and small restaurants are proliferating, as well as sari and spice shops and similar ethnic specialties. They are also prominent operators of the City's larger newsstands, major concessionaires of the Metropolitan Transit Authority, the Long Island Rail Road, and City-leased sidewalk kiosks. From newsstands, they are expanding into greeting card and stationery shops.

Many non-Asians are likewise determined micro-capitalists. Caribbean and Central American Hispanics have captured a large portion of the metropolitan home improvement, house-cleaning, and lawn-care service industries. An overwhelming proportion of the 30,000 self-employed drivers of New York's 11,700 medallion taxis are immigrants. A survey of applicants for the training course preparatory to a taxi-driver's license indicated that 73 percent were foreign-born, originating in 82 countries. Haitians were by far the most numerous, followed by Dominicans, Africans, and Middle Easterners.[27] They are replacing Israelis and Soviet émigrés, who had in turn replaced an aging generation of (largely) Jewish drivers since retired on the proceeds of high-priced medallions. The incidence of immigrants as owner-drivers of the 30,000 or more non-medallion taxis is reported to be even higher, with West Indians and Haitians predominating.[28]

In addition to small garment factories, Dominicans are acquiring (frequently from Puerto Ricans) the bodegas and service and repair shops in Hispanic neighborhoods, a trend observable in Sunset Park (Chapter 7). And proprietors from every ethnic group operate the driving schools, beauty parlors, and travel and real estate offices that cater to their compatriots. Greeks and Italians are prevalent in food vending, notably pizza counters and fast-service establishments that are often steppingstones to the ownership of full-service restaurants.

At the "penny capital" end of the entrepreneurial chain is the

---

27. Anne G. Morris, "Taxi School: A First Step in Professionalizing Taxi Driving," unpublished report, Center for Logistics and Transportation, City University of New York, 1986. Under current industry practices, the majority of drivers are self-employed, leasing medallion vehicles for a fixed fee.
28. Cf. Elizabeth A. Roistacher, "The New York City Taxi Industry: What Price Medallions," *City Almanac* (New York: J. M. Kaplan Center for New York City Affairs of the New School for Social Research, 1988), Vol. 20, No. 3, p. 7.

street peddler. Though not at the density of Chinatown's Canal Street, New Immigrants are converting the sidewalks of New York into a Third World bazaar, an open-air mall of watches and bijouterie, toys, flowers, and incense. By what miracle there appears, at the first drop of rain, a legion of umbrella vendors, only heaven knows. Also on the peddlers' stands is "brand name" merchandise with logos of doubtful provenance—handbags, calculators and cassettes, and sports shirts emblazoned with that celebrated crocodile, taken at face value only by the incurably gullible.

The new entrepreneurs are remarkably industrious. As had earlier generations of immigrant proprietors, they toil exceedingly long days and weeks, though perhaps not as frequently into the late night as the Jewish candy store owner or German delicatessen owner in an era less riddled by crime and possessed of an unlimited supply of retail help.[29]

## WAGE AND SALARY EMPLOYMENT

The wage and salary jobs of New Immigrants are likewise ethnically differentiated. Immigrants, as ever in history, are disproportionately represented in manufacturing and the lower echelons of the service industries (Table 3–6). New York's garment manufacturing is becoming once again an industry of immigrants, with Chinese and Hispanic women the predominant labor supply. In 1980, 36 percent of those employed in New York City in apparel manufacturing were post-1965 foreigners. A group of male immigrants from one locale in Greece have made a place for themselves in fur manufacturing. In eating and drinking places, a category that spans the immensity from Burger Kings to the Four Seasons, New Immigrants accounted for 33 percent of all workers. In hotels and motels, the figure was nearly 31 percent.

---

29. A study of retail stores in Jackson Heights found that 54.8 percent of the Korean establishments were open on Sunday as were 47.6 percent of the Hispanic stores compared to 35.4 percent of white-owned stores. Roger Waldinger, "Immigrant Enterprise: A New Test of Competing Theories," Symposium on Hispanic Enterprise, Arizona State University, April 3, 1987. National data on ethnic differences in small-business working hours are reported by the U.S. Bureau of the Census, 1982 (Washington, D.C.: Superintendent of Documents, U.S. Government Printing Office, August 1987), pp. 50–51. See also the findings in the retail survey of Sunset Park (Chapter 7 and Appendix E).

TABLE 3–6
New York City Industries with Concentrations of New Immigrants, 1980*

| Industry | Total Employed | Post-1965 Immigrants Employed | Total Employed |
|---|---|---|---|
| Total for all industries | 2,897,880 | 492,760 | 17.0 |
| Apparel manufacturing | 118,540 | 42,760 | 36.1 |
| Hospitals | 185,820 | 41,660 | 22.4 |
| Eating and drinking establishments | 110,640 | 36,820 | 33.3 |
| Banking | 125,320 | 21,540 | 17.2 |
| Construction | 77,960 | 15,120 | 19.4 |
| Real estate and building management | 71,660 | 11,540 | 16.1 |
| Private households | 30,620 | 11,520 | 37.6 |
| Nursing facilities | 30,960 | 9,820 | 31.7 |
| Miscellaneous manufacturing | 32,080 | 9,520 | 29.7 |
| Grocery stores | 47,040 | 8,920 | 19.0 |
| Insurance | 76,980 | 8,720 | 11.3 |
| Motels and hotels | 25,420 | 7,860 | 30.9 |
| Printing and publishing | 74,820 | 7,760 | 10.4 |
| Total, 13 industries | 1,007,320 | 233,560 | 23.2 |
| All other industries | 1,890,560 | 259,200 | 13.7 |

Source: Elizabeth Bogen, op. cit., p. 85, derived from 1980 Census, U.S. Public Use Microdata File.
* In rank order by number of post-1965 immigrants employed.

## BENEFITS AND COSTS

A preponderance of research indicates that the New Immigration has conferred a substantial net benefit on New York, the undisputed gains overbalancing the undisputed costs.[30] One is their sheer numbers. Thomas Muller has estimated that without the presence of the new foreigners, the City's population would have shrunk to below 6 million.[31] In a New York of 6 million, much of Brooklyn, Queens, and the Bronx would resemble deserted villages. It is noteworthy that urban centers such as Cleveland, Pittsburgh, Buffalo, and a score of others that had not been major catchment areas for immigrants have all continued to lose people.

30. Bogen, op. cit., p. 9.
31. Muller, op. cit.

To the labor force and the economy, the New Immigrants have brought not just their numbers and aspirations but their skills as well. Though most are disadvantaged in one respect or another, generally speaking, they enter better prepared than did the pre-1924 immigrant waves. Since educational standards have risen in most of the sending countries, higher proportions bring job skills or are at least job-ready. Most new Asians are not the land toilers of the past. South Korea has a higher rate of literacy and college enrollment than does the United States. The average schooling levels of all foreign-born Asian groups—with the notable exception of rural Vietnamese—exceed the average for non-Hispanic whites.[32] Contrast, too, the Russian newcomers of recent years with their counterparts a century ago; today's settlers come from large cities, have high school or advanced diplomas, and bring children proficient in math and science (many also in English and all in rock music). The earlier immigrants came from small shtetls, the males with little more than a religious education, most women and girls without even that.

Third World physicians dominate the City's hospitals (including Sunset Park's principal medical center), psychiatric wards, nursing homes, and any number of poverty areas abandoned by American doctors. Chinese and Asian professionals increasingly populate architectural and engineering offices, laboratories, pharmacies, and similar technical workplaces.

Philippine and West Indian women are extensively employed in hospitals and health care. The bottom of the service sector—home care and household domestics—depends heavily on Caribbean and Central American female immigrants, many of them doubtless undocumented.

The infusion of new residents with a profusion of skills at every level challenges the validity of the "labor mismatch" thesis, namely, that the declining educational attainments of New York's youth in the face of steadily higher job qualifications will be destructive of the City's economy. That gloomy thesis contains large grains of truth, but obviously not its full measure. The unprecedented rise in private employment indicates that employees have been able to surmount labor-supply difficulties, though not in every sector or occupation. The concept does not allow sufficiently for the fact that a local labor pool draws from many sources other than local high schools. The foreign-born are apparently filling the technical and skilled jobs be-

---

32. U.S. Commission on Civil Rights, "The Economic Status of Americans of Asian Descent" (mimeo), June 1988, p. 10.

yond the reach of the high school dropout and undereducated locals. The computer rooms and teller windows of business and financial establishments draw heavily from the newcomers. And while New York is, on net balance, still losing white population, the entry of large numbers of young native-born careerists has narrowed the balance.[33]

Without that huge influx of human capital, the pessimists might have won the day. But, whatever the residual skill deficits and other imperfections in the labor supply, there is obviously a sturdy job market in which supply adjusts tolerably well to demand. Notwithstanding the existence of the hard-to-employ, a mass of employables has provided sufficient numbers, versatility, and productivity to support a thriving economy. Average weekly earnings have risen substantially more than in the nation as a whole. Approximately 400,000 more people are now employed than a decade ago, of whom 200,000 are City residents. That is scarcely the performance of a failed labor force.

The foreign-born have also been a prop for New York's faltering subways. To the New Immigrants as to the old, the subways are a lifeline, heavily utilized not only for the journey to work but for all other trips as well. Though it seems to have gone unnoticed, it is no coincidence that subway ridership began its recovery during the years of recent immigration. Traffic on the New York subway system had been on a free fall since 1947, the annual totals dropping by more than half from 2 billion to less than 1 billion. Between 1977 and 1988, despite repeated fare increases and a disastrous decline in quality of service, the annual turnstile count increased by more than 7 million and is still going up. The bulk of the increase is accounted for by subway lines and stations proximate to immigrant concentrations, such as the Jackson Heights stations on the No. 7 line in Queens and

---

33. One must leave for another occasion an account of how effectively New York's labor force has also been enhanced by its ambitious young strivers. The obligatory word is yuppies; a recent runner-up is dinkys, double-income-no-kids-yet. Both terms and their variants are straight pop sociology; given the infinite variety of the generational cohort, they obscure more than they inform. But because they are now so ingrained as shorthand description, they will be used here without further apology.

Yuppies and dinkys, both the locally grown or the migrants from other regions, are a traditional component of New York's work force. Their numbers as well as their opportunities seem to have increased relative to decades just past. New York's economy has gained from these young careerists who are drawn here from the nation's top universities, and who reinforce the City's primacy as a financial and business center.

the Eighth Avenue station on Sunset park's N line that serves the Asian newcomers.

The newcomers have also repopulated a shrinking public school system. There are, and will continue to be, heavy costs in absorbing those enrollments. But against those costs are innumerable positive outcomes as well. The good discipline and classroom performance of scores of thousands of young immigrant children are generally acknowledged. Many, because of aptness and motivation, gladden the hearts of teachers. After they overcome the language barrier, even the children of the poorest and least-educated Indochinese refugees soon attain the performance levels of other Asians. Muller states:

> The perception that immigrant children in schools are considered a benefit is shown in surveys. When parents in the Washington, D.C., area were asked whether these students have helped or hurt the school their child is attending, 39 percent responded that they improved the school, and only five percent indicated a negative impact. Three out of five of those polled had a preference that their children attend a school with some children of immigrants. Only four percent said they would prefer a school with no immigrants, the same percentage that expressed a preference for a school where most students are foreign born. It is important to note that only about half of the new immigrants in the Washington area are Asian. These results suggest that immigrant children in general are thought to improve the school system.[34]

In New York's schools where the immigrant enrollment is considerably more Hispanic than Asian, the verdict is not quite as favorable as Washington's. As the 164,000 children enrolled in the special-language program attest (Table 3–7), the New Immigration thrusts a major pedagogical burden upon the City's public schools, already staggering under the weight of the educational problems of the indigenous poor and underclass youth. But few principals believe that their schools would now be better off without the new children, and many have publicly declared their delight in having them. Some believe that the upward drift in test scores of recent years is in large part attributable to immigrant children. The fact that the math scores seem to have risen more than reading scores may indicate the presence of children whose minds can more readily grasp the universal language of numbers than an unfamiliar tongue.

The City University of New York has once again become the "im-

34. Muller, *op. cit.*

**ABLE 3–7**
**irthplace of Children Enrolled in Special Language Programs,**
**lew York City Public Schools, 1987**

| ountry | | Country | | Country | |
|---|---|---|---|---|---|
| fghanistan | 538 | Ghana | 64 | Panama | 612 |
| lbania | 30 | Greece | 449 | Papua New Guinea | 50 |
| rgentina | 234 | Guatemala | 828 | Paraguay | 80 |
| angladesh | 228 | Guyana | 1,008 | Peru | 832 |
| elize | 26 | Haiti | 6,753 | Philippines | 282 |
| olivia | 128 | Honduras | 1,267 | Poland | 318 |
| razil | 161 | Hong Kong | 1,503 | Portugal | 96 |
| ritish Virgin Islands | 36 | Hungary | 53 | Puerto Rico | 20,690 |
| ritish West Indies | 35 | India | 1,104 | Romania | 423 |
| urma | 95 | Indonesia | 96 | Saudi Arabia | 42 |
| ambodia | 991 | Iran | 163 | Spain | 238 |
| anada | 99 | Israel | 777 | Sudan | 28 |
| hile | 143 | Italy | 711 | Syria | 32 |
| hina | 7,852 | Jamaica | 235 | Taiwan | 1,283 |
| olombia | 3,328 | Japan | 273 | Thailand | 219 |
| osta Rica | 142 | Jordan | 63 | Trinidad and Tobago | 56 |
| uba | 289 | Korea | 2,742 | Turkey | 178 |
| ominican Republic | 16,702 | Laos | 57 | USSR | 543 |
| ominica | 33 | Lebanon | 89 | United Kingdom | 29 |
| cuador | 2,951 | Liberia | 64 | United States* | 70,451 |
| gypt | 186 | Macao | 28 | Uruguay | 55 |
| Salvador | 1,803 | Malaysia | 55 | Venezuela | 318 |
| hiopia | 59 | Mexico | 1,216 | Vietnam | 1,378 |
| ance | 75 | Nicaragua | 683 | Yemen | 198 |
| ench Guiana | 47 | Nigeria | 77 | Yugoslavia | 429 |
| ermany, West | 66 | Pakistan | 640 | | |

*urce:* Special Tabulation, Board of Education, Office of Educational Assessment.

*ote:* New York City's Special Language program serves children from a total of 148 countries, cluding those who are native-born Americans. We have eliminated those countries represented by wer than 25 children. Of the countries excluded, 51 comprised 10 children or fewer; 20 comprised tween 11 and 25 children.

*rimarily native-born children of foreign parents.

migrants' Harvard." Its engineering, business administration, and professional schools are Third World academies, as are their science and, increasingly, their social science departments. Thus, in education one sees the bimodality of outcomes earlier noted; foreigners contribute to both high rates of school dropouts and high rates of graduate degrees.

The newcomers' burden on public services other than schools is mixed. From the beginning of the New Immigration, in both the congressional hearings and floor debates, there was fearful testimony that poor immigrants would tax the nation's health and welfare services, imposing heavy costs on public budgets. A number of studies, however, have shown that immigrants tend to use public services less frequently than does the native population.[35] One reason is their higher work-participation rates. A second, some believe, is a reluctance to apply for public aid lest they be disqualified as a public charge in some subsequent application for citizenship.

Still other studies have indicated that the net fiscal contribution of the new foreigners is positive, that is, their taxes and Social Security deductions exceed the public costs imposed.[36] The same research, however, points out considerable variability in types of services and among types of immigrants. On the whole, refugees, who more often arrive penniless, impose higher costs than do regularly admitted immigrants; and among the latter, Asians have the least inclination to seek public assistance.

In New York, which tends to be more generous than other jurisdictions, registered aliens are eligible for all social services including cash grants for home relief; they have full access to health care and hospitals, housing, schools, libraries, and the like. The undocumented also have access to most public services, though not to cash grants.[37] Immigrants also add to certain administrative costs. City agencies that deal with the public need a battery of interpreters, not least the courts and hospitals where instant and accurate communication is vital.

Then, of course, there are the costs for police and the criminal justice system, in pursuit of transgressors with a foreign accent. Crime, someone said, is an equal opportunity employer. Even the champions of the New Immigrants will freely concede that many operate deep in the underground economy, a choice made also by prior generations of foreigners. The Dominican drug dealers of Washington Heights and the Caribbean auto chop shops in every borough bespeak the temptations of twisted pathways to status and affluence.

---

35. Leif Jensen, "Patterns of Immigration and Public Assistance Utilization, 1978–1985," *International Immigration Review*, Spring 1985, pp. 51–83. See also Marta Tienda and Leif Jensen, "Immigration and Social Service Participation: Dispelling the Myth of Dependency," *Social Science Quarterly*, Vol. 67-1, pp. 3–20.

36. Muller, *op. cit.*

37. For a good discussion of how immigrants use New York City public services and of the taxes they pay, see Bogen, *op. cit.*, Chapter 9.

It is not possible, though, to measure the extent to which immigrant crime is incremental or substitutive; as with legal labor markets, it is probably some of both. Apparently the Italian Mafia has ceded some franchises to Chinese and Hispanics just as they had earlier pre-empted some from the Irish and Jews. But it would be folly to wear blinders. Absent the New Immigration, only the naive would believe that New York's vast and ever-proliferating drug "economy" (second only to Miami's, where drug-trafficking is likewise a prime immigrant specialty) would be at today's scale. One must frankly acknowledge that part of the money that helped revive the City's housing stock and retail streets was derived from employment that escapes the notice of the Bureau of Labor Statistics and from income that escapes the notice of the Census Bureau and Internal Revenue Service.

A nonbudgeted cost stems from the tensions of clashing life-styles. The host population is as wary of cultural inundation as foreigners are of cultural contamination. The indigenous may resent the blasting radios, the added street litter, the indecipherable store signs, and the overcrowded dwelling units. Asians, Russian Jews, and Middle East-erners worry that their children will become "badly" Americanized, tempted by premature sex or drugs and other vices that can deflect them from educational pursuits.

For all that, anti-immigrant bigotry is a good deal more subdued in New York than elsewhere in the region and nation, and bears utterly no resemblance to the violent communal strife in other parts of the world. Nonetheless, ethnic frictions are scarcely unknown here. Among the more publicized are episodic boycotts of Korean retailers in black neighborhoods, who seldom live there or employ local youth. Koreans, in turn, speak their fears and anger regarding theft, vandalism, and personal assault. In 1988, unidentified residents of Bensonhurst distributed a hostile leaflet warning against the conse-quences of Asian entry. In Sunset Park some long-established retail-ers make no secret of their displeasure over the lower prices and longer hours of competing Chinese stores. But so far such sentiments have not had serious overt consequences, though ethnic defense organizations like the Chinese-American Planning Council maintain a hotline to ward off impending conflicts and to defuse those that occur.

The attitudes of New Yorkers toward the New Immigrants range across the spectrum from affirmative hospitality to indifference to explicit rancor. Usually, ethnic antipathies are limited to hard looks and words. At other times they may be expressed by exit: The middle class relinquishes to the newcomers the schools, housing, churches, and local institutions. The surrender may be grudging and contested. Or it may be willing, even eager, as exemplified by the sales of homes at good prices to upwardly mobile immigrants, transactions observable throughout Brooklyn, including Sunset Park.

For whatever reason, the City's New Immigrants have not provoked anything like the clashes between whites and native-born blacks that periodically scarred New York's social history and that episodically still flare up, most conspicuously in Howard Beach and Bensonhurst. Most of the officially recorded intergroup incidents in New York in 1988 were between whites and native-born blacks or desecrations of Jewish cemeteries and synagogues rather than against immigrant populations as such.[38] Certainly, nothing resembling a "Stop Immigration" movement has surfaced in New York as occasionally appears elsewhere in the country. The strength of New York's economy has so far blunted one traditional source of friction—competition for jobs. That problem could erupt in some leaner future. Recall, however, that it did not arise during New York's years of high unemployment in the seventies and early eighties despite the entry by then of more than a million immigrants.

If anything, judging from the ceaseless quest for nurses, foreign-language teachers, retail clerks, chefs, and domestic help, more rather than fewer immigrants would be welcome both in the City and the nation. The Port Authority labor survey cited earlier forthrightly acknowledged that the New York region cannot "grow" a sufficient labor force and must look to migration if the economy is to remain vigorous. It is generally agreed that as the baby boomers age the United States will not be able to enjoy further economic growth without substantial infusions of labor from abroad. Muller concludes his comprehensive study of the economic consequences of the New Immigration with a recommendation that, because of labor market needs, legal admissions to the country should be raised from the current level of about 600,000 per year to 2 million.[39]

Legislation introduced in the Senate and House since 1988 would add upward of 100,000 per year to present statutory quotas and more than half again for additional refugees. Thus, immigration is more likely to increase than not, indicating that congressmen, highly attuned to the public will, do not discern a strong groundswell for restriction. That would hardly be the case were there not a belief that the New Immigration, on net balance, is serving the public weal.

---

38. From unpublished data provided by the Police Department's Bias Incident Investigating Unit, September 1, 1988.
39. Muller, *op. cit.*

# CHAPTER 4

# Other Factors
# in Neighborhood Revival:
# Economic Boom,
# Housing Shortage,
# Community Organization

## NEW YORK'S RESURGENT ECONOMY

A major contributor to neighborhood restoration was the stunning rebound in New York's economy. It was accompanied by an unprecedented increase in private employment, rising real income, and a modest gain in population and households. One should caution that good times do not inevitably generate neighborhood revival. Indeed, they may have an opposite effect, witness the pervasive decline of New York's neighborhoods during the long period of economic growth in the sixties. That prosperous era nourished the new suburban communities in New York's metropolitan ring (and the Sunbelt), not the older neighborhoods of the inner rings. What is exceptional about the recent boom is that the housing markets of both the core and the environs have simultaneously flourished, something true across most of the Northeast region.

From its nadir in the mid-seventies, New York's economy made a spectacular return, recapturing after the mid-eighties nearly all of the lost ground and, in key sectors, breaking through to new heights. Though Tokyo and London nip at its heels, Manhattan remains the capital of an expanding global commercial and financial system, a gigantic centrifugal pump spewing jobs, purchasing power, and housing demanders into every part of the metropolitan area. New York's recovery—its economy and its morale—was all the more grati-

**TABLE 4–1**
**Selected Economic Indicators, New York City, 1976 and 1986**

|  | 1976 | 1986 | Percent Change |
|---|---|---|---|
| Payroll employment (thousands)[a] | 3,210 | 3,539 | +10.2% |
| Unemployment rate (percent) | 9.6[b] | 4.5 | −53.2 |
| Assessed values of taxable |  |  |  |
| real estate (billions)[c] | 39.7 | 52.6 | +32.5 |
| Retail sales (billions)[d] | 26.5[b] | 33.9 | +27.9 |
|  |  |  |  |
| Taxes (millions of dollars)[d] |  |  |  |
| Real estate | $2,967 | $4,600 | +55.0 |
| Sales | 828 | 1,909 | +130.6 |
| Personal income and earnings | 592 | 1,816 | +207.8 |
| Business taxes | 920 | 1,914 | +108.08 |

Source: New York City Department of Finance.
[a] 1982.
[b] Calendar year.
[c] Fiscal year ending June 30.
[d] General corporation; financial corporation; unincorporated business; commercial rent.

fying because it was so little expected. It confounded the skeptics who, a short decade ago, confidently declared that New York's future was to have no future. Few in 1975 spied the phoenix amid the ashes.

*New York Ascendant* is the triumphant title of a 1987 report of the Commission on the Year 2000. The commission's buoyancy was affirmed by extraordinary improvements in virtually every statistical indicator—employment, wages and earnings, per capita real income, retail sales, tourism, hotel occupancy, commercial construction, assessed values, municipal tax revenues (Table 4–1). The report was issued shortly before the stock market crash of October 19. But the dampening effects, though evident, have not proved significant; jobs in the financial sector went down but aggregate employment continued to grow before stabilizing in 1989.

## THE CITY'S REGAINED POPULARITY

By 1988, the visual evidence of New York's decade-long renaissance was as telling as the statistical. What struck the eye was a dense skyscape of new office and apartment towers in Manhattan, river to river, Battery to 96th Street: if New York had an official bird, it would be the crane. What struck all the senses was New York's recharged street life, masses of people enjoying masses of people; a half-million more individuals entered the Central Business District each day than a decade ago. And they seemed less in a hurry to leave: Both the happy hours in the taverns and the evening rush hours on trains and bridges stretched longer into the evening.

The teeming out-of-doors was reflected in a kaleidoscope of street scenes—a reanimated Central Park, wall-to-wall crowds at the Trump Tower, the Fifth Avenue Library, the South Street Seaport, and Battery Park City; hordes of tourists checking in and out of hotels, a profusion of amiable block fairs, a sprawl of al fresco lunchers in every office plaza and public space, street musicians, and sidewalk cafés. Broadway was relighted and so was off Broadway. The proliferation of small dance companies and art galleries appeared to be limited only by high rents and a shortage of space. Equally conspicuous were the exuberant shopping corridors—downtown, the Nassau Street mall by weekday and SoHo by weekend; uptown, the glitz of Columbus Avenue and the ritz of Madison Avenue; and, in between, the inexhaustible enticements of Fifth Avenue.

Thus, to understand the revival of New York's neighborhoods one must look beyond the measurable indexes of employment, income, and retail sales. One has also to pay heed to an elusive but momentous factor—a reglorification of the cosmopolitan cities. In places like Boston, San Francisco and, of course, New York, middle-class out-migration rates have fallen and in-migration rates have risen. Every one of Manhattan's private universities has enjoyed a swelling flood of young applicants, a trend not entirely attributable to their academic luster. New York's profuse street life and the magnetic pull of its urban delights testify to a significant attitudinal change, a reattachment some would date back to the Tall Ships of 1976. That mood had eroded in the fifties and sixties. One recalls the cover of a national magazine with a confected picture of grass sprouting in Manhattan's core.

The Big Apple had once again become a desirable living experience. Without that rekindling of affection, one would be hard put to explain the extraordinary sacrifices of money and housing standards that residents endure to be at the core, in Manhattan preferably, but if not, as close as possible. To many of the young, a tiny hovel on the Lower East Side is preferable despite a monthly rent that would easily pay for a spacious two-bedroom apartment in Queens or a three-bedroom duplex in Sunset Park. For all that, center-city housing demand vastly exceeds supply at rents within the range of New York's income levels. The uplift of Brooklyn and Queens, of Hoboken and Jersey City, is in large part a consequence of market realities, the compromises of frustrated would-be Manhattanites driven to second and third choices.

## NEW YORK'S DARK SIDE

The renewed appetite for New York City residence was not curbed by the City's undisputed disadvantages. If the Sunset Parks shared New York City's refound health, they also shared its concurrent illnesses. As counterpoise to its cheer, the Commission on the Year 2000 reported—candidly and poignantly—that New York was also a badly wounded city and that not all of its wounds would be soon cured. The City's malaise is reflected in innumerable environmental defects and, worse, a weakening social order. As is discussed at some length in Chapter 7, Sunset Park's resurrection is diminished, as is New York's, by interminable lags in the restoration of a long-neglected infrastructure, especially a malfunctioning subway system, a crowded, obsolescent school plant, pitted streets, antediluvian water mains that periodically turn diluvian.

More ominous, by far, than the failings in infrastructure is the deepening shadow of a hard-core underclass. Its consequences have spared few neighborhoods, certainly not Sunset Park. Rates of school dropout, teenage pregnancy, and long-term welfare dependency continue dismayingly high. After a few years of what seemed like a subsidence in drug abuse and a steady decrease in crime rates, there was a sudden recrudescence of addiction. Added to the insidious poison of heroin (the principal factor in the spread of AIDS) was the explosive power of crack.[40] Homicide rates went sharply up by 1989, headed for a new record. Drug-felony arrests once again multiplied, from 5,000 in 1985 to more than thrice that in 1987. Drug-related crime, on a steep growth curve, adds new recruits each year. The proportion of felons convicted for the first time of drug-related crimes

---

40. Between 1974 and 1986, among convicted felons who were under the influence of drugs at the time of their arrest, the use of cocaine (increasingly in the form of crack) multiplied tenfold while the use of heroin declined. Crack has now overtaken heroin among the users of hard drugs. Bureau of Justice Statistics, "Drug Use and Crime," July 1988, p. 2.

steadily grows and so does the geographical spread. Most neighbor-hoods are within easy proximity to a more or less organized drug distribution system, and some have become major wholesale and retail markets. That is now the case in many or most public housing projects, notwithstanding the vigilance of what is, arguably, the nation's strictest housing authority.

The fact that such thick and threatening clouds did not obliterate the luster of New York's renaissance was testimony to the strength of the recuperative forces. But the balance of light and dark may be shifting: No one can foretell whether the degenerative forces may not in the end defeat the progenerative economic forces, already weakening. The rampant contagion of crack, a substance whose addictive potency per dollar of cost is beyond compare and whose pharmacological properties are less well known than are its frightful consequences, looms as a greater danger than anything experienced during the juvenile "crime and delinquency" era of the fifties and sixties when marijuana, angel dust, and heroin agitated the big cities. Sunset Park, too, has learned to fear crack. As later discussed, a reinforced narcotics squad is now its leading priority.

## THE HOUSING SHORTAGE

The Commission on the Year 2000 pointed to yet another egregious weakness: a chronic and worsening shortage of affordable housing. Its most brutal manifestation is homelessness—the hotel families and the pavement dwellers. But they are merely the visible tip of a submerged mass of housing stresses and dissatisfactions. Paradoxically, that housing shortage, for all its dislocations, has also conferred a pervasive benefit: It is the proximate cause of community revival, as will be elaborated below.

The volume of house building in New York has fallen to levels reminiscent of the Great Depression. New dwelling units completed, which averaged 32,300 per year in the fifties and 34,700 in the sixties, declined to 16,570 in the seventies. Over the first half of the eighties, the average tumbled to 8,500.[41] Stimulated by heavy subsidies, the figures have improved only modestly since. In 1989 no one believed that improvement would last. The precipitous decline in the output of

---

41. New York City Department of City Planning, "New Housing in New York City 1985," November 1986, p. 15.

affordable housing has greatly exacerbated the shortage and virtually guarantees its perpetuation.

The fall in the market for new housing has a longer list of explanations than remedies. Foremost is a merciless escalation in the price of unsubsidized new housing, driven by secular trends in land and labor costs, a dense web of mandated regulations, and the high real price of mortgage capital. In New York City, the development cost of a square foot of new housing is at vertiginous heights, having risen far faster than household income. Nor is there any sign that public policy is able to do much to bring it down. Indeed, whatever their justification, public interventions—zoning and historic landmarking, Byzantine administrative procedures, and hardening rules governing the standards of structures and materials—are all formulas for higher costs. The exceedingly high costs of new unsubsidized apartments have drastically narrowed their market. The collapse of private unsubsidized construction represents a failure of demand, not supply. Developers would gladly produce more. But they cannot build—or finance—any more than will be bought or rented. Judging from expensive advertising, desperate promotions, and lengthening absorption periods, there is a surplus rather than a shortage of market-rate housing.

To comprehend the deterrent effects of soaring construction costs on housing demand, two related but distinguishable factors must be considered. One is the cost of new housing relative to income; the other is the cost of new housing relative to its nearest substitute, which is existing housing. It is the first factor that dominates the familiar "affordability" issue. New housing, which many decades ago was within the reach of the working class, is increasingly beyond the reach of the middle class, even its upper range. Because of "income-bracket creep" (i.e., the tendency for prices and rents of new housing to rise faster than income), public-policy makers have been compelled to expand eligibility limits for subsidized housing. Programs once confined to families in the middle third of the income distribution now extend to the top quintile, even higher. At the same time, the monthly burden for new occupants has multiplied. In the sixties, rent-income ratios of 12 to 16 percent were the rule in middle-income programs. The ratios are now 30 percent for all units covered by public programs.

Seldom considered is a second market deterrent, namely, the price of new housing relative to its nearest alternative—existing housing. Because of the various systems of rent and occupancy regulations that govern New York's existing housing stock,[42] the gap in rents and prices between the new and the old is at an all-time high. To hark back to an earlier era, the monthly costs of the small homes and Federal Housing Administration (FHA) apartments erected in New York City and its environs during the building surge of the first two postwar decades were usually not much more than 50 to 75 percent above the prevailing average for existing units. Currently, the differential for a new unsubsidized two-bedroom apartment compared to a regulated one is in the 400 to 500 percent range, even in Brooklyn or Queens.

Because of the enormous premium for "newness," the new-housing market is doubly squeezed. The market dropouts are not solely those who lack means but also those who do not. Consumers do not buy a product merely because they can afford to. They have also to want to. Affluent occupants who rent more or less satisfactory older units have far less reason than their pre–rent control counterparts to become customers for new housing; the jump in costs is simply too great compared to the increment in space and quality (if any). Thus, compounding the affordability factor is the rejectability factor. That is the basic reason why the turnover rate in the existing rental inventory has plunged precipitously, dragging vacancy rates down with it and generating a fierce competition for the relatively few affordable units that become accessible.

These dismal market circumstances are likely to prevail indefinitely. That is so because public policy in New York seeks to reduce the price gap between new and existing housing neither by allowing the price of the old to rise (e.g., rent deregulation or, more gradually, vacancy decontrol) nor by driving down the costs of the new. Virtually the sole gap-closing instrument of housing policy is an array of subsidy programs that redistribute costs from occupants to public budgets. But subsidy resources are chronically in short supply and would be so even if the current federal retrenchment is mitigated. The City's own subsidy programs are extraordinarily expensive (ranging up to $100,000 per unit in the case of low-income occupants). They are also perennially beset by divisive controversies over target populations, site selection, and building densities. It is not surprising that

---

42. That stock of 1.6 million units, well over one-half of New York's total housing inventory, consists of 1.2 million rent-controlled and rent-stabilized private rental units, plus 400,000 units of public housing, Mitchell-Lama, and Redevelopment Company rental and cooperative apartments.

in the City's announced ten-year program of 250,000 low- and moder-ate-income units, the new-construction goal is only 6,000 units per year; few cognoscenti believe that even that target will be hit. For these reasons, too, giant projects like Starrett City and Co-op City in the outer boroughs and Stuyvesant Town, Penn Station South, and Morningside Gardens in Manhattan seem a thing of the past; certainly none has been built recently, excepting Brownsville's Nehemiah project, a deeply subsidized development on a site too wasted to be fought over. Unlike prior eras in New York's housing history, there is trifling prospect of a mass building boom.

## RECYCLED HOUSING, RECYCLED NEIGHBORHOODS

The limping supply of new housing measured against ten years of gains in households and employment created a profound disequilib-rium. Inevitably, the burgeoning demand was deflected to existing housing. Almost all who searched for affordable housing had to find it within an existing, rejuvenating inventory erected by prior genera-tions of builders in now mature neighborhoods. That circumstance has had the utmost consequences for the older stock. It stimulated a widespread preservation and rehabilitation movement: the extensive reconstruction of ancient brownstones and apartment buildings; ex-pansion of one-family homes into two-family and two- into three-family; the conversion into housing of such nonresidential structures as lofts and other industrial buildings, shops, and garages. Even roof-tops were not overlooked. In prime market areas, old buildings were crowned with expensive new penthouses. In recent years, additional housing demand has been accommodated by the recycling of older structures at a rate twice that of new construction.[43]

The intensified demand for older housing resulted, willy-nilly, in an intensified demand for older neighborhoods. The failure of new construction has thus been a critical, if unacknowledged, stimulus for the revitalization of New York's stricken neighborhoods. The bright

---

43. Though to a lesser extent than in New York, the rising real costs of new construc-tion have had similar consequences throughout the United States. According to the Joint Center for Housing Studies at Harvard University, national expenditures on residential improvements and remodeling are a steadily rising fraction of total residen-tial investment outlays; they are now approaching one-half, compared to one-tenth in the earlier part of the century.

side of the Law of Unintended Consequences once again revealed itself. That remark is meant as irony, not cynicism. No one would responsibly propose the suppression of new construction as a rational way of renewing declining neighborhoods. New housing, too, has a valuable role in any policy for neighborhood revival. It serves segments of housing demand not readily accommodated in recycled buildings, replaces hopelessly blighted eyesores, and adds to the net supply. As a matter of fact, most of the small quantity of new housing built in recent years has been on infill sites in mature neighborhoods (though not, in every case, to the latter's delectation). Still, a pervasive benefit is not to be spurned because it is the unexpected outcome of adverse trends in housing costs or flawed policies, laws and regulations that contribute to deficits in the housing supply.

## RISING DOMINOES

The relentless demand for housing in settled neighborhoods touched off a remarkable geographic sequence. As successive cohorts of unlucky housing demanders failed to find affordable accommodations in the choicer neighborhoods of Manhattan, they swooped down upon the less choice, descending step by step the gradient of market preference. The tide of housing demand swept north from Lincoln Center (itself not so many decades ago a decidedly unchoice neighborhood) to Upper Broadway to Morningside Heights, to Manhattan Valley, from Chelsea and Greenwich Village east to Union Square and Alphabet City, from SoHo to Tribeca. It crossed the river from Manhattan to Brooklyn, a generation ago to Brooklyn Heights, then afterwards to Cobble Hill, Carroll Gardens, and Park Slope, then to Boerum Hill, Flatbush, Prospect Heights, Fort Greene, and Greenpoint. On its southward sweep through Brooklyn, the tide rolled over Sunset Park. To switch metaphors, a reverse domino game was in play. Each area's uplift became the lever that uplifted a more affordable neighbor, the mirror image of the process by which New York's neighborhoods fell.

The progressive, demand-driven revaluation of New York's housing submarkets has not yet run its full course; it continues to spill over into hitherto neglected neighborhoods, even those once deemed moribund (e.g., South Williamsburgh and Bushwick and even sections of Brownsville and the South Bronx). The elevation of bypassed areas was evidenced by rising property prices and by their return to the classified pages and brokers' listings. It was directly observed at the periodic auction sales of City-owned real estate where demand meets supply, freely and openly. There, the bidding for property in downfallen neighborhoods, once muted, had become spirited. At successive auctions, the winning bids penetrated ever-higher levels, the crestfallen losing bidders matched by delighted City property-disposition staff.

So long as the City's economy remains tolerably healthy, even if below the peaks of recent years, and the number of households continues to rise (which seems likely), the foreseeable future should see, to one degree or another, virtually all the City's flattened dominoes upended. The exceptions will be the precincts of the underclass, and not every part of those.

An inevitable corollary of a persistent housing shortage is that there will be little reprieve from the mounting burden of displacement and homelessness, a tormenting problem that can be relieved only by the production of costly special dwellings, whose placement is furiously contested almost wherever proposed. A second corollary is a denser utilization of existing sites and structures. The sliver apartment buildings of Manhattan are perhaps the most publicized example of the overutilized site. One already sees in Brooklyn and Queens more and more three-story structures on two-story blocks, encouraged by new (and disputed) zoning regulations. The transformation of nonresidential buildings into residential space (the SoHo phenomenon), once confined to Manhattan, has spread throughout the metropolitan area. And there is more than a strong likelihood of increased sharing of dwelling units, that is, average household size may well rise in the future, reversing a long downward course. New York's Housing Authority reports a sizable volume of unauthorized doubling up, in perhaps as many as a third of their units; very large households are also a commonplace in New Immigrant enclaves where apartment subdivision, often prompted by the undocumented, is a local folk art. Since much doubling up is illegal and therefore clandestine, actual increases in household size may not be fully reflected in official surveys.

The nature of the housing shortage—its causes and consequences—is a devilishly complex subject, one that deserves more than the brief comments above. For assessing the causes and prospects of neighborhood revival, it suffices to say that an enduring shortage of moderate-price housing can be taken as a given.

## THE ROLE OF COMMUNITY ORGANIZATIONS

Still another factor in neighborhood comeback is organized community development. Grass-roots groups have labored strenuously to arrest the downward spiral of their neighborhoods. By rallying residents and by mustering public and private resources for targeted reconstruction programs, they provided a favorable setting though, one must quickly add, not the surety of revival. As decades of experience show, absent adequate levels of central-city housing demand of sufficient strength to spill over into less-preferred sites, community development, with occasional exceptions, can be a Sisyphean task of inch-by-inch gains and discouragingly large setbacks. In the weak big-city housing markets of the sixties and seventies, the national failure rate of subsidized housing, including those sponsored by local nonprofit groups, was staggering. By 1974, the Department of Housing and Urban Development (HUD) had acquired 364 multifamily projects through foreclosure and had been assigned the mortgages on another 1,798 projects. A total of 200,000 units, mostly subsidized, were thrown back into HUD's lap, exposing it to $2 billion in losses. Nonprofit organizations were well represented among the failed and failing. At that time, private foundations, including the Ford Foundation, were induced to set up rescue operations in New York, Boston, and the San Francisco area, which aided nonprofit housing sponsors in arranging workout plans. Foundations, together with HUD, also provided emergency relief to numerous community development corporations threatened by building foreclosures.

Faith and good works are seldom dependable substitutes for a robust housing market. Conversely, where strong housing markets returned, many declining neighborhoods staged comebacks without reliance on community development organizations other than in the paler version of local booster associations. A crucial role for effective organized community development is to foster a firmer market. By dint of persuasion and subsidy incentives, it induces responsible but hesitant residents to remain and encourages their counterparts to come in. Its second, perhaps more indispensable, role is to minimize the disruptions and inequities if and when housing reinvestment returns. By directing subsidy funds to poorer residents who might otherwise be displaced and by exacting concessions from private investors and services from public agencies, they soften the impact of "gentrification." In Sunset Park, for example, it is more than likely that the home ownership market would sooner or later have re-covered absent an organized community development movement. But, without the latter's intervention, it is unlikely that the commu-nity would have retained so large a base of poor families. As will be seen, it was largely the efforts of Sunset Park's community develop-ment organization that preserved and rehabilitated much of the low-rent apartment inventory that served low-income families (and still does). There were then (and are now) strong voices in Sunset Park that would cheer the departure of the poor.

# CHAPTER 5

# New People
# in Old Neighborhoods

The housing shortage in the New York area was reinforced by demographic factors—a large inflow of new people, mainly foreigners. Because of their very sizable numbers, the New Immigrants have reversed New York's drastic population decline of the seventies. Without them, it is estimated that, notwithstanding all the baby boomers, the City would now have no more than 6 million people.[44] So staggering a shrinkage would have been accompanied by further drains in most neighborhoods. Instead, the City's population increased from a little over 7 million in 1980 to 7.3 million (more likely 7.5 million) in 1987.

Outside the yuppie strongholds of Manhattan and other favored areas in Brooklyn and Queens, immigrants have been the leading factor in neighborhood revitalization. Owing to their high employment rates and multiple wage earners, the new foreigners have injected large doses of new purchasing power into the rehabilitation of an aging housing stock and the resurrection of inert retail streets. Their presence has been visible not only in the demand for housing

---

44. Muller, *op. cit.* Such calculations, of course, abstract from the interdependence of events. Immigrants and yuppies doubtless influenced each other's numbers since both have been significant to the growth of New York's economy. And, conversely, the economic expansion increased the flow of both groups.

but in the supply as well, displaying a willingness to undertake the disagreeable, if potentially profitable, tasks entailed in fixing up and managing decaying buildings. In great numbers, too, they have accepted the arduous hours (and the dangers) of operating small retail stores. Here and there, they have also restored the semblance of a long-absent night life, for example, Brooklyn's Brighton Beach and the Ironbound section in Newark.

In any number of derelict places once given up for lost, from the Bronx to Brooklyn and across the Hudson in the worn-out industrial cities of New Jersey, vital signs have reappeared along with the immigrants. Newark, trapped for decades in an apparently inexorable downward spiral, was widely viewed as a telltale of urban trends, as is New Hampshire's Dixville Notch of presidential elections. "Wherever cities are heading," grieved a former mayor, "Newark will get there first." The mayor's subtext was that his benighted city was fated for one triumph—a first in the race to the bottom. There is now evidence that Newark's descent has been arrested, if not yet halted. Writing ten years after the mayor's gloomy assessment, Thomas Muller, a leading analyst of urban immigration, noted:

> The Portuguese community in Newark, New Jersey, less than a dozen miles from midtown Manhattan, recalls the entry of European immigrants to the area in the late nineteenth century. These immigrants, predominantly from rural areas of northern Portugal, now occupy housing in neighborhoods where Irish railroad workers lived and attended churches a century ago. Most Portuguese immigrants came, legally or illegally, since the 1960s, and currently form two enclaves within the city. In the Ironbound section of Newark, an estimated 30,000 reside in renovated and well-maintained small houses they purchased. A considerable proportion of Portuguese males are skilled construction workers; women work in factories or as homemakers.
>
> Dozens of Portuguese-owned restaurants, bakeries, grocery stores, and travel agencies line the commercial corridors. This almost totally self-sufficient section of Newark is a striking contrast to an area only a mile or two north, where massive public housing projects, now mostly abandoned, await demolition. Newark is beginning to recover from the stigma associated with its name. The Portuguese and less numerous other immigrants are contributing to this economic recovery.[45]

Muller's vignette has counterparts everywhere, few of them adequately examined. Because of the imbalance in media reporting, the

---

45. *Ibid.*

public has been well supplied with stories about the new panache in the City's trendier places—Chelsea, the Upper West Side, the East Village, SoHo, Carroll Gardens, and Brooklyn Heights. But only of late, and still inadequately, was there attention to the improving status of the more workaday communities that constitute the vast bulk of New York. The dazzle and astronomical rents of Columbus Avenue's boutiques in what had been, in the sixties, an avenue of forlorn tenements, are a hardy newspaper perennial. What is as crucial to New York's future is reblooming commerce on the Bronx's Third Avenue and Fordham Road, on Brooklyn's Flatbush Avenue, Bensonhurst's 86th Street, and Sunset Park's Fifth Avenue. In Queens, the new bustle on Main Street, Steinway Street, Junction Boulevard, and a multitude of other local shopping promenades owes little to baby boomers on a buying spree. The crowds are preponderantly immigrants giving patronage to immigrant storekeepers. A restaurant owned by a Lebanese immigrant catering to Hispanic and Asian immigrants is an unremarkable sight in the ethnic quiltwork of contemporary New York.

Throughout the metropolitan area, especially in its déclassé sections, the revitalizers have tended to be New Immigrants. It was they, not yuppies, who first chanced Flushing and Ridgewood, Brighton Beach and Greenpoint. In a recent sale of new houses in Bedford-Stuyvesant, a majority of the buyers were Asian; none was white middle-class. The City's small-home neighborhoods have a special attraction for many immigrants. The Asian home ownership rate is now equal to that of whites and bids fair to exceed it. West Indians and Haitians also exhibit relatively high property ownership rates, higher than for native-born blacks and Hispanics. For immigrants the home ownership goal is achievable mainly in lower-end markets, often by dint of overcrowding; friends and relatives pool their money to buy a house and to share it with co-ethnics. Tightly packed dwelling units are characteristic of immigrants, the stuff of the sociologists' horror stories during the great European migrations. The newly arrived, with thinner pocketbooks and other cultural values, are typically less reverent of privacy and space than is America's middle class.

None of this is to slight the significant role of baby boomers—the singles and the doubly employed childless couples—in neighborhood revival. Their consumer prowess in the markets for housing and sumptuary goods is legendary. In neighborhoods with claim to status or chic, the energizing role of yuppies has been as decisive as the immigrants' energizing role in areas yuppies shun. But in a city as big and heterogeneous as New York, comprehensive five-borough revival requires larger numbers and less fastidious choices than one associates with young professionals. In many places, of course, the New Immigrants and yuppies merge forces in neighborhood uplift. In Sunset Park, as will be seen, they stand side by side. Indeed, to a degree (as was famously the case in Greenwich Village during the twenties and thirties), it was the ethnics who drew the yuppies. That has again happened in Astoria, Sunnyside, Greenpoint, and the Lower East Side. Some of the first yuppies in those areas valued their non-middle-class status; it fed their self-image as "urban pioneers." Those pioneers sometimes resented the intrusion of following waves of their fellows who would, they feared, unlike themselves, violate the neighborhood's "soul." To long-settled residents it was, of course, the pioneers who were perceived as intruders. "If they were the pioneers," snapped an elderly Italian inhabitant of a now-fashionable yuppie retreat, "what were we—the Indians?"

## GENTRIFICATION AND ITS DISCONTENTS

Compared to their fallen circumstances in the sixties and seventies, a majority of New York City's older neighborhoods now appears to be in one phase or another of recovery. In not much more than a decade, community after community traversed a cycle from depopulation and the stresses of market failure to repopulation and the stresses of market success. The latter is usually condemned as gentrification, a pejorative term that obscures as much as it illuminates. The subject is worth a few comments.

One is that gentrification is rarely perceived as a beneficial process, as an indispensable counterpoise to the "degentrification" that wreaked incalculable harm upon New York's neighborhoods during the dark decades of middle- and working-class exodus. Another is that the phenomenon is almost always cast as a morality play, a tale of gratuitous injury inflicted on the innocent and powerless by the powerful and callous, if not the downright wicked. The villains in the piece are real estate developers, often allied with uncaring or venal public officials. No one doubts that hard-charging developers make tempting (and, in many cases, deserving) targets. But the deeper truth is that private developers are no more than the intermediaries of change, striving, selfishly to be sure, to satisfy families and individuals in a legitimate quest to better their housing circumstances. Were that not the case, developers would soon go bankrupt and drag their mortgage lenders down with them. That was a common occurrence during the heyday of the federal urban renewal era when thousands of private new projects failed because of an insufficency of people willing to move into inner-city areas.

A genuinely balanced account of the costs and benefits in neighborhood renewal would have many more sides than is suggested by simple victimization models. That account would give weight to the churches and shops that, without new clients, would close their doors; to property owners who, without added rent rolls, must let their buildings run down; and to the elderly, who have waited achingly for buyers to give them the means to retire.

Seemingly, those uncompromisingly opposed to gentrification would forever congeal a neighborhood's status quo. The unexpressed premise is that the present socioeconomic composition of a neighborhood, whatever it may happen at some particular moment to be, is unassailably optimal. That is a premise to be proved rather than asserted. Another premise, this usually forcefully expressed, is that today's residents (some who may have moved in only yesterday) have a nonrebuttable entitlement to permanent possession, or at least an entitlement superior to that of new entrants. Needless to say, there is no such entitlement either in law or equity.

There is much more to say about the complexities that swirl over gentrification and its correlate—neighborhood diversification. The issue will arise again in the final chapter when Sunset Park's future is examined.

## IMMIGRANT SETTLEMENTS

New York's New Immigrants are settled throughout all five boroughs and within every type of housing. Consistent with historical experience, they have tended to concentrate in ethnically distinctive enclaves. In several respects, however, the landscape of recent ethnic settlement differs from that of past eras. For one, as indicated earlier, Brooklyn and Queens, rather than Manhattan, have absorbed a majority of newcomers. For another, immigrant enclaves are now multiple rather than singular, forming numerous clusters of satellite settlements apart from the primary concentrations. Third, because more come with money and education, many immigrants move directly into middle-class neighborhoods, rather than progressing there by stages. At the turn of the last century, New York's East European

Jews, nearly all poverty-stricken, settled almost exclusively on the Lower East Side (and, to some extent, after the bridges and Brooklyn subway lines were built, in Williamsburgh and Brownsville). Typically, long years went by before the odyssey started that led first to East Harlem, the Bronx, Flatbush, and Borough Park, then to West End Avenue, Forest Hills, and Canarsie, and then to Scarsdale, Great Neck, the Five Towns and, of course, Miami Beach, which became New York's unofficial sixth borough. Similarly, Mulberry Street, East Harlem, and Red Hook were the first habitats of poor Italian immigrants before the leap to the North Bronx, Corona, Bensonhurst, Staten Island, and then to the suburbs. Now, new Chinese or Koreans go directly to Flushing, Bay Ridge, or Sunset Park, Jamaicans to Springfield Gardens, and Haitians to Flatbush.

The increased locational options of New Immigrants reflect important changes compared with the pre-1924 immigrant experience. One is that many more New Immigrants come with capital and education permitting early entry into the mainstream. Another is the City's unparalleled public transit system which, notwithstanding operational lapses, serves an immensely larger territory than before World War I. As previously noted, for immigrants, more so than for the indigenous population, public transit is a life support. It would be an instructive exercise, beyond the bounds of this study, to correlate the routes of particular subway lines with the distribution of particular ethnic settlements. What the Seventh Avenue IRT, which joined the Garment District to the Bronx, was for the Jews, the BMT's N line, which links Chinatown to Sunset Park, now is for a multitude of Chinese immigrants.[46]

Another reason for the multiplication of locational options is that the virulence of ethnic bigotry has dissipated, at least compared with the past. (Charles Abrams's waggish definition of neighborhood in the immigrant years was the street boundaries within which one could walk without being attacked.) The antipathy to "dirty foreigners," the insults, and physical assaults one immigrant group inflicted upon another, are now much less evident.

Testimony to New York's greater ethnic tolerance is the general acceptance of Asians throughout New York. There are few white

---

46. In Sunset Park, it is, as will be later shown in considerable detail, the section centered on Eighth Avenue in the Fifties that has become the principal settlement for Chinese newcomers. The Eighth Avenue station of the N line that runs underground directly from Manhattan's Chinatown first emerges into daylight at that stop. To new Chinese, insecure about subway signs, it became the "blue sky" station.

working- or middle-class (or for that matter, affluent) neighborhoods without an Asian presence. That includes the Chinese, a people once condemned to the pit of the ethnic hierarchy ("a town populated by 1,200 souls and two Chinamen," was a typical locution in older popular literature along with the opium dens, pigtails, coolie pidgin, and an appetite for rats). Chinese were excluded decades earlier and more ruthlessly than southern and eastern Europeans; indeed, until the fifties, those already here were (with certain exceptions) denied naturalization.[47]

## THE IMMIGRANT ATLAS

New Immigrant settlement patterns are a kaleidoscope of mass and movement. An accurate map would be profusely dotted and require yearly updating. A 1988 ethnic atlas would have disclosed the following:

• Concentrations of Koreans are in Flushing and adjacent areas in Queens.
• Chinese, though more dispersed than Koreans, have also formed a major enclave in Flushing. They are still enlarging the traditional boundaries of Manhattan's Chinatown, which has exploded from a tight enclave of 25,000 people in 35 small blocks to over 100,000, preempting much of the Italian and Jewish Lower East Side. It is said that were Flushing and Chinatown independent cities, they would be among the fastest-growing urban areas in the United States. The new concentration in southeast Sunset Park will be later described.
• Indians and Pakistani are also concentrated in Flushing and nearly all parts of Queens, where they were among the first Asian settlers. But because so many are educated professionals they are more widely scattered; many are settling in industrial cities across the Hudson.
• West Indians are in East Flatbush and southeast Queens, especially Laurelton, Springfield Gardens, and parts of Jamaica.

---

47. For a fine account of the long years of anti-Chinese discrimination see Shih-Shan Henry Tsai, *The Chinese Experience in America* (Bloomington: University of Indiana Press, 1986).

- Haitians are in Crown Heights, East Flatbush, and portions of the Upper West Side.
- Dominicans are the main new ethnic group in Washington Heights and are prevalent in Corona and Sunset Park.
- Greeks have made Astoria an Hellenic-American center, with Bay Ridge a popular second move for the assimilated.
- South and Central Americans have favored Jackson Heights and Elmhurst but are also quite dispersed.
- Soviet Jews are, of course, Brighton Beach's well-publicized newcomers. But many of the better educated went to Washington Heights in proximity to the City's universities and museums. Later on, the Rego Park–Kew Gardens corridor of Queens Boulevard became a popular choice.
- Poles are heavily concentrated in Greenpoint, which (along with Buffalo, Chicago, and Detroit's Hamtramck) is one of America's principal outposts of the national homeland, sufficiently so to have been visited by their compatriot, Pope John Paul II. They have also spilled over into nearby Bushwick, and some have joined their assimilated kinsmen in Sunset Park.
- Irish, many of them undocumented and scattered, have a pronounced presence in Inwood, Woodlawn, and Woodside, with a cluster, too, in Sunset Park.

The listing above is no more than a rough approximation of actual metropolitan patterns of immigrant settlement. A detailed map would be marked with a multitude of nuclei and subnuclei that extends well into the suburban rings. For Cubans, New Jersey's Union City and environs constitute a satellite of Miami. A substantial number of Asian Indians are in Jersey City. The most prosperous are in the affluent suburbs, Asians in Westchester and Long Island, Iranian Jews in the "gilded ghettos" of Great Neck and the Five Towns. Ridership on metropolitan commuter railroads and buses is slowly approaching the ethnic configurations of New York's subways.

Within the larger ethnic settlements, considerable mixing takes place as various immigrant groups intersperse with older residents as well as with each other. The New Immigrants have woven a tapestry of many colors, languages, and ancestries along both flanks of the No. 7 subway in Queens, polyethnicity magnified to its highest power; it has no parallel in previous waves of migration. Even at the time of its densest settlement, the Lower East Side, the historic exemplar of immigrant New York, was a cross section of European nationalities plus a sliver from one Chinese region. The Flushing–Corona–Elmhurst–Jackson Heights cluster approximates an ethnic cross section of the planet. Several Brooklyn neighborhoods (Sunset Park included) are rapidly catching up with Queens.

The New Immigrants have so profoundly altered the ethnogeography of New York and other big cities that it will become necessary to devise new concepts of discrimination and more sophisticated instruments to measure segregation. Currently, the best known calibrator—the Taeuber Index—is biracial, confined solely to the disparate proportions of blacks and whites within a given census tract. For our time, more comprehensive and finely grained multiethnic indexes will have to be invented and applied to areas smaller than tracts. The appropriate models may come from forestry, where naturalists have constructed measures to denote the spatial dispersion of the multifarious species of trees.[48]

---

48. For a recent effort in constructing multiethnic indexes, see Michael J. White, "The Segregation and Residential Assimilation of Immigrants" (Washington, D.C.: The Urban Institute, 1988). The author confirms the general perception that blacks are more segregated than are Asians and Hispanics.

# CHAPTER 6

## Sunset Park: Growth and Decline

It is time now to turn to the heart of the study, a narration of how successive waves of immigration have affected the rise, decline, and comeback of Sunset Park. The biography of a living community, like the biography of a living person, is, inevitably, an unfinished one. Sunset Park's repopulation and recovery are still in process so that it is easier to look from the present backward than from the present forward. Tomorrow may bring changes that will mock the projections and speculations ventured here.

Every urbanist knows that to venture into a study of neighborhoods is to wander into a statistical wilderness. Whatever the shortage of reliable data for thorough analyses of major urban agglomerations, it is as nothing compared to lacunae in the data base of micro areas. A collateral, and by no means subordinate, goal of this study was to rummage about the storehouses of data, to ascertain their accessibility and utility, and to identify lines of inquiry that would lead to deeper understanding. The consequences of that search are set forth in Appendix A, a series of extended statements on data sources and data gaps that informs the Sunset Park account.

## SUNSET PARK DEFINED

Sunset Park's history as an identified neighborhood is not, by New York's standards, very old. It lacks the venerability and pedigree of such other Brooklyn neighborhoods as Williamsburgh, Flatbush, or Bushwick, whose origins and delimitations are certified by ancient writs inscribed on parchment. No neighborhood called Sunset Park appears in old maps or chronicles. In former times, most of the northern and southern sections of today's Sunset Park were in the domains of the original Dutch towns and later considered parts of the better-known adjacent communities, Red Hook, Gowanus, or Bay Ridge. In the biography of a nurse dispatched from Norway in the 1880s to minister to the health needs of Norwegian immigrants (the prelude to the founding of the neighborhood's first hospital), the geographical references are solely to Brooklyn, or to South Brooklyn, or to specific streets.[49] Likewise, in an affectionate history of the Norwegian settlement of southwest Brooklyn, references to Sunset Park denote the public park per se, and the area immediately surrounding it. It was not until some time after 1910, when considerable numbers of Norwegians from other sections of New York City settled there, that the name Sunset Park entered common usage to denote the stretch of blocks from Greenwood Cemetery southward to Bay Ridge.[50]

The Scandinavian community took that name from its park, a splendid 23-acre expanse of rolling greenery, developed in the 1890s and completed in 1903. It occupies 41st to 44th streets, Fifth to Seventh avenues. The Park's promontory is the second highest in Brooklyn. It offers magnificent views of New York Bay across to Staten Island and New Jersey, as well as a panoramic sweep of Manhattan's skyline; on a clear day the Citicorp Building on 53rd Street in Manhattan is in easy sight. That elevation—terminal heapage of the glacial age—runs along most of West Brooklyn. It gives honest entitlement to the present names of such neighborhoods as Bay Ridge, Cobble Hill, Prospect Heights, and Brooklyn Heights, all once known by less lofty denominations. The Park has special appeal at day's end when its vistas are enhanced by the setting sun. Long before it became a public park, the site was a popular gathering place for Scan-

49. Erling N. Rolfsrud, *The Borrowed Sister* (Augsburg: Augsburg Publishing House, 1953).
50. Christen T. Jonassen, "Cultural Variables in the Ecology of an Ethnic Group," *American Sociological Review*, Vol. 14, February 1949, pp. 32–41.

dinavian, Irish, Italian, and other immigrants to whom it was village green and playing field. A large pond that anteceded today's Olympic-size swimming pool was favored for fishing and swimming and its grassy grounds for sports and national pageants.

Sunset Park as a formally designated community was born in 1966, a boom time for neighborhood birthrates. In the sixties, the idea of neighborhood had become a leitmotif in national policy and, for the votaries of the organized grass-roots movement, a sanctity. The concept burst into full flower, fertilized by such emerging ideals as participatory democracy and empowerment of the poor. Neighborhoods and communities were enshrined as the fourth layer of governance in the federalist structure; there were populists and decentralists—radical and conservative—who would joyfully have made it the first.

As Sunset Park fell on hard times in the sixties, the case for official community status grew urgent. More was involved than local esprit and more, too, than a mimicking of the current vogue (though it was that, too) of bestowing a prettified nomenclature on grittier places (e.g., Red Hook–Gowanus transmuted to Carroll Gardens, much of the Lower East Side to East Village, and Hell's Kitchen to Clinton Hill). Independent and official neighborhood status was a predicate to money, for a myriad of federal, state, and municipal grants and loans. Sunset Park was invented out of sober necessity, its elevation to official standing an act of statecraft.

In ordinary discourse, the boundaries of Sunset Park, as of other neighborhoods, are variously defined; no single set of boundaries serves every purpose nor conforms to available data. For much of the research in this study the boundaries established by the Department of City Planning were accepted. So delimited, Sunset Park is bounded on the north by the Prospect Expressway (approximately 15th Street), on the south by 65th Street (the Bay Ridge Freight Line), on the west by Upper New York Bay and Gowanus Bay, and on the east by Eighth Avenue. When necessary, however, those boundaries are stretched or narrowed to conform to census tract, zip code, health area, and community district data.

Sunset Park occupies the larger part of Community District 7, one of the 59 official jurisdictions established by New York City to strengthen local planning and administration. District 7 incorporates also Windsor Terrace, a small neighborhood of generally higher socioeconomic status that lies to Sunset Park's northeast athwart Greenwood Cemetery and extending to the outer edges of Flatbush. Sunset Park, so defined, comprised 100,000 people in 1987, accounting for more than 80 percent of the District 7 total. Immediately to Sunset

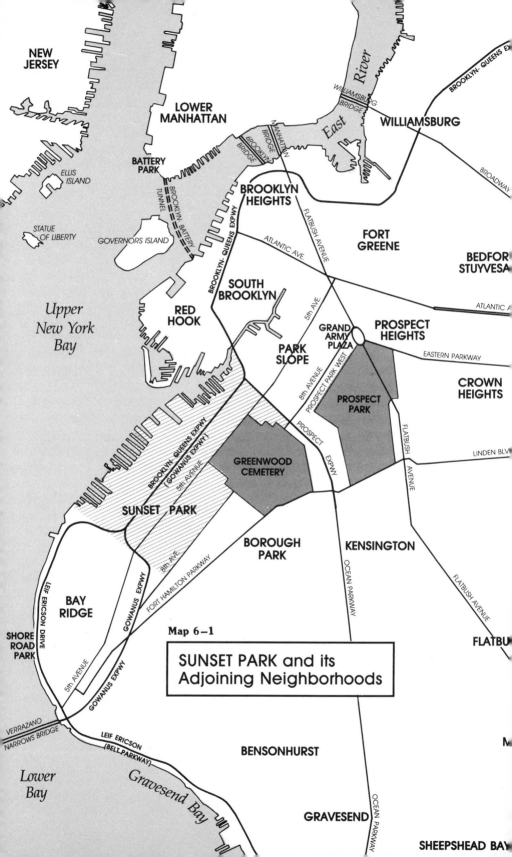

Map 6–1

**SUNSET PARK and its Adjoining Neighborhoods**

Park's north is Park Slope, a community of much superior status and an exemplar of gentrification. To its south is Bay Ridge, an attractive, solidly middle-class community with traces of affluence, especially on the streets facing the Narrows. To its east is Borough Park, the habitat of Orthodox and Hasidic Jews and, in many respects, now the "Jerusalem" of Jewish New York as once was the Lower East Side. Thus, Sunset Park is encircled by neighborhoods of considerably greater socioeconomic standing, with higher house prices and rents.

Sunset Park is distinguished from the typical community by its extensive Industrial Zone. The Zone encompasses the entire waterfront between Red Hook and Bay Ridge as well as the streets upland from the Bay to Third Avenue. It is part of the industrial littoral that arches north and east around Red Hook, Williamsburgh, and Greenpoint, and past Newtown Creek into Queens. As will be seen in the historical summary coming next, the Zone was a pivotal factor in Sunset Park's urbanization and, subsequently, no small contributor to its decline.

That history begins with the formation of Sunset Park's waterfront economy, proceeds to the sequences of immigrant settlement, and to the development of its housing, public transit, and religious institutions. Following that is the sad story of its decline. The chapter ends with a profile of Sunset Park's fallen status, as depicted in the 1980 census. The happier story of its post-1980 revival is deferred to Chapter 7.

### Sunset Park's Genesis

Like most of Brooklyn, the terrain that is now Sunset Park was, until the end of the nineteenth century, mainly rural and agricultural; most of its area was divided between two of the original Dutch towns, New Utrecht to its south and east and Breuckelen (Brooklyn) to its north. The nearest settlement was Gowanus (founded in 1636), a hamlet centered on what is today Third Avenue and 27th Street. In 1834, when the town of Brooklyn was chartered as a city, Gowanus plus a large expanse of today's Sunset Park were annexed as a ward. In the new City of Brooklyn that ward was customarily referred to as South Brooklyn. (Nowadays, South Brooklyn denotes a cluster of neighborhoods much farther south, abutting the Atlantic–Jamaica Bay–Narrows littoral, including Coney Island, Brighton Beach, Sheepshead Bay, Canarsie, Mill Basin, Bensonhurst–Bath Beach, and Bay Ridge–Dycker Heights.)

The area's urbanization commenced in the second half of the

nineteenth century following the establishment of small shipbuilding and boat repair facilities along its waterfront. A signal date was the completion of the Brooklyn Bridge in 1883, permitting overland and transit connections between Brooklyn and Manhattan. The new connection immensely enhanced Brooklyn's potential for residential and industrial growth, not least that of the close-in waterfront area across the East River and along the Upper Bay.

In 1890 a Brooklyn businessman, Irving T. Bush, espied in that waterfront an opportunity to compete with Manhattan's shipping and dock facilities, then already locked in a long—and ultimately hopeless—struggle with encroaching real estate development and gridlocked streets. Bush undertook the construction of what is called today an industrial park. Starting with a pier, a warehouse, an old railroad engine, and a tugboat, Bush Terminal gradually spread over nearly two miles of shoreline. At its peak, the terminal comprised 150 building units, eight large piers, and a railway.

World War I catapulted the Industrial Zone to new levels of activity. Bush Terminal was further expanded, and the War Department completed construction of its massive Army Port of Embarkation, now Brooklyn Army Terminal (BAT). BAT lies south of Bush Terminal, extending from 58th Street to 64th Street. It was designed by Cass Gilbert, celebrated for his Woolworth Building and U.S. Customs House. BAT consists of two massive 8-story buildings of exceptional architectural quality plus three large enclosed piers. Taken together, these structures contain more than 5 million square feet of working space. BAT occupies its own place in the memory books of 3 million World War II servicemen for whom it was the last American footfall before debarkation in a foreign land. It was declared a national landmark in 1975. It reappears at several places in this narrative.

The shipyards, piers, and industrial buildings were interconnected by a 14-mile railroad—The New York Dock Railway. Via a fleet of lighters (rail barges), it linked Brooklyn to New Jersey and thence to the transcontinental trunk railroads. It also provided a linkage to New England via a branch rail line on 65th Street. Industrial development bred further industrial development. The two terminals—Bush and the Army's—were soon augmented by such large establishments as the Bethlehem Steel Shipyard, the American Can Company, American Machine and Foundry, and Colgate-Palmolive-Peet; contiguous to the big-name establishments were hundreds of small machine shops, truckers, repair shops, and a miscellany of suppliers and servicers to the waterfront trade.

## THE EUROPEAN MIGRATIONS

From the dawn of its history Sunset Park was a catchment for newly landed immigrants. Transplanted Europeans were its community builders, literally as well as figuratively. The first large stream of settlers (skipping past the original Dutch and English farmers) were the Irish of the hungry years; some 5,300 were enumerated by 1855. It was Irish hands and shoulders that built the area's industrial structures and piers, excavated the Gowanus Canal, paved its streets, and set down its trolley and transit lines. The Irish were soon joined by Scandinavians and still later by Italians and Poles. Each wave was attracted by the plentiful jobs generated by the expansion of the industrial waterfront and the accompanying development upland. The unskilled became laborers and cargo handlers, the skilled were employed in ship repair and building construction.

Norwegians, whose merchant seamen had become familiar with Brooklyn's waterfront, were Sunset Park's second large stream of settlers. A small pocket of Norwegians had colonized North Brooklyn's waterfront as early as 1830 in the area between where the Brooklyn and Manhattan bridges now stand. By 1890, there were nearly 5,000 Norwegians in Brooklyn, most of them living in or just upland of Brooklyn's waterfront from Hamilton Avenue to Greenpoint.[51] Many had been attracted by the Atlantic Dock in Red Hook, the eastern seaboard's primary exporter of grain brought down via the Erie Canal. In contrast to their rural compatriots, who migrated to the Upper Midwest and Northwest as farmers and dairymen, the Norwegians who settled in Sunset Park had been engaged in maritime employments as seafarers, boat builders, and dockyard craftsmen. When steam displaced sail, thousands of unemployed Scandinavians and North Germans emigrated to America's port cities in search of jobs. They were attracted to Sunset Park by its shipyards and building boom, a ready market for their skills. Many of their young women became domestics in the homes of Brooklyn's gentry.

Next came the Finns, though in lesser numbers than the Norwegians. The first substantial flow arrived in the 1880s, forming a distinct cultural group. By 1910, 1,000 Finns had colonized "Finn Town" whose hub was Eighth Avenue and 43rd Street. On still-unpaved streets these skilled workers erected sturdy homes with their own hands. "They felt," said a descendant, "that they were carpenters;

---

51. Jonassen, *op. cit.*, pp. 266–267.

why should they live in other people's houses?" Finn Town, encompassing Fourth to Eighth avenues, 40th to 45th streets, remains one of Sunset Park's better sections. It borders the Park (which the Finns called "Pukin Maki" or Goat Hill, a reference to the time when the site was used by farmers to run their animals). In 1916, a second wave of Finnish migrants, infused with socialist-labor ideology,[52] erected on 43rd Street next to the Park what is generally counted as New York's first working-class housing cooperative, "Alku I" (The Beginning). By the 1920s it was followed by a score of others, each designated by what was deemed an appropriate, if somewhat whimsical, name, among them "The Poorhouse," "The Old Maid's Home," and "Drop of Sweat." In keeping with the Finns' strict aversion to debt, the cooperatives were financed entirely out of savings, spurning the mortgage loans then used by every apartment builder and most home purchasers. These cooperatives survive as affordable housing, passed along in good repair from generation to generation of ancestral Finns. Occasionally, some go on the open market whence they are eagerly snapped up. (A study consultant, Daniel McCarthy, managed to acquire one, to his evident content.) The co-ops are still debt-free, and even now no purchaser, Finn or non-Finn, is permitted to borrow against stock shares.

Italians and Poles were likewise late-nineteenth-century settlers. Italian laborers gravitated toward the docks and longshore jobs. Initially, they congregated around Red Hook's piers but soon spread out along the waterfront south to Sunset Park, forming residential enclaves in the blocks west of Third Avenue.[53] They were later to organize one of the most powerful and turbulent waterfront unions, starkly portrayed in *On the Waterfront* (filmed, however, in Hoboken).

Polish immigrants clustered in northern Sunset Park, close to Greenwood Cemetery, where many found jobs as grave diggers and

---

52. Many became radical labor activists, some prominent in the Wobblies (Industrial Workers of the World). A schism developed early between them and the "patriots" (i.e., conservative nationalists) that led to many lively debates and feuds not ended until the Soviet invasion of Finland. Katri Ekman, Corinne Olli, John B. Olli (eds.), *A History of Finnish American Organizations in Greater New York, 1891–1976* (New York: Greater New York Finnish Bicentennial Planning Committee, Inc., 1976).

53. One of Red Hook's first Italian residents went farther afield. Local legend has it that the area served as a training ground for the young Al Capone. It is there he acquired that eponymous scar, before departing for Chicago to pursue his own inglorious vision of the American dream and to enter American mythology as the city-gangster counterpart of the Wild West desperado. Red Hook is also the setting of Arthur Miller's *The View From the Bridge*, the now-classic drama of scenes from the domestic life of an Italian waterfront laborer's family.

landscape workers, thanks to a compatriot who was a supervisor; co-ethnicity in employment has deep roots. Other European immigrants included modest numbers of Greeks and Russians; most of the latter were Jews, many becoming Sunset Park's small retailers.

## Residential Development

Sunset Park's long era of immigrant settlement was marked by three waves of residential construction: (a) the early years; (b) a burst in 1914–1917 that accompanied the waterfront frenzy of World War I; (c) 1922–1929, when employment in the Industrial Zone, though down from the war peak, was sustained by national prosperity and an immense expansion in America's world trade; U.S. import tariffs were then nominal and export demand was fueled by the reconstruction of war-torn Europe.

As a major employment center, the Zone generated a keen demand for housing; residential sites built up house by house were increasingly developed by the block and half-block. Vacant tracts to the east of the industrial waterfront were soon covered with low-cost frame homes for blue-collar workers. Brick and masonry homes were built upon the slope running up from the Bay to its crest on Sixth Avenue and beyond for skilled artisans, local proprietors, and a rising middle class. Most of Sunset Park's prime inventory of owner-occupied homes, those in its so-called brownstone belt, date back to that hectic urbanization period. These (typically) attached row houses were, unabashedly, inexpensive imitations of the stately four- and five-story townhouses then going up in the posh blocks of Brooklyn Heights, Carroll Gardens, Fort Greene, and Park Slope. Sunset Park boasts few of the mansions common to those areas. To fit the purses of the less affluent, most homes were built on small lots as two- and three-story structures, with two dwellings, one for rent to help with the mortgage. Typically, each unit contains five or six rooms of fairly modest dimensions.[54]

Many of Sunset Park's apartment buildings were constructed during the second and third waves of the residential cycle. All the avenues, from Third through Eighth, were developed partly or wholly with retail stores, usually with residential units on top. Fifth Avenue, accessible to most residents and especially convenient to the better-off on the heights of the slope, became the community's retail spine.

---

54. An excellent architectural account of these early buildings is rendered by Andrew Scott Dolkart, in support of the Sunset Park Restoration Committee's petition for historic landmarking (unpublished manuscript). (Cf. Chapter 7.)

Sunset Park participated in New York's housing boom of the twenties though, with little vacant land left, to a lesser extent than did the open areas of Brooklyn, Queens, and the Bronx. Because sites in Sunset Park had become scarce and costly, most of the additions in that period were relatively large apartment buildings (a few with elevators but most of them walk-ups) and numerous commercial structures. New York's new subway system (next discussed) spurred additional residential development, much of it eastward to Seventh and Eighth avenues and southward to Bay Ridge.

**Public Transit**

New York's neighborhoods are, in the main, the creatures of its unparalleled network of public transportation. Sunset Park, where public transit came early, is no exception. In 1885, the tempo of its residential development accelerated following the construction of a steam rail line that linked it to the 39th Street ferry, the primary passage to lower Manhattan.[55] A short while later, the area was accommodated by cable car and steam rail running across the new Brooklyn Bridge from Manhattan's Park Row. By the turn of the century, following the electrification of the Brooklyn Rapid Transit System, residents were further served by an elevated railroad from the tip of Manhattan and over the Brooklyn Bridge, continuing along Brooklyn's Fifth Avenue. At 38th Street the El forked, one leg turning west to Third Avenue and then south to 65th Street, the other, the Culver Line (whose wooden cars, open platforms, and folding gates are still fondly recalled by transit buffs), proceeding southeast to Coney Island. Coney Island had become, by the end of the nineteenth century, New York's most popular play area, drawing thousands by rail and boat.

Between 1910 and 1915 a new subway was added, the Fourth Avenue local (now the R line), running from lower Manhattan through Borough Hall under Fourth Avenue to 95th Street. By 1920, the full BMT system was in place. Coney Island was the primary terminus of the new lines, its attractions now accessible to the millions instead of the thousands. Since several of the lines en route to Coney Island pass through part or all of Sunset Park, the area's locational advan-

---

55. Long before that, a stagecoach service connected the town of Brooklyn with Yellow Hook, which, following the yellow fever epidemic in mid-century, was given the less menacing name of Bay Ridge. The prettification of place names has a venerable history. The stage was later replaced by horse-drawn carriages on fixed rails.

tage was immeasurably enhanced. A new Sea Beach Express (now the N line), running beneath Fourth Avenue to 59th Street before turning southeast to Coney Island, gave Sunset Park's residents speedy access to Manhattan's Central Business District, Herald Square, Times Square, and beyond. To accommodate the underground rail expansion, Fourth Avenue, which had been laid out in the 1870s as a parkway, was enlarged to boulevard width, embellished with a landscaped median, alas, has long vanished. Even so, the new avenue was not then (and decidedly not now) the rival of such other landscaped Brooklyn streets as Ocean and Eastern parkways.

As Sunset Park's urban infrastructure developed, so did a Sunset Park community. More accurately, Sunset Park became an ensemble of variegated social, religious, and political communities. Ethnic pluralism is more often marked by passive tolerance than by ethnic camaraderie or perfect tranquility. The social distance that separated the various immigrant groups was considerable though, apparently, unmarred by any excess of hostile confrontations; at least few such episodes are recorded in the (generally nostalgic) histories that come to notice. The newspapers of the time, however, might have had other stories to tell. Epithets—Mick, Dago, Squarehead, and Kike—bawled or whispered were then common discourse in immigrant neighborhoods. It is known, too, that in the thirties a strain of anti-Semitism developed, stirred by adherents of the Christian Front and Father Coughlin's Social Justice movement. By the end of the fifties, most of the relatively small number of Jews who had settled in Sunset Park since the turn of the century left for other places, including Borough Park, their synagogues sold to other institutional users.

### A Community of Churches

For immigrants, after job and home comes church. It is typical of the immigrant experience that once a settlement attains threshold scale, the first makeshift places of worship give way to large permanent structures, built to whatever scale and quality the parent hierarchy will support or collection plates can tease from parishioners' pay envelopes.

Brooklyn had long been dubbed the City of Churches and the new European immigrants reinforced that characterization. As early as 1848 Sunset Park's Irish immigrants had acquired some land on Fifth Avenue and 21st Street on which they later built their first church, St. John the Evangelist. St. John's soon became the mother church for

Catholics of other nationalities who came later—German, Scandinavian, Polish, Italian, and Ukrainian.[56] In 1870, a site for St. Michael's was purchased on Fourth Avenue and 42nd Street on which a small church and school were placed. By the 1890s, the Irish had grown in population and affluence; many had graduated from pick and shovel to become contractors, publicans, lawyers and, unnecessary to say, politicians, policemen, and firemen. They expressed their rising status in ever-grander churches. In 1894, Irish parishioners dedicated a small but attractive church on Fifth Avenue between 59th and 60th streets—Our Lady of Perpetual Help (OLPH). In 1905, the present edifice of St. Michael's was dedicated, supplanting a modest predecessor. St. Michael's soaring campanile topped by an egg-shaped dome still dominates Sunset Park's skyline. As their numbers further increased, the Irish built in 1912 their fourth church—St. Agatha's—on 49th Street and Seventh Avenue. In 1924, the original OLPH was replaced by an imposing basilica of cathedral dimensions, Brooklyn's largest Roman Catholic place of worship. It also provides Southwest Brooklyn with a major secondary school. Unlike other Irish churches, which became heavily Hispanicized, OLPH remains a bastion of the Irish middle class, though nothing like before: Its elementary school is now more than 40 percent Hispanic.

In keeping with the traditional ethnic separations within Roman Catholicism, Poles and Italians soon built their own churches. The Poles organized in 1896 Our Lady of Czenstochowa, a parish in the northwest quadrant of Sunset Park. On a large site between Third and Fourth avenues, 24th and 25th streets, they erected a church by that name as well as a rectory, convent, and school. Though diminished in membership, the church remains the seat of the community's "Polish town."

Sunset Park's Italians, after some years of uncomfortable attendance at Irish churches, organized in 1902 St. Rocco's Church, first in a small chapel on 22nd Street, then in a much larger building on 27th between Fourth and Fifth avenues, formerly a Norwegian Lutheran church.

A Greek church on 18th Street west of Second Avenue and a Ukrainian church on 19th Street east of Fifth Avenue also still stand. B'nai Israel, an imposing Greek-style temple built in 1917 on 54th Street and Fourth Avenue, is now the Salem Gospel Tabernacle, a Seventh-

---

56. Robert J. and Alice Walsh, *Sunset Park, a Time Remembered* (Brooklyn: Sunset Park Restoration Committee, 1980).

Upper
New York
Bay

Map 6–2

SUNSET PARK
Principal Institutions

Our Lady of Czestochowa

BMT
25th

Post Office
11232
St. Rocco's

72nd Pre
Station

P.S.
172

BROOKLYN–QUEENS EXPWY

P.S.
371

BMT IND.
36th St.

GREENWOC
CEMETERY

Center P.S.
For Family Life 136

St. Michael's Church
and School

Transit Yard

P.S. 1

BMT
45th St.

GOWANUS EXPWY

SUNSET
PARK

Lutheran
Medical Center

Imatra H

New
South Branch
Library

BMT
53 St.

Health Center

P.S. 169

P.S. 94

Brooklyn
Army Terminal

P.S.
140

BMT
59th St.

St. Agatha School

P.S.
118

Our Lady of
Perpetual Help

Post Office
11220

Fatih Camh
(mosque)

BMT
8th Ave.

Day Adventist church. The cornerstone is still engraved with the Hebrew date, 5678.

The Scandinavians, numerous and denominationally diverse, planted a veritable forest of churches. It included the Bethelship Norwegian Methodist Church (founded in 1872), Trinity Lutheran (1890), the First Evangelical Free Church (1897), Zion Lutheran Church (1908), Christ United Methodist Church (1908), the Fifty-ninth Street Lutheran Brethren Church (1912), and the Second Evangelical Free Church (1913). The Finns, too, established their own, the Finnish Evangelical Lutheran Church. The first, in 1897, was in a converted building on 23rd Street near Fourth Avenue. In 1909, a new and larger one was built on 44th Street between Seventh and Eighth avenues; to widen its ethnic outreach its name was later changed to Gloria Dei Evangelical Lutheran Church.[57] The Finnish Golgotha Congregational Church at 733 44th Street, after a sequence of improvised habitats, also opened its doors to others. Eventually, the Scandinavian churches, their original membership declining, became multiethnic, which is to say, largely Hispanic and Asian.

Norwegian Lutherans founded yet another institution, a hospital destined to play a towering role in Sunset Park's communal history. The hospital began life in 1889 as the Norwegian Lutheran and Deaconesses' Home and Hospital in a frame house with 30 beds on Fourth Avenue and 45th Street.[58] Initially it ministered to the health needs of Norwegian immigrants but soon opened its doors to all comers. Fund-raising, mostly coins and dollar bills, was likewise ecumenical; the larger contributions tended to come from Brooklyn's social elite, including $50 from a wealthy executive to purchase Freya, the hospital's first ambulance horse. In 1903, the structure was replaced with a new, then up-to-date facility with 200 beds, large enough to serve most of Southwest Brooklyn. In a manner of speaking, the hospital became Sunset Park's totem; on it every community event was recorded. The hospital grew as Sunset Park grew, suffered as Sunset Park suffered, aligning and realigning its health-care programs with the changing population. In the course of time, it was to become a prime mover in the neighborhood's recovery. Along the

---

57. Ekman, Olli, and Olli, *op. cit.*, pp. 46–50.
58. Actually, that house was the successor to a still smaller facility to the north, acquired in 1883. The origin and early success of that institution owe much to the efforts of a dedicated Lutheran nurse-deaconess, Sister Elisabeth Fedde; her inspirational story is related in Rolfsrud, *op. cit.*

way, it renamed itself Lutheran Hospital and still later, as had become the fashion, Lutheran Medical Center.

## Little Scandinavia

Though, in the aggregate, there were more Irish, Italians, and Poles than Scandinavians, it was the latter who gave Sunset Park its distinctive persona. That was so because the Scandinavians were concentrated in the neighborhood's core rather than, as were other ethnics, dispersed over a large terrain that only later was brought within the official boundaries. Also, Scandinavian settlements in New York City commanded a certain scarcity value. Throughout the flood years of immigration, New York had acquired any number of Italian and Irish neighborhoods. But enclaves of Norwegians, Swedes, and Finns were rare. Containing the largest concentration of Norwegians this side of Minneapolis, Sunset Park became a center of America's Norwegian culture, acknowledged as such by touring compatriots from other regions and the home country. The list included Roald Amundsen, Sonja Henie, and the king of Norway who, in 1939, visited to celebrate Leif Ericson Day.

Sunset Park's Scandinavian flavor was intensified by a multitude of cultural institutions. It was the locus of every Scandinavian branch of the Lutheran Church, the center of Scandinavian national heritage societies and home-language newspapers. The *Nordiske Tidende*, first published in 1891, became the leading Norwegian newspaper of the eastern United States. It publishes still, though as a weekly with sections in English; its office, however, has moved to Bay Ridge. The Finnish-language newspaper, *New Yorkin Uutiset*, continues to publish at Eighth Avenue and 44th Street though, like the *Tidende*, only as a (part-English) weekly. Its circulation, once above 10,000, is now a mere 3,000; more of its aging subscribers live in the retirement havens of California and Florida than in Sunset Park.

Another relic is Imatra Hall, established by the Finnish Aid Society as a social and recreational center; it still stands on 40th Street, a place for a neighborly cup of coffee or to raise a friendly glass or two. Each year ethnic Finns gather there to recount old times and to recite their celebrated epic poem, "The Kalevale" (whose meter was borrowed by Longfellow for "Hiawatha"). Few of the once-abundant Scandinavian delicatessens and none of the Scandinavian restaurants have endured. Olsen's on Eighth Avenue is still the spot for Scandinavian bread and cakes, and local Finns can still buy herring and lingonberries at specially stocked superettes. But, on the whole, the remainders of the Scandinavian legacy are more in evidence within the Bay Ridge–Fort Hamilton area, long a magnet for Sunset Park's assimilated Norwegians. The symbol that memorializes the Norwegian settlement of America, a stone monument with Runic lettering at which Norway Day is annually celebrated, is in Bay Ridge's Leif Ericson Park just beyond Sunset Park's southern boundary.

### Post-Maturity

Sunset Park, no more than a fledgling urban area in 1880, was by 1930 a fully matured one. By then, foreign immigration had virtually ended and nearly all the vacant land was gone. With most of today's industrial, residential, and institutional buildings in place and all of the subway lines installed, Sunset Park's development was substantially complete. Thereafter, it might have looked forward to an era of stable equilibrium. What it got, instead, was a sequence of volatile fluctuations, first the anguish of the Great Depression, then the excitements of the Second World War, and later a procession of postwar shocks and aftershocks.

The Depression of the thirties brought grave hardships. With the world economy in retreat and the forbiddingly protectionist Smoot-Hawley now law, foreign trade disintegrated; seaports all along the East Coast competed fiercely for the remnants. Activity at the docks dropped. The morning shape-up of longshoremen for a day's pay was at its cruelest, a work-culture made graphic to the world's moviegoers in *On the Waterfront*, an only mildly fictionalized account of the harsher realities of Brooklyn's underemployed docks.

Manufacturing fared as badly, with severe layoffs in all the local industrial plants. As unemployment soared, family income evaporated and house vacancies increased. To eke out the weekly budget, many families, renters as well as owners, were compelled to take in roomers. Deprivation was widespread. But, as older residents like to recall, impoverishment did not equate with poverty, as the concept is applied today—often a code word for the breakdown in individual behavior and the social order. Family ties held, communal sanctions prevailed, doors were left unlocked, stores kept open late, and none feared a midnight walk from the subway. These recollections of a golden past were to be hurled like missiles against a later generation of Hispanic newcomers whose poverty was adjudged to be of a different kind. Memory is selective. Forgotten or suppressed were the interethnic frictions, the brute violence and organized crime at the docks, the youthful delinquents, the heavy incidence of alcoholism. Much of the pastoral duties of the Scandinavian ministers revolved around temperance campaigns or attending to the inevitable consequences of drink—dissipated pay envelopes, abused wives, and abandoned families.

Europe's World War II rescued Sunset Park's Industrial Zone from its slump, even prior to U.S. entry. In 1939, America became the Allies' arsenal and had itself begun to rearm. Activity at the waterfront and in the local shipyards picked up sharply. After Pearl Harbor, the uplift was seismic. The Brooklyn Army Terminal was retooled for production levels far above those of World War I. Bush Terminal and every plant in the Industrial Zone were strained to full capacity, most on a round-the-clock schedule. Sunset Park's vacancies and its Depression survival kit, the rooms-to-let, were rapidly filled by a horde of production workers drawn from every stagnant region in a depressed national economy. Home owners created additional dwelling space by converting one-family homes into twos, and twos into threes. Family income recovered and mortgage arrears were paid off. An active sales market for older houses returned, at smartly rising prices. Rents, too, began to climb, but that ascent was quickly stayed by new federal ceilings. The rent-control system, later inherited by state and city government, was to have lasting effects on Sunset Park's housing future. It benefited those tenants whose dwellings were kept in tolerably good repair. And it placed a protective mantle over statutory tenants that was later to shield the poor from the hazards of gentrification. But it also was to harm large numbers of others—tenants, owners, and mortgage holders—whose buildings lapsed into decay, abandonment, and often uninhabitability.

## THE FALL OF SUNSET PARK

By war's end, Sunset Park was afflicted by every species of calamity—environmental, economic, and social. Earlier, a swath had been cut out of its heart by that master builder of highways, Robert Moses. A drastic cutback in jobs occurred and the waterfront fell quiet. The City imposed an extremely adverse change in local zoning regulations. A massive turnover of population shredded the social fabric.

### The Gowanus Expressway

A neighborhood that had been given coherence by one mode of transport—the subway—was to be split by another—a huge elevated highway. The Gowanus Expressway, much of it placed on the columns of the defunct Third Avenue El, was a shuddering environmental shock. Though most of the expressway was built before the war, its full effect did not strike the community until after the return to postwar normalcy and a major expansion in the roadway.

The expressway interconnects the Brooklyn-Battery Tunnel, New York's airports, and Long Island's arterials and provides, via the Verrazano Bridge and Staten Island, a route to New Jersey and the continent. Its importance to the metropolitan movement of cars and trucks was no doubt justified. But only its staunchest defenders could justify the engineering and location. It is a poorly designed arterial without shoulders or service lanes. Its placement was something of an improvisation. To acquire the right-of-way, Moses, then New York's panjandrum of urban development, condemned the entire frontage along Third Avenue between Hamilton Avenue and 39th Street; more than 100 stores were removed and 1,300 families displaced. Later, to widen the expressway and to transform Third Avenue beneath it into a ten-lane road, the eastern frontage from 39th Street to 63rd Street was likewise demolished. The physical scars of that surgery are still visible in Third Avenue's frontage, a jumble of unsightly lots and truncated structures. Piling insult on injury, the expressway offered few convenient entry or exit points for the vehicles of Sunset Park's residents and businesses.

The expressway darkens and blights Sunset Park. It is a permanent disfigurement not only of the built environment but also of the community's internal unity. To be sure, there was a large measure of social and ethnic separation between the laborers who lived downslope in the cheaper frame houses and the more affluent in the masonry houses upslope. But the separations of social history were now physical as well, reified by a perilous chasm. Third Avenue is a ten-lane user-unfriendly crossing that carries double the traffic of the expressway above it. School children, in their twice-a-day negotiation of this crossing, require the assistance of two guards. At other times, pedestrians cope unaided, a hazard few care to chance. The expressway and the highway beneath it form a structural divide, reminiscent of nineteenth-century railroads that ushered into America's urban history the "this side, other side of the tracks" social construct.

### Shrinking Jobs and Population

Soon after the war, activity at the Brooklyn Army Terminal abruptly halted. By 1950 its roster, 40,000 at the peak including 10,000 civilians, shrank to little more than 1,100. Ship movements, freight tonnage, and ship repairs went into a free-fall. As New Jersey, Baltimore, and other eastern ports took Brooklyn's business away, the Bethlehem Steel yard, stripped year by year to a skeletal work force, shut down in 1963 for good. In 1968, after a bitter strike, American Machine and Foundry (AMF) abandoned its building, a loss of another 1,300 jobs. (Later, as will be seen, this building was resurrected for a second life.) Seven of Bush Terminal's eight piers closed. Thousands of local residents, their livelihoods gone, forsook the area. The housing market faltered and vacancies abounded. It was a replay of the thirties, only worse, since the decline tore apart Sunset Park's entire institutional and social system, not solely its economy.

The postwar suburban explosion was a trauma that spared few of New York's mature neighborhoods. The period between 1950 and 1980 was the age supreme of the mass rush to the outer rings (and, for lesser numbers, to the Sunbelt). Brooklyn's population declined during those decades by a half-million, from 2.7 million to 2.2 million. For many Brooklynites, the suburban move was a pull, the realization of a long-deferred American dream; for others it was a push, a flight from deterioration, crime, and ethnic change.

Sunset Park's younger households and elderly retirees joined the trek. Bay Ridge represented the shortest and least disruptive move. Semirural Staten Island—New York's own suburb—was another favored destination as, of course, were Nassau County and New Jersey. The neighborhood's population, already reduced by the shrinkage of industrial employment, dropped further. Sunset Park's population fell from a prewar level of nearly 104,000 to a little over 97,000 in 1950, to 87,000 in 1960, and despite the huge influx of Puerto Ricans, to even less in 1970 (Table 6–1).

The old housing stock, expanded and refitted to accommodate wartime production workers and later the family formations of young veterans, provided ready-made opportunities for the newcomers. But the in-movers were simply too poor to sustain a stable market. The housing sector went into a tailspin marked by plummeting sales prices, rising mortgage defaults, and curtailed maintenance. A régime of disinvestment set in, though not as severe as the devastation that ravaged other New York neighborhoods. Only a fraction of Sunset Park's housing stock was permanently destroyed or irredeemably damaged, thus preserving the seeds of future revival.

### The 1961 Zoning Resolution

The already parlous state of the housing market was exacerbated by the City's enactment in 1961 of a comprehensive set of new zon-

**TABLE 6–1**
**Selected Characteristics, Sunset Park, 1940–1970ª**

|  | 1940 | 1950 | 1960 | 1970 |
|---|---|---|---|---|
| Total population | 103,718 | 97,471 | 87,648 | 86,874 |
| Number of households | 28,327 | 28,158 | 28,600 | 28,862 |
| Average household size | 3.9 | 3.4 | 3.1 | 3.0 |
| Number of families | n.a.ᵇ | 26,065 | 24,949 | 24,294 |
| Median income—families and unrelated individuals | n.a. | $3,112 | $6,281 | $8,000 |
| Total dwelling units | n.a. | 28,427 | 29,213 | 29,886 |
| Median contract rent | $32.34 | $37.47 | $54.76 | $63.420 |

*Source:* Decennial Censuses of Population and Housing.
ª Because of difficulties in assembling historical data, the tabulations are limited to 25 tracts rather than the 27 occupied tracts Sunset Park currently comprises.
ᵇ Not available.

ing regulations. Most vulnerable were the residential blocks in and around the Industrial Zone. Unlike the former zoning map, which authorized a mix of industrial and residential development, the new zoning resolution reserved the blocks west of the expressway almost exclusively for manufacturing. The resolution's intent was to add to the supply of land area available for "as of right" industrial expansion by reducing the intrusion of incompatible uses, especially housing. The competition between the two land uses is an enduring one: The specter of abattoirs in residential neighborhoods was the classic justification for the first zoning laws, the minatory lessons of urban-planning textbooks. Industrial users fully reciprocate their dislike of residential neighbors. They, too, have a repertory of horror stories that tell how aggressive residents file unreasonable complaints of exaggerated nuisances. And usually with effect. To any hand-to-hand conflict with local industry, local householders bring the power of their votes.

The zoning amendments were an act of long-deliberated public policy. City Hall and its Planning Commission, dismayed by the chronic hemorrhages in manufacturing and longshore jobs, were resolutely determined to arrest or reverse the attrition, undaunted by the deep-seated economic trends that had prompted it. During the sixties, the City adopted a series of pro-industry measures. They included financial incentives—tax abatement and concessional loans to expanding firms—and the acquisition of large sites in each outer borough for development into industrial parks. Pro-industrial zoning was thus one in a broad array of program instruments.

Whatever its rationale, the 1961 zoning resolution dealt the community a drastic blow. Overnight, it cast some 2,000 Sunset Park residences, containing an estimated 10,000 people, into nonconforming status. The resolution not only compromised the affected dwellings' marketability but, by limiting permissible repairs and improvements, also undermined their very viability. Ironically, the Industrial Zone, a community-building force during the decades of Sunset Park's urbanization, was now contributing to community-unbuilding. The once-symbiotic relation between Sunset Park's residential and industrial sectors had long ago become frayed. By the sixties, only a moderate and steadily declining fraction of residents were employed in the Zone. The large corporate establishments with a tradition of good community relations and local benefactions had left, or were poised to. They were replaced by small, often fly-by-night, firms in quest of cheap labor and cheap rents, whose sense of obligation to the community was as fragile as their capital.

In short, by the sixties the residents of Sunset Park had much less reason than did their predecessors to support or defend local industrial interests—industrial real estate owners and occupants, public-development agencies, or even the local maritime unions. Indeed, some would have willingly surrendered parts of the Industrial Zone for some combination of new housing and waterfront parks. Such a trade-off even then had a strong appeal to urban planners who were less sanguine than the City Planning Commission about New York's maritime and industrial future.[59] That appeal is even stronger today, as will be said later.

## THE PUERTO RICAN MIGRATIONS

By the end of the fifties Sunset Park had once again become a catchment area for a new wave of migration. With the gates to foreigners virtually closed (the special exceptions—Europe's war displacees and political refugees—did not bring large numbers), the primary source of overseas newcomers was Puerto Rico. In 1917 its people had been elevated to U.S. citizenship. After the economic boosters of World War II flamed out, the commonwealth lapsed into a severe depres-

---

59. Cf. Urban Design Associates, *Sunset Park West Study*, May 1970, pp. 4–5. The analysts were an outside group of urban planners recruited to review land use patterns in the community. The report, in two volumes covering industry, housing, and traffic, forcefully recommended a major residential redevelopment of the Industrial Zone.

sion. High birthrates and falling death rates brought overpopulation. Too few jobs and too many mouths to feed induced a mass movement from island to mainland, the largest inflow to New York since the European migrations. By 1960 the census counted 1.2 million Puerto Ricans in New York; because of circular migration, the gross intake was substantially greater. The newcomers settled wherever low-cost housing could be found. Manhattan, particularly East Harlem, the Lower East Side, and the Upper West Side, experienced the initial impact. Pushed out by urban renewal projects—then at their peak—or spontaneously attracted by better housing opportunities, Puerto Ricans fanned out to the South Bronx, Williamsburgh, and countless other places in the outer boroughs, including Sunset Park.

A colony of Puerto Ricans had lived in Sunset Park since the twenties, many, like their Scandinavian neighbors, dockworkers and seafarers. But as late as 1950, Hispanics constituted only 2 percent of the community. During the next 20 years, however, the freshets swelled to streams as tens of thousands of Puerto Ricans moved into the dwellings of tens of thousands of departing Sunset Park residents. To the newcomers, Sunset Park's abundant vacancies at favorable low rents were irresistible lures. So, too, to rural islanders, was its lowrise ambiance. Equally attractive were the unskilled jobs available in the factories and sites abandoned by more productive industries. Another attraction was the area's excellent public transportation. For those without automobiles (the circumstance, even as late as 1980, of a majority of Sunset Park's Hispanic families) it provided speedy access to jobs, friends, and relatives everywhere in New York.

The newcomers came not only from the commonwealth but also from the more crowded and turbulent parts of the City. Many were the uprooted of the extensive urban renewal programs of Manhattan's Columbus Circle, Morningside Heights, and the Lower East Side. Others were the evictees of apartment buildings undergoing renovation everywhere in old neighborhoods. The allegation that Sunset Park was being used as a dumping ground had some basis in fact, but only to a degree. Sunset Park was not conspicuously among the City areas consciously and consistently turned into endpoints for urban renewal's displacees. Those were Coney Island and the Rockaways with their large inventory of vacant seasonal homes as well as the low-rent apartment houses of the South Bronx abandoned by their long-time residents.

Within short years, Hispanics were to become Sunset Park's predominant ethnic group. By 1970, they accounted for nearly 40 percent of all residents and for more than half of the population downslope from Fourth Avenue. In some census tracts near the waterfront, more than seven out of eight residents were Hispanic, nearly all Puerto Rican.

Sunset Park's distinctive ethnicity, once Scandinavian, had become Latino. Every local institution was to reflect that transformation. The most consequential was in Sunset Park's schools. In 1957, according to one unofficial estimate (official ethnic counts were not allowed in those days), the proportion of Spanish-speaking children was only 10 percent of local school enrollment.[60] By 1973, now based on official data, the proportion of Hispanics in the local elementary schools rose to 70 percent (Table 6–2). White enrollment had plunged to less than 27 percent. By 1975 Hispanic enrollment grew to 75 percent and by 1980 to nearly 85 percent. By then the share of white children tumbled to 11 percent. Schools that had been operating below capacity were now overshooting capacity. Ethnic trends in the junior high schools were similar. But, since these schools drew from adjacent white areas, the share of Hispanics was lower and the share of whites was higher. Also, during the seventies, Sunset Park's Asian children had begun to leave their first faint mark on the public schools.

The area's Catholic schools, even more drained than the public schools by the exodus of whites, began also to enroll Hispanics, though not in compensatory numbers; parochial schools entered a long period of below-capacity operations—fewer and fewer seats occupied by more and more Hispanics—that continues to this day (Chapter 7).

Hispanics were also absorbed into Sunset Park's Catholic churches and many of the Protestant. Pentecostal churches soon appeared, mostly storefront congregations. To minister to the newcomers, a reconstituted clergy emerged, Hispanic or Spanish-speaking and versed in Hispanic culture. Other institutions likewise adapted to the social transformation. Lutheran Medical Center established a network of clinics and outreach services to the poor, who would soon be its largest clientele. Retail ownership and merchandise were rapidly Latinized. Fifth Avenue became a Caribbean marketplace of supermercados, bodegas, carnicerías, and fruterías. Non-Hispanic merchants acquired a smatter of pidgin Spanish, enough to bark "mira, mira," "descuentos," and "precios bajos."

Unlike prior waves of European migrants who gave added thrust to the development of a yet-unshaped community, the new Puerto

---

60. *Brooklyn Communities, Volume II* (New York: The Community Council of New York, 1959), p. 51.

**TABLE 6–2**
**Enrollment by Ethnicity, Sunset Park's Public Schools, 1973–1980[a]**

| School Year | Asian | Puerto Rican | Total Hispanic | Black | White | Total Number[b] |
|---|---|---|---|---|---|---|
| | | | *Elementary Schools* | | | |
| 1973–1974 | 1.4% | 65.6% | 70.2% | 1.5% | 26.8% | 7,136 |
| 1974–1975 | 1.5 | 65.2 | 71.6 | 1.2 | 24.4 | 7,134 |
| 1975–1976 | 1.6 | 69.5 | 76.6 | 1.5 | 20.3 | 7,253 |
| 1976–1977 | 2.5 | 69.2 | 77.8 | 1.6 | 18.0 | 7,099 |
| 1979–1980 | 2.6 | n.a. | 84.4 | 1.9 | 11.0 | 6,355 |
| | | | *Junior High Schools* | | | |
| 1973–1974 | 1.7 | 47.9 | 51.8 | 10.0 | 36.4 | 4,564 |
| 1974–1975 | 2.0 | 48.6 | 53.9 | 9.8 | 34.3 | 4,516 |
| 1975–1976 | 1.8 | 51.5 | 56.4 | 9.3 | 32.3 | 4,674 |
| 1976–1977 | 2.4 | 54.6 | 59.9 | 9.1 | 28.4 | 4,268 |
| 1979–1980 | 3.9 | n.a. | 64.8 | 8.8 | 22.5 | 4,103 |

*Source:* Board of Education of the City of New York.
[a] The data are based on the five elementary and three junior high schools located within the study area. Six schools are in School District 15 and two in School District 20. No figures are available for academic years 1977–1979.
[b] Inclusive of a small number of American Indians.

Ricans entered a Sunset Park well past its prime. It was their fate to depress more deeply an already depressed community. The metaphor of New York as the economic escalator of masses of poor newcomers connotes a general, not universal, truth. Nothing in urban history suggests that all immigrants carry in their baggage a ticket to early success. Each ethnic group, each member of each group, brings particular strengths and weaknesses. The path to the mainstream may be fast, slow, or a road to nowhere.

A crucial circumstance is the economic and social milieu at the time of arrival. New York's economy had radically changed since the twenties, when the last of the Europeans streamed in. The kinds of employment that most Puerto Rican men and women were fitted for—goods handling and low-skill manufacturing—were precisely those in precipitous retreat. To be sure, many of the earlier immigrants, especially Italians and Poles, had also been handicapped by lack of English, education, or job skills, or all three. But the Europeans came in an age when such lacks mattered less. Moreover, Kennedy Airport was not a final terminus as Ellis Island had been for the preponderance of Europeans. For many Puerto Ricans it was a commuter station. Cheap airfares and easy circulation between island and mainland sapped the commitment to assimilation, the will and time to acquire proficiency in English, and new job skills.[61]

Another drastic change since the great trans-Atlantic migrations was the decay in social controls. The pre-1924 immigrants had come into an urban society of stable families and home-centered life, governed by strict behavioral codes enforced by the authority of parent, church, teacher, and police. The Europeans had come, too, long before the rot of powerful, mind-altering killer drugs. To be sure, alcohol was a chronic problem, but it did not destroy adolescents at the precocious ages at which they now succumb to drugs. Alcoholism ruined individual families, but heroin (and, now more appallingly, crack) ruins entire communities; because of crack the one-parent family has been superseded by the no-parent family. Drug-induced AIDS and abandoned children threaten to crush the public welfare and hospital systems beyond anything ever witnessed in an alcohol culture. The Red Hook public housing projects, not far from Sunset Park, were exemplary communities throughout the era of whisky, beer, and gin, generally regarded as paragons of New York's public housing inventory. In today's age of crack, Red Hook Houses have become one of Brooklyn's hellholes, its Pruitt-Igoe. Once, too, the instruments of street conflict were fists and baseball bats. Now, as in an arms race, the homicidal power of weaponry has multiplied exponentially. The spring-blade knives à la West Side Story were replaced by Saturday night specials, then by Magnums, and then by an arsenal of lethal automatic firearms. The bruises and black eyes of teenage encounters became manslaughter and murder.[62]

---

61. A lessened commitment to permanent settlement is a trait not confined to Puerto Ricans. The "circular flow" hypothesis seems also to apply to other immigrants from the Caribbean, such as Dominicans, also now prominent in Sunset Park, whose rate of naturalization is far lower than that for South Americans and Asians. Cf. Demetrios G. Papademetriou and Nicholas DiMarzio, *Undocumented Aliens in the New York Metropolitan Area: An Exploration Into Their Social and Labor Market Incorporation* (Staten Island, N.Y.: The Center for Migration Studies of New York, Inc., 1986), p. 114. See also the retail survey (Appendix E), which indicates that a third of the Hispanic population plans to return to their native lands and only half of those who are not citizens (a large minority) want to become so.

62. For a graphic account of the precocity and "banality" of deadly street violence see Claude Brown's "Manchild in Harlem," *The New York Times Magazine*, September 16, 1984. Five years later, even that chilling account no longer seems exceptional.

In the face of a collapsing blue-collar economy, the average incomes of New York City's Puerto Rican families dropped to the lowest of any ethnic group. With the disintegration of the inner city, their social structure collapsed. Female headship rates soared to levels above those of other ethnic groups. By 1980, more than 43 percent of Puerto Rican families were headed by women, compared to 32 percent for other Hispanics and 21 percent for all families. Overwhelmed mothers, working or not, left fatherless children to fend for themselves in a street culture of gangs, crime, and drugs. The results were predictable.

Rising female headship was accompanied by high rates of welfare enrollment, higher than for other Hispanics and blacks. It has commonly been observed that the welfare system is driven by its own dynamic. For most, it is a welcome refuge to weather occasional and brief intervals of joblessness or family distress. For others, it is entrapment in a lifetime of dependency with unwholesome consequences for them and for the life chances of their children.

The socioeconomic indicators of Sunset Park's new Hispanics were soon reflected in the socioeconomic indicators of the community. Between 1960 and 1970 the community's real income declined (Table 6–1). Poverty and public-assistance rates climbed. Nearly 60 percent of the poverty families were female-headed with young children, and 22 percent of its households were on public assistance. School achievement scores in reading and mathematics likewise declined; several of Sunset Park's elementary schools ranked in the lowest 15 percent in the City.

As local purchasing power shrank, the neighborhood's retail trade, already buffeted by competition from shopping malls, also declined. During the sixties and seventies, vacancies appeared in all the commercial avenues, some even on Fifth Avenue. Because of the redundancy of retail frontage, Seventh Avenue was rezoned from commercial to residential; more than 50 of its empty stores and others on Eighth Avenue were bricked over and converted to dwellings.

The rapidity of these demographic and social changes bewildered and disturbed long-term residents. It provoked a counterreaction. The amnesia of history is such that the descendants of Sunset Park's immigrants had suppressed the memories of ethnic insults hurled against their forebears. Many looked upon the newcomers not as community builders but as community wreckers, as parasitic males living off welfare females, as parents who produced nothing but more children and more dependency, as depressants of the quality of everyday life. In the words of James Blaine, a chronicler of the neighborhood's history, they viewed the Puerto Rican newcomers "not just as another wave of immigration but as the final tsunami." By the midsixties, the temperature of anti-Hispanic feeling mounted. The smolder was fanned into flame by real estate "blockbusters," who stirred the fears of every property owner.

Arrayed against these hostile attitudes were Sunset Park's beleaguered liberal forces, notably the churches, the Lutheran Medical Center, Hispanic leaders and, generally, the coalition that would later give rise to the Sunset Park Redevelopment Committee. They welcomed the newcomers with gestures of friendship—proffers of help and a place in the community's councils. Threatened Hispanics regrouped their own forces and established in 1970 an ethnic-defense federation, UPROSE (United Puerto Rican and Spanish Organizations of Sunset Park–Bay Ridge, Inc.).[63]

### Distress in the Home Ownership Market

The ethnic turmoil was exacerbated by a sharp decline in property values that jeopardized the life savings of Sunset Park's older residents. In actuality, a market decline had set in well before the peak Puerto Rican entry, brought on by the misfortunes earlier recited— the dying waterfront, the blight of the expressway, and the suburban exodus of the fifties.

Exacerbating matters was the 1961 Zoning Resolution. As said, in most of the blocks west of Third Avenue, the housing inventory had been declared nonconforming, subject to rigid prohibitions against reconstruction, or improvements, even against certain kinds of repairs. Under the circumstances, a galloping disinvestment was inevitable. Mortgage lenders cut off loans to property owners within the

---

63. The network of constructive relations forged between progressives and Puerto Ricans within Sunset Park later reached out to take in nearby Borough Park, where similar interethnic conflicts raged. Clashes between Borough Park's Jews and Sunset Park's Hispanics had been fomented by the former's anger over assaults by Puerto Rican youth (one, in 1978, fatal) and by the latter's anger over the perceived mistreatment of Puerto Rican tenants by Jewish landlords. To mediate tensions, and to cooperate on common goals, Sunset Park's St. Agatha's Church, situated on Borough Park's border, and Borough Park's St. Catherine's helped to create an organization called Sunbro, melding the two communities' names. Giving substance to this effort were the two communities' local development organizations, the Sunset Park Redevelopment Committee (SPRC) and Southern Brooklyn Community Organization (SBCO). Later, SPRC was to assist SBCO in the management of apartment properties along the Eighth to Tenth Avenue corridor that links the two communities. They also merged political forces to lever additional government resources.

rezoned area; title and casualty insurance became hard to get. From the standpoint of banks and insurance companies, nonconforming housing is an unacceptable legal and economic risk, irrespective of the creditworthiness or ethnicity of owners. But affected property owners perceived the withdrawal of mortgage lenders as a clear case of redlining. Mortgage lenders rebutted the allegation, pointing out that the investment quality of housing had been impaired by overt (and legal) public actions, not by any private conspiracy. No matter where guilt lay, the withdrawal of financial intermediaries dooms a housing market: buyers evaporate, old mortgages cannot be renewed, and loans, even for necessary repairs, dry up.

Thus, the area was destined for a downhill slide, with or without Puerto Rican entry. Indeed, it was observed that much of the Puerto Rican migration was induced by that decline. Cause and effect were further confused by a deliberate and organized blockbusting campaign. Real estate speculators played on every home owner's anxieties. "The neighborhood is gone. Sell now, tomorrow will be too late," went the dread warning. The blockbuster's whisper amplified to full-throated volume. Fear turned to panic.

Conspiring with the blockbusters were corrupt FHA officials, enticed by the handsome profits to be derived from frightened sellers and ignorant buyers. Under a special program, the FHA was enabled not only to underwrite home mortgages but to make them available to the working poor, to buyers well down the income scale. The magic was Section 235.[64] Promulgated by Congress as a benign innovation, Section 235 proved a near disaster. By the early seventies the national default rate was prodigious, presenting President Nixon with a plausible excuse for his stunning moratorium of January 1973—a complete shutdown of every housing-subsidy program.

Ironically, the Section 235 difficulties between 1969 and 1972 owed something to the fact that it evolved into something very nearly the reverse of redlining: It provided more mortgage money to the poor than the poor could beneficially absorb. The origin of the problem was in lax lending standards, compounded by outright fraud. The scam, in Sunset Park as elsewhere, was a combination of panic selling, blatant over-appraisals, and shoddy merchandise. Typically, speculators contrived the purchase of a house from a distressed

---

64. Section 235 of the National Housing Act, enacted in the last days of the Great Society, provides special incentives to low-income families to become home owners. The aid is twofold—a sharply reduced-rate mortgage, as low as 1 percent, and the waiver of all but a token down payment.

owner for $5,000 or less. After cosmetic touch-ups, the property was sold for $20,000 to be financed by an FHA-approved mortgage of nearly equivalent amount. The buyers of these overpriced and over-mortgaged houses were usually the new Puerto Ricans, unwary families who lacked the means to meet monthly financial charges plus the costs of keeping oft-defective homes in good repair. Substantial numbers of properties went into default, turned back to mortgagees and eventually to FHA.[65] In Sunset Park, nearly 100 were boarded up, to become the prey of vandals, drug dealers, and weather. The notoriety brought Section 235—a potentially useful program—into disrepute and, for some years thereafter, into discard.[66]

Chastened by the public uproar, FHA's policy swung to the opposite extreme. It turned off its underwriting spigots, either summarily rejecting applications or capping appraisals at impractically low levels. A consequence of FHA's new "religion" (it will figure in a later discussion) was to retard Sunset Park's organized community renewal programs: HUD officials were loath to transfer FHA-held property in sufficient volume and with mortgages high enough to cover reconstruction costs. They were unpersuaded that even a responsible nonprofit community organization could make a go of the area's depressed housing market.[67] Much time would be expended and much political capital exhausted before FHA could be coaxed back into Sunset Park's stricken areas.

In the interim, disinvestment accelerated. By 1977, the abandonment total included more than 200 small properties and 40 apartment buildings. On street after street the building line was punctured by empty lots as owners, to save on taxes and insurance, demolished uneconomic structures; the lots were quickly littered with the debris of a dismantling neighborhood. The blocks below (and often above) Fourth Avenue were defaced by the stigmata of dereliction—boarded-up and abandoned housing, shuttered industrial plants, the carcasses of junked cars.

---

65. A scandal erupted. In the New York area, 40 real estate brokers and FHA officials and 10 corporations were implicated. Among the latter was Dun & Bradstreet, which had spuriously enhanced borrowers' credit ratings. The *New York Times*, April 5, 1972, p. 47.
66. It has been advantageously reintroduced in New York—notably in the renewal of Brownsville (the Nehemiah project) and the South Bronx (the Charlotte Street project). The program was strengthened by more stringent controls and deeper subsidies.
67. As expressed by HUD's regional director, the objections were that "the industrial stretches were blighted, visually depressing and show no signs of improvement." The *New York Times*, December 26, 1976, Section 8, p. 1.

Those sections of Sunset Park unaffected by rezoning and the Section 235 ripoffs or that were distant from poverty concentrations were less environmentally impaired, though by no means spared. Even the prime blocks—many with decaying multifamily buildings on their avenues and corners—were not immune to market penalties as crime and drug trafficking increased and as schools, shopping, and public services deteriorated. As their prices tumbled, some homes on the better blocks were purchased by a trickle of middle-class bargain hunters, those more needful or less risk-averse than their fellows. They were, to apply a word now in disrepute, the pioneers, the pathfinders for a larger number to follow.

### The Collapse of Multifamily Housing

Whatever the vicissitudes of Sunset Park's home ownership market, the collapse of the multifamily sectors was far worse—and, in the event, more enduring. Those buildings were afflicted not only by intractable financial burdens but by social and political ones as well. The financial problems were bad enough. Although the rents in most larger multifamily buildings were legally fixed at low levels, they were still high relative to the incomes of their poorer occupants, mainly Puerto Ricans with low earnings and frequent bouts of unemployment, many on welfare.

With rent collections inadequate for proper upkeep, responsible landlords soon gave way to a horde of "slash and burn" speculators. These speculators, their skills honed to a fine edge in a host of failing neighborhoods, followed a familiar script. Commonly, they sold and resold the properties at artificial prices to inflate the value base, thereby obtaining higher mortgage loans and fire insurance coverage. Others were adept at skimming profits off the multifarious subsidies made available by City and federal agencies. Too many concentrated on milking their properties until the eve of abandonment, applying none of the rent money to repairs and as little as possible to bare-bones maintenance. Code-violation notices showered upon them were wantonly ignored. Mortgage and tax arrears mounted. Buildings, delinquent in debt service and taxes, were forfeited to mortgages or simply abandoned. Overinsured buildings were irresistible temptations to professional torchers; arson was rife. Both the City and mortgage holders to which many properties had reverted—the Anchor, Dime, and Lincoln savings banks among them—deemed it essential that management be contracted out. The contracts were sometimes let to commercial firms, but frequently to community organizations. The latter was to be the case in Sunset Park.

## A COMMUNITY ORGANIZATION IS BORN

By the middle of the sixties, Sunset Park's residents and institutions, inundated by a sea of troubles, were forced to a classic choice in governance—voice or exit. Should they resolve their problems by confronting them or by fleeing? Thousands of families, some as early as the fifties but more in the years that followed, elected to flee. But what of the others, the engagés who would not (or could not) join the exodus?

Those who chose voice over exit initiated over the next several years a series of meliorative steps. The two most consequential were a 1966 petition (soon granted) for the designation of Sunset Park as a poverty area and the launching of a community development program. The poverty designation made the now-established neighborhood eligible for special aids from the Office of Economic Opportunity (OEO) and other federal and state agencies. But that was a remedial, not a developmental, tactic—the stanching of a hemorrhage, not an advance toward health. Three more years were to pass before the community was moved to a proactive stance—organized programs that would not merely arrest the excrescences of Sunset Park's decline but restore its lost vitality.

The birth of Sunset Park's community development organization was stimulated by unique circumstances, though not a unique process. The annals of community action amply demonstrate that effective grass-roots organizations are seldom the creatures of calm planning or high-minded motives. More often they are spawned by the common perception of some impending and widely shared threat. Saul Alinsky, the evangel of neighborhood organization, had mastered that lesson. He lay down the two transcendent commandments in community action's bible. One is that neighborhood coalitions are forged in the crucible of anger. The other is that protest is precedent to program; indeed, according to the most fundamentalist version of Alinsky orthodoxy, protest matters more than program.[68]

---

68. An intriguing thought springs to mind: Had Alinsky and his disciples been in Sunset Park at the time Moses initiated the Gowanus Expressway, would it have been stopped? Perhaps. At any rate, a match between those two redoubtable figures might have rewarded New Yorkers with a marvelous spectacle.

The call to arms in Sunset Park was sounded during the summer of 1969. The rallying event was a proposal to drop upon the community a major meat-packing distribution plant, Brooklyn's largest. It transpired that the City's economic development authorities had decided to move the Fort Greene wholesale meat market within the Industrial Zone. The City owned there a large site at First Avenue between 54th and 57th streets formerly occupied by Bethlehem Steel's shipyard. The background for the City's decision was this: The facilities of the antiquated Fort Greene Meat Market, a century and more old, had fallen out of compliance with the rigorous sanitary standards promulgated by Congress in 1967. The Fort Greene site, just off the crowded intersection of Atlantic and Flatbush avenues, was hopelessly unsuited to any redesign consistent with the new standards. The practical choice for the market's proprietors was extinction or relocation. The City was determined on relocation and, moreover, within Brooklyn. It persuaded the merchants to transfer operations to a large new cooperatively owned facility in Sunset Park, available on advantageous terms.

The community's response to the proposal was instant fury. It saw in the meat market a noxious producer of stink and vermin, of truck-clogged streets, and predawn din. Once again a mindless bureaucracy was converting Sunset Park into a dumping ground. Once again it was blight-by-public-policy, a replay of the Gowanus Expressway and the Zoning Resolution. What made the offense more galling was that the meat market was to be placed hard by a site that the Lutheran Medical Center (LMC) had under consideration for its new hospital.

In August 1969, a mass protest meeting was mobilized under LMC's aegis. At the end of that meeting Sunset Park's first community development organization came into being—the Sunset Park Redevelopment Committee (SPRC, pronounced spark). SPRC was thenceforth to be Sunset Park's principal instrument for urban renewal. To the organizing effort, LMC contributed leadership and staff, among them a young and committed community organizer, Kathryn Wylde. She was to perform a key role in bolstering the fledgling organization with purpose, program, and resources.

SPRC encompassed a cross section of the neighborhood—churches, ethnic organizations, local businesses, civic and block associations. A significant gesture was to draw in the new Hispanics who, as noted earlier, had formed UPROSE, an autonomous ethnic organization, to represent their interests and to press for programs attentive to their special needs. The organization was headed by Gonzalo

Plasencia, the "Mayor of Third Avenue," the street given over to the first Puerto Rican bodegas.

The realists in SPRC's ranks were aware that the community would never again be what it had been. Too much had changed—demography, the waterfront, the lure of the suburbs. But Sunset Park could try to achieve something resembling stability, a neighborhood able to retain and attract upwardly mobile and community-minded people, no matter how different their heritage from those of the past. Values and behavior were what mattered, not ethnicity.

As it happened, the community lost its battle to block the meat market. The City proceeded with unaccustomed efficacy to implement its relocation plan. But the victors awarded the losers three consolation prizes. One was a commitment to an early study by outside professionals of ways to amend the hateful zoning regulations and, more broadly, to improve conditions in the industrial area. Second was a promise of generous access to the City's pool of urban renewal aids, not merely those accessible to all but also those for which only selected neighborhoods were eligible. The third was assurance that the City would affirmatively abet LMC's quest for a new hospital.

At the center of LMC's community activities was its recently appointed chief executive officer, George Adams. Adams, a man of commanding manner and resolute mission, had come to LMC in 1966 at a critical stage in the institution's history. What Adams inherited was an outmoded, financially troubled hospital, locked into a debilitated community abandoned by many of its traditional clients, attending physicians, and financial backers. LMC itself had reason enough to leave Sunset Park for more congenial surroundings. Indeed, some years before Adams's arrival, there had been sentiment among LMC's directors for a move to Bay Ridge. In 1960, not yet Sunset Park's darkest hour, LMC had acquired rights to a 3-acre site on 91st Street and Shore Road, a location attractive in every respect except that it was a good deal more convenient to the middle-class residents of Bay Ridge than to the poor residents of Sunset Park; the latter would have received there an uncertain, if not downright unfriendly, welcome.

To Adams and others on the LMC board, the Bay Ridge option was problematic. Several practical concerns had to be factored in. One was that a move to Bay Ridge could prove financially hazardous. Since Sunset Park was a designated poverty area, LMC was entitled to substantial federal funds; between 1967 and 1969, nearly $4 million had flowed in and larger amounts were in sight. Those funds were not likely to be transferred to affluent Bay Ridge. Second, Bay Ridge was not only middle-class but solidly Republican. Reflecting their conservative constituents, Bay Ridge's elected officials had no overwhelming desire to turn prime land over to a hospital with a poverty clientele. Their political opposition was not to be ignored since the immense sums of money needed to build a new hospital required the goodwill of a Republican-dominated state government.

Finally, the Bay Ridge option was morally unappealing. LMC had occupied a salient and honorable position in Southwest Brooklyn for upward of three-quarters of a century. That was so despite the fact that it was not universally held in high affection; many Puerto Ricans believed LMC slighted their health needs with second-rate service. Nonetheless, the hospital symbolized Sunset Park's Scandinavian heritage as much as did the Lutheran churches or the monument in Leif Ericson Park. LMC's desertion of the community could be a fateful signal, a vote of no-confidence that would further sink the neighborhood's ebbing prospects for a comeback. Moreover, it would leave Sunset Park's poorer residents without medical services of any kind, however much some deprecated its quality. Virtually all Sunset Park's private practitioners had departed the area, so that LMC had become, for all practical purposes, the neighborhood's family physician.

In view of these financial and moral imperatives, Adams and LMC voted for voice over exit. LMC elected to stay in Sunset Park and to redouble its commitment to community renewal. LMC's role in Sunset Park had to be much more than that of a hospital and provider of medical care. It would also become the guardian of the wider interests of the community and of its disadvantaged members. The hospital's more prestigious functions—teaching and research—would have to give way to other priorities. And so they did throughout the seventies.[69]

LMC was determined to bring to the community—and to its new SPRC—every federal, state, and City subsidy within reach, a full harvest of loans, grants, and contracts from OEO, HHS (Health and Human Services), HUD, City, and State. To accomplish that, Sunset Park needed a strong political base. But influential political allies could be dependably enlisted only by demonstrating community cohesion. Sunset Park had to become more than the formal name of a heterogenous assortment of people residing on a cobbled piece of

---

69. Robert J. Walsh, "Creating a Unique Identity for a Community Hospital," Community Relations Study, September 1987.

geography. It had to be made into a neighborhood conscious of itself, prepared to mobilize and to wield its power. With Adams and Wylde in the lead, LMC worked zealously to instill a spirit of neighborhood unity, of shared effort and shared goals. To a degree it succeeded. In a few short years, the political system came to acknowledge Sunset Park as an identifiable unit in Brooklyn's governance, an entity to be reckoned with in the competition for public resources. SPRC also became a formidable fund-raiser. With private foundation grants, it acquired its own budget and staff whose primary responsibility was the reconstruction of the housing stock.

## A New Hospital for LMC

Sunset Park's flag lofted, Adams and SPRC moved on the Lindsay administration to cash in the IOU's collected in settlement of the meat market controversy. At the top of LMC's agenda was a replacement hospital. In Adams's view, LMC could not offer effective leadership unless it remade itself into an effective institution. By the sixties, the hospital's facilities were woefully obsolete, too old, too cramped, and falling away from the best standards of medical care. Modern medical economics dictated a much larger hospital—more beds, outpatient facilities, customized spaces for high-tech equipment and, not least, a sufficiency of parking space for staff and visitors. LMC's very survival depended on building an up-to-date medical complex. The goal, though, was clearer than the means.

A new medical center on LMC's existing site was plainly unfeasible. Health-care service would be disrupted during the long years of reconstruction. Worse yet, the existing site was much too cramped. An expansion into adjacent sites, however, would cause the displacement of many families and small businesses, an unpalatable option forthwith rejected. Somehow, somewhere, a more appropriate parcel would have to be found. But large developable sites were not plentiful in Sunset Park's residential areas; nor, were one found, did LMC possess an overflowing bank account to pay for it. And without good title to an appropriate site, government funds for hospital construction would be denied.

The resolution was as daring as the dilemma was deep. It was an idea that had occasionally flitted past the mind's eye of LMC's leadership. Why not build the new hospital in the Industrial Zone, thereby embedding an anchor of strength in that stricken area? Why not acquire the abandoned AMF plant on Second Avenue and reconstruct it into a state-of-the-art medical center? The vacant AMF structure, a full square block in size, was capacious enough. It was also structurally sound, with solid walls and floors, built to exacting industrial specifications.

The abandoned AMF building had come into City ownership in 1968, conveyed gratis by the departing company. Since it had cost the City nothing, LMC sought to obtain the property at a concessional price or, better yet, for nothing. The Lindsay people rejected LMC's appeal, pointing to a prohibition in the city charter that barred preferential property transfers to private parties. The City counteroffered, proposing a long-term lease at an advantageous rent. The counteroffer was unsatisfactory to LMC; it needed fee ownership to qualify for the government loans to pay the immense costs of reconstruction.

LMC mustered its political allies and ultimately won its case. A special act of the state legislature legitimated the transfer of the property to the hospital at a nominal figure, demonstrating, not for the first or last time, the indispensability of political clout to effective community development. Quickly, a hospital loan of more than $30 million was obtained from the state. More loans were to follow, $65 million in all. By 1977, a brand-new hospital within the walls of an old factory was in full operation. Somewhere in heaven, Deaconess Fedde, for whom improvisation had been a way of life, was surely smiling at this latest example, her 30 beds now more than 500 and her one-horse ambulance a fleet of charging vehicles. As astonishing for her would be the radically altered world of hospital economics. Her dime and dollar private solicitations had been supplanted by multimillion dollar infusions from public agencies. De facto if not de jure, government had superseded the Lutheran Church as master of LMC's destiny.

The solution to its hospital plant in sight, LMC turned undivided attention to community development. By the end of 1973, SPRC obtained a Ford Foundation grant of $150,000 for program implementation, to be administered by LMC. With these and other donated funds it recruited a small full-time staff. The first director was Eugene Murphy, a former congressional aide and legislative representative of the National League of Cities. Wylde left LMC to join SPRC as Murphy's community organizer, neighborhood activist, and program factotum. Murphy remained SPRC's head until 1979 when he was succeeded by Wilfredo Lugo, a Puerto Rican on LMC's community staff assigned to youth employment and related social programs.

During the Murphy-Wylde-Lugo years, SPRC obtained grants from ten foundations, though Ford remained its largest private do-nor.[70] In addition to seeking cash gifts, it enlisted the financial co-operation of several banks (Citibank, Banco Popular, and Anchor, notably) as well as Brooklyn's leading utilities, Con Edison and Brooklyn Union Gas.

Throughout SPRC's life, housing was the principal preoccupation—programs to rehabilitate, finance, and subsidize the community's worn-out residential inventory. But housing was only one of three tasks on LMC's community agenda. The two others were (a) a comprehensive reformulation by the City of its plans for the Industrial Zone, and (b) programs for human renewal, among them job training, health care, and drug prevention and treatment.

### Replanning the Industrial Zone

From the outset of its 1969 plunge into community action, LMC sought the removal of constraints on residential property owners in the manufacturing zone. More affirmatively, it urged a comprehensive program to harmonize industrial uses with the residential community, the key bargaining points in the meat market controversy. The Lindsay administration paid off this IOU with dispatch, though not without misgiving, since it was an invitation to a clash with private and public economic-development constituencies for whom jobs were a higher priority than housing.[71] Before the end of 1969, LMC and the City Planning Commission jointly engaged a team of urban professionals who drew up a plan to mesh the City's goal of industrial renewal with Sunset Park's agenda for community renewal.[72]

---

70. The others were the Consumer Farmer Foundation, Edna McConnell Clark Foundation, Fund for the City of New York, Local Initiatives Support Corporation, Robert Sterling Clark Foundation, Scherman Foundation, Stewart Mott Foundation, The New York Community Trust, The Vincent Astor Foundation.

71. Conflicts between industrial and residential land use are a hardy perennial in New York City, and not only in waterfront areas. In its zeal to protect a vanishing blue-collar sector, the City Planning Commission has been extremely loath to open industrial zones to housing use. The conversion of loft buildings to artists' housing in the manufacturing area now known as SoHo triggered a long and ferocious battle not yet satisfactorily resolved. The same was true of its grudging surrender of Manhattan's waterfront, which no longer has a single working pier. Generally speaking, the City is overzoned for manufacturing in the sense that it would take some unimaginable reversal of economic trends to develop industrially zoned areas to their capacity. As will be discussed later, the Commission on the Year 2000 has urged the City to reconsider its protective stance and to embark on a comprehensive replanning of the 500-plus miles of New York waterfront.

72. Urban Design Associates, *Sunset Park West Study*, May 1970. The report is in two

Guided in large measure by the planners' recommendations, the City embraced a plan to reconcile the community's grievances with its own commitment to the Industrial Zone's perpetuation. The high points included:

- A series of zoning changes to guarantee the integrity of the industrial mapping but also the continuance of residential use under less severe restrictions; new construction was still forbidden but specified kinds of repairs and improvements were to be allowed.
- A rearrangement of street signs and traffic patterns to facilitate the flow of vehicles and to lessen the disruptive impact on residential blocks.
- A ratification of the decision to construct the Brooklyn Meat Distribution Cooperative on First Avenue between 54th and 57th streets.
- To foster industrial revival, the establishment of a Northeast Terminal Container Port Corporation and the reconstruction of the shipping and cargo loading and unloading facilities along First and Second avenues; to advance that goal, the City purchased the Bush Terminal piers and turned them over to the Container Port Corporation; the City likewise acquired the railroad yards and leased them to the New York Dock Railway Corporation.

**Social Programs**

The physical replanning agenda was supplemented by an array of social programs, directed principally to the disadvantaged newcomers. They included most of the contemporary antipoverty agenda, for example, primary health-care services, manpower development, job training, Head Start, community action, a mental health program (in conjunction with Borough Park's Maimonides Hospital), and drug-abuse prevention and cure.

The social programs were noteworthy less for their content—conventionally Great Society—than for their divisiveness. The programs had no easy sledding. The community action component touched off a contentious welfare-rights movement that inflamed much of the Sunset Park community; a popular bumper sticker of those years was: "I fight poverty. I work." Matters were further exacerbated when, to implement the antidrug program, it was decided to establish a methadone treatment center in the middle of Sun-

---

volumes and covers industry, housing, traffic, plus a review of the feasibility of the AMF structure as an LMC replacement.

set Park's most vulnerable area. Given the City's mounting addiction rates, it doubtless fulfilled an urgent need. But it earned no plaudits and was looked upon by the people in the vicinity with utter repugnance.

Those who had opposed the 1966 poverty designation recalled their grim warning that LMC's pro-poor agenda, however well-intentioned, would reduce Sunset Park to a welfare colony. They regarded their case as proved when, during the 1977 blackout, extensive looting occurred, some of the worst in Brooklyn. It devastated the neighborhood's retail streets and was viewed as an assault on the neighborhood's civil order, of a sort never before experienced.

### SPRC's Housing Programs

The bedrock of Sunset Park's programs was its "brownstones," a large inventory of moderately priced row houses for owner occupancy that constituted its singular advantage in the inter-neighborhood competition for young middle-class households.[73] At a time when the brownstone movement was attracting a strong following, with beneficial results for several of Brooklyn's older neighborhoods, that inventory was perceived as the key to the community's future. SPRC's highest priority was the restoration of a stable market for owner occupancy. It moved quickly. Acting through an affiliated organization (Sunset Bay Housing Corporation), SPRC launched a program to salvage the 100 or more derelict structures that blighted their surroundings and, by contagion, the entire neighborhood. To prospective buyers and mortgage lenders, Sunset Park's abandoned eyesores were portents of irreversible slumhood.

SPRC's plan was to acquire, at minimal prices, the discarded properties, most of them in FHA's possession. The buildings would be rehabilitated and resold to responsible owners under new FHA mortgages, Section 235 for low-income buyers and Section 203 (FHA's basic program) for middle-class buyers. In those straitened years, FHA was a sine qua non. Uninsured private mortgages were unavailable or available only on impossible terms. The success of SPRC's program was dependent on FHA's willingness to yield its properties at nominal prices and to appraise and mortgage them at a figure sufficiently high to pay the heavy rehabilitation costs.

---

73. By then the term "brownstone" had become an honorific, applied to every manner of row house whatever its building material. Only a fraction were true brownstones, that is, with a façade of reddish-brown sandstone; most were brick of various hues, and some of limestone or other masonry.

FHA was anything but forthcoming. Its underwriters saw no market for the properties in the industrial area and balked at the idea of jacking up their appraisals to accommodate SPRC. Still scarred by the Section 235 misadventure, they refused to make a distinction between speculation and community investment; no such distinction existed in the FHA underwriters' manual, its appraisers' bible. After much political tugging and hauling, SPRC succeeded in acquiring 20 FHA-held houses at an average price of $1,900 per property but without any open-ended mortgage commitment. Unfortunately, rehabilitation costs proved a good deal higher than anticipated in the negotiated transfer, above $30,000 per property. In the mid-seventies, a selling price of $32,000 was a vain hope, except in Sunset Park's prime blocks. Even with the most generous mortgages FHA was prepared to offer, SPRC was able to sell fewer than half.[74] Sunset Park's weak housing market dashed another wistful hope—cross-subsidy. Without forfeiting its commitment to low- and moderate-income families, SPRC once believed it could sell its very best houses to affluent buyers at high enough prices to apply some of the profit to marking down the inferior properties.

The only realistic answer was capital write-down, a selling price set below costs. Portions of the Ford grant and other foundation grants went into a pool to absorb such write-downs. Private gifts, however, could not begin to meet total capital requirements. Access to public subsidy was essential. Moreover, for efficiency's sake, SPRC sought to advance from retailer to wholesaler, to acquire and rehabilitate properties in sufficient volume to achieve economies of scale. That meant not only a large flow of public subsidies but an assured and continuous one as well.

Toward that end, SPRC persuaded the City in 1976 to designate Sunset Park as a Neighborhood Preservation Area, thereby eligible for enriched subsidies. The pivotal aid was a newly devised Small Home Improvement Program (SHIP). SHIP was funded through federal Community Development Block Grants; block grant money could be applied to a broad range of purposes including whatever write-downs were needed to close the gaps between cost and price. To accommodate low-income purchasers, SPRC was able to tease out another (by then) scarce subsidy—Section 235. To avoid the booby

---

74. That problem was to persist throughout the inflationary period of the latter seventies. By that time market prices had risen to $40,000 but the costs of reconstruction had risen to $80,000. Cf. Sunset Park Redevelopment Committee, "Ten Years of Growth, 1975–1985," p. 17.

traps of the 235 fiasco, SPRC carefully screened every purchaser. It provided counseling in financial management as well as workshops in home repair and maintenance. None of the homes sold by SPRC experienced mortgage delinquency.

By the end of the seventies, as SPRC was still coping with its most problem-ridden properties, small numbers of yuppies and immigrants were beginning to buy houses in the better blocks, in straightforward transactions with no special assistance other than market-rate loans from sympathetic banks. The seeds of a private housing and mortgage market were beginning to germinate.[75]

If the home ownership market appeared pointed to recovery, the opposite was true of the multifamily sector. The rescue of Sunset Park's decaying and financially distressed apartment buildings was to be a lasting predicament for SPRC. What made the problem so daunting was not only the financial impediments but, as will be seen, deep social and political ones as well. Policies involving occupancy in the multifamily stock were riven by controversy.

The economic impediments to renewing multifamily housing were formidable enough: how to pay for the substantial costs of rehabilitation and adequate maintenance without raising rents beyond the means of low-income occupants, some the elderly but most of them Puerto Ricans. To ease that impasse, the City's most popular J-51 subsidy was available, an aid utilized over the years by apartment owners with hundreds of thousands of tenants.[76] The second most frequent subsidy was an array of concessional mortgage aids, some that reduce or eliminate equity requirements, some that reduce interest rates, and others that insure part or all of the risk; several mortgage formulas do all three. Since the gap between costs and affordability can be disheartening, community-development organizations with a very poor clientele are forced to twist every dial in the subsidy system—capital grants, low interest rates, blended private-public mortgages, mortgage insurance, a variety of rent-assistance aids, property-tax concessions, and management contracts on liberal terms. No municipality in the United States approximates the range and liberality of housing aids available in New York City. Table 6–3

---

75. As is noted in Chapter 8, by the time the last SHIP house was sold in 1983, there was no further need for the program and it was discontinued. See SPRC, *op. cit.*, p. 18.

76. J-51 defrays the bulk of the costs of rehabilitation in two ways. First, it does not assess the value of improvements for 20 years; second, it forgives part of the annual pre-rehabilitation tax liability, in an amount that would reimburse the investor over a 12-year period for 75 percent of certified costs.

**TABLE 6–3**
**Selected Subsidies and Aids Employed in District 7 Housing Programs, 1960–1985**

| Types of Programs | Number[a] of Units | Types of Programs | Number[a] of Units |
|---|---|---|---|
| FHA, all sections[b] | 473 | Alternative management, | |
| Section 8, new construc- | | no rehabilitation | 334 |
| tion | 503 | Neighborhood housing serv- | |
| Section 8, substantial re- | | ices[c] | 34 |
| habilitation | 501 | Sweat equity | 26 |
| Section 8, moderate re- | | City loans | 177 |
| habilitation | 125 | Section 312 loans | 58 |
| Participatory loans | 192 | SHIP and HIP | 501 |
| Article 8A, alternative | | J-51 tax abatement | 2,550 |
| management | 360 | 421a tax abatement | 152 |

*Source:* New York City, Department of City Planning, *Housing Database: Public and Publicly Aided Housing in New York City*, 1985, Tables C1–C5.
[a] Some properties obtain more than one aid, hence the actual number of aided units is smaller than indicated here.
[b] Includes period prior to 1960.
[c] Windsor Terrace only.

summarizes the lengthy roster of subsidies employed in Sunset Park's (District 7's) housing programs.

The deepest, and often the only workable, subsidy for low-income people is federal Section 8.[77] After a strenuous and bitterly opposed effort, Sunset Park was designated in 1979 as a Neighborhood Strategy Area (NSA), thus giving it access to a special allotment of Section 8. SPRC managed to pry loose more than 600 of these coveted certificates for its multifamily rehabilitation program (Table 6–3). But the political costs of doing so were enormous.

The application for NSA designation and Section 8 pinched a painful community nerve and was ferociously assailed. It was construed as another stigmatizing label, a depressant not only to Sunset Park's self-image and hopes for recovery but, more seriously, to future property values. The action reignited the rancorous conflict of a dozen years earlier when Sunset Park was designated as a poverty area.

---

77. Under Section 8, HUD pays, for an extended contractual period—up to 20 years for rehabilitation and 40 years for new construction—the difference between the fair market rent of a dwelling unit and an occupant's ability to pay, defined as 30 percent of family income. To qualify, income cannot exceed 80 percent of the area median, with adjustments for family size.

Indeed, some regarded NSA status as even more disfiguring than poverty status. Most poverty aids were based on annual appropriations. But Section 8 subsidies carried a long contract term, stretched out for decades. It guaranteed the perpetuation of a nonrepresentative tenantry, the behaviorally unwanted along with the deserving needy. To its opponents, Section 8 was the equivalent of a low-income public housing "project," in blue-collar communities an epithet synonymous with "cesspool." A neighborhood that throughout its life had been spared by the Housing Authority was now to be visited with a backdoor variant.

To Sunset Park's Puerto Ricans the attack on Section 8 was blatant prejudice. Little or no opposition to Section 8 had surfaced when several hundred certificates were sought and granted to the Marian Heim apartment complex for the elderly, developed on the former LMC site. The Marian Heim residents were, of course, largely of European heritage. How could Section 8 be praiseworthy succor when applied to one ethnic group and a pernicious transaction when applied to another? What possible explanation was there but raw bigotry?

To resolve such interclass, interethnic conflicts, SPRC was forced to expend energy and goodwill, lest a fractious community be hopelessly splintered. If one dilemma of grass-roots renewal is community apathy, the other is community arousal. To target resources on the needy without provoking a counterreaction from the non-needy and political vetoes, more is required than money, technocratic wizardry, and access to public agencies and elected officials. It requires also the capacity to weave—and preserve—consensus among disputatious and mutually hostile groups. The word "community" in community development is something of a misnomer. It implies a harmony rarely present in a pluralistic society.

The scars of the Section 8 conflict have not fully healed, though interethnic tensions have subsided. Antipathies toward Sunset Park's Hispanic welfare dependents are no longer overtly vented, but neither have they been extinguished. Even now, as will be seen, local political leaders tread warily around proposals involving subsidies for Sunset Park's multifamily housing.

## SUNSET PARK: THE 1980 CENSUS PROFILE

By 1980, Sunset Park's worst days were over and a better era was poised to begin. That, however, was not at all clear at the time, when most social and economic signals were flashing danger. The picture of Sunset Park drawn by the 1980 census takers carried little good news. A plethora of new statistics confirmed the exacerbation of the adverse trends recorded in prior censuses and observed in everyday experience. Over the decade, reflecting the massive exodus of people from New York—a net loss of nearly 800,000—Sunset Park's population had grown smaller, poorer, and considerably more Hispanic. The community was still in the grip of hyperactive population turnover; half its 1980 householders had lived somewhere else 5 years before. The average age of its housing stock had increased, unrejuvenated by new construction, of which there was precious little. The increasing volume of rehabilitation already under way was not capturable in the static format of the decennial questionnaire. But there was evidence in census tabulations that the neighborhood was acquiring an Asian subcommunity, still tiny and barely visible.

Measured from a constant set of census tracts, the neighborhood had lost, over the decade, another 9 percent of its people, declining to 86,700. The decline in households, however, was only 3 percent, from just under 32,000 to just under 31,000. The lesser shrinkage in households was due to a decline in household size. It fell from 3.0 to 2.8, extending the long-term trend shown in Table 6–4.[78] Given so massive an influx of large Hispanic families, the further drop in household size was somewhat unexpected. It bespoke the departures of additional thousands of young families and the further graying of the community's European residents, a large proportion of whom were now one- and two-person households.

Thus, despite the massive ethnic succession by poorer and more fertile people, in 1980 Sunset Park was not afflicted by the intense crowding characteristic of prior eras of immigration. Its reduced population was accommodated by a residential inventory almost unchanged in size, the losses approximately matched by additions, mainly by the conversions of older structures.

---

78. To facilitate comparisons with prior censuses going back to 1940, the 1970 data presented in the earlier historical table were based on a somewhat narrower set of neighborhood boundaries. The 1980 tables shown here and in Appendix B comprise 28 census tracts as follows: 2, 20, 22, 72, 74, 76, 78, 80, 82, 84, 86 (the public park), 88, 90, 92, 94, 96, 98, 100, 101, 102, 104, 106, 108, 118, 122, 143, 145, 147. Six of the tracts—90, 92, 94, 104, 106, 108—extend to Ninth Avenue, one block beyond Sunset Park's official Eighth Avenue boundary. A rough estimate for the overage was made from the block tabulations. By today's official boundaries Sunset Park's 1980 population would have been approximately 10,000 smaller, and its households 4,000 fewer, than here shown. Owing to differences in subject coverage and inconsistencies in the published figures, no other adjustments were attempted.

**TABLE 6-4**
Selected Characteristics, 1970 and 1980

|  | 1970 | 1980 |
|---|---|---|
| Population | 95,660 | 86,720 |
| Households | 31,888 | 30,971 |
| Average household size | 3.0 | 2.8 |
| Median income of families and individuals (current dollars) | $8,000 | $9,042 |
| Consumer Price Index, New York area (1967 = 100) | 119.0 | 237.2 |

Source: U.S. Census of Population and Housing, 1970 and 1980, Statistical Abstract of the U.S., 1987.

Over the decade, Sunset Park underwent a further decline in economic status, despite New York's recovering economy. Median income of families and unrelated individuals increased by 13 percent in nominal dollars, from $8,000 to $9,042. But the doubling of New York's consumer price index over the decade caused a deep erosion—approximately 42 percent—in the community's real purchasing power. By 1980, nearly 30 percent of the study area's population were in families below the poverty level. One out of four households obtained part or all of its 1979 income from public assistance. Sunset Park was poor not only measured against New York City as a whole (a median household income of $10,200 compared to $13,850) but also measured against Brooklyn (a median of nearly $12,000). The community's slide, however, was no plunge to the bottom. Sunset Park was still well above the bleakest poverty areas such as Williamsburgh ($8,880), Bedford-Stuyvesant ($7,857), Bushwick ($6,955), and most of the South Bronx (a range of $6,400 to $7,000).

The distribution of income of Sunset Park differed strikingly by tenure and subneighborhood. Sunset Park's home owners, a quarter of all households, reported incomes double those of renters.[79] But, even home ownership did not imply remarkable affluence; less than 5 percent of Sunset Park's households reported an income of $35,000 or more compared to more than 14 percent in New York City as a whole.

---

79. The income disparity between owners and renters, citywide, had generally become wider than in the past. The phenomenon reflects a pervasive national trend that sees the rental inventory more and more occupied by the poorest segments, broken families, and minorities. Cf. Anthony Downs, *Rental Housing in the 1980s* (Washington, D.C.: The Brookings Institution, 1983), p. 3.

As throughout its historical development, Sunset Park's poorer areas, with occasional exceptions, were below (i.e., west of) Fifth Avenue, and the poorest below Third Avenue. As displayed in Maps B–1 to B–3 (Appendix B), the relatively prosperous areas were in the upland tracts containing the brownstone blocks.

Needless to say, the geographic distribution of Sunset Park's poor and near-poor households conformed closely with the geographic distribution of its Puerto Rican population. Over the decade, Sunset Park had grown even more Hispanic, intensifying the trend that began in the late fifties. In 1980, half of its residents reported Hispanic ancestry compared with less than 40 percent in 1970.[80] Like the Irish, Scandinavians, and Italian immigrants who preceded them and the Chinese who came after, Hispanic in-migrants sought out the places where co-ethnics had taken root. They provided a ready-made support system of language, culture, and kinship. There was this difference, however. In 1970, Sunset Park's Hispanicity was almost entirely Puerto Rican, more than 90 percent of the total. In 1980, by contrast, non-Puerto Rican Hispanics of Caribbean, Mexican, and Latin American origin accounted for more than one out of five (Table B–2). As will be shown in the next chapter, the incidence of non-Puerto Rican Hispanics has steadily risen.

Spatially, Sunset Park's Hispanicization had grown both deeper and wider. Census tracts with large concentrations in 1970 became still more concentrated and tracts previously unoccupied acquired substantial numbers. As Map B–4 indicates, in 1980 the population of 9 tracts was 60 percent or more Hispanic and 18 had at least 40 percent; in 1970, the corresponding figures were 4 and 9. In only two tracts, 104 and 106 at Sunset Park's southwest corner (occupied principally by Irish, Italians, and Asians) did Hispanics constitute less than 20 percent of the total.

Though Puerto Ricans share a common language and other cul-

---

80. It should be noted, however, that intercensal ethnic comparisons are problematic. The 1980 questions differed significantly from those of 1970. In 1970, for example, language and birthplace of respondent and parent were the principal definers of Hispanicity. In 1980, the respondents could report themselves as Puerto Ricans or other Hispanics even if they had been U.S. residents for several generations and spoke no Spanish. These definitional changes affect even more the study of Sunset Park's European ethnics, in particular Irish, Italians, and other descendants of the great historic immigrations. The great-grandson of a pre-1900 Irish immigrant could in 1980 identify himself as of Irish ancestry; in 1970 he would have been reported as a native of native parentage and excluded from any ethnic category. Thus, detailed statistical analyses of Sunset Park's changing ethnic composition are not feasible. The figures that appear here should be regarded as only rough approximations.

tural features with non-Puerto Rican Hispanics, there are many significant differences among the various subgroups. On the average, Puerto Ricans occupy the lowest levels in the social and economic hierarchy, followed by Dominicans, then by Mexicans and Central Americans. Cubans and South Americans are at the upper levels. Though census data do not permit a comparative analysis of the differential traits of Sunset Park Puerto Ricans and non-Puerto Ricans, a City planning study highlights those differences for the City as a whole. Puerto Ricans ranked below other Hispanics in income and attachment to the labor force, and higher in female-headedness and welfare dependency (Table B–1).

Sunset Park's Puerto Ricans were burdened with all the problems and disabilities characteristic of Puerto Rican areas throughout the City—street gangs, a drug subculture, chronic unemployment, teenage pregnancy, and transmitted poverty. It could be said at the time what Sunset Park's Center for Family Life was to say later. The Center, whose devoted nuns, trained social workers, minister to the local poor, most of them Hispanic, was moved to these words:

> For many [of the poor in Sunset Park] poverty as well as lack of parental and marital supports have become intergenerational. There is the experience of living with minimal or very restricted expectations and of being outside the possibilities for most other Americans. For some there are special burdens of conflict within the family itself, and serious problems impact on children from the very beginnings of childhood. By the time some youngsters reach the age of 5 or 6, the combined effects of parental uprootings and many kinds of deprivations thwart cognitive and emotional development to such an extent that they will have a hard time "catching up" with other children at school and meeting later social and developmental needs. Some of our "underparented" parents need to overcome problems of alcohol or substance abuse or learn to reverse neglect or abuse or other maladaptive patterns of behavior which expose their children to grave risks.[81]

Sunset Park's ancestral Europeans dwindled in number. By 1980, Italians, though still the largest European-origin group, were less than 11 percent of the total compared to more than 15 percent a decade earlier. Because of changes in ethnic classifications (cf. footnote 78), the actual decline was almost certainly considerably greater.

---

81. Robert J. McMahon, Sister Mary Geraldine, Sister Mary Paul, *A Progress Report* (Brooklyn, N.Y.: Center for Family Life in Sunset Park, July 1987).

The proportions of other once-prominent ethnic groups, notably Irish and Scandinavian, were now in single digits. The category, "Other Ancestries," is the catchall that combines the lesser European nationalities and those of undetermined origin. The latter reflects the inherent perplexities of ethnic classification—both for the Census Bureau and for respondents—in a society where processes of assimilation and intermarriage are powerful and where ancestral trees ramify into every conceivable configuration.

Asians, too few in 1970 for separate tabulation, in 1980 earned a line of their own. Overwhelmingly Chinese, they accounted for 2.8 percent of the population, not much below that of Sunset Park's long-established Polish enclave. As the Europeans had before them, they, too, were forming a community within a community.

As is shown in the ethnic-distribution maps in Appendix B, ethnicity was unevenly concentrated within Sunset Park's subneighborhoods. Though, as said, every tract was occupied by Hispanics, the incidence ranged from a low of 10 percent in the southeast sector, bordering on Borough Park and Bay Ridge, to 86 percent in Tract 20, west of the expressway. The spatial distribution of the various European ethnics was significantly influenced by the location of their parish churches. Italians (Map B–5) were the most broadly dispersed, though few any longer lived below the expressway; the heavier concentrations were in the northerly tracts (101, 145, and 143) nearest to historically Italian Red Hook and adjacent to St. Rocco's. The tracts (84, 88, and 90) close to St. Michael's constituted another Italian enclave. Sunset Park's remaining Irish were thinly dispersed. There was, however, a solid concentration in the cluster of tracts abutting on Our Lady of Perpetual Help (102, 118, and 122) (Map B–6).

The community's new Chinese adopted Tract 104 (Seventh to Eighth avenues, 56th to 60th streets) as their initial center, with tendrils trailing into adjacent blocks (Map B–7). Those tendrils were soon to thicken, as will be seen in the next chapter.

Remarkably, Sunset Park was in 1980, as throughout its century of growth and decline, an essentially non-black community. That fact was unaffected by dramatic increases during the second half of the century in the proportion of blacks in New York and even more so in Brooklyn; in 1980, the City's and borough's respective proportions of non-Hispanic blacks were 24 and 31 percent. By contrast, in 1980 blacks in Sunset Park represented only a minute 2 percent of the community, a proportion associated more with exclusionary suburbs than with older, nonaffluent New York City neighborhoods.

Why so is not altogether clear. The insidious workings of racial prejudice leap soon enough to mind. New York is not Chicago or

Detroit, but it contains any number of white ethnic neighborhoods famous for preserving a monoracial character even when surrounded by racial minorities. The Lower East Side's Little Italy, the Belmont section of the Bronx, Howard Beach in Queens, and Greenpoint and Bensonhurst in Brooklyn are ready instances.[82] Unlike Sunset Park, however, those neighborhoods have not accommodated many Puerto Ricans, either. Why was it that the inexpensive housing opportunities and vacancies that made Sunset Park so inviting to so many Puerto Rican and other Hispanics did not also attract New York's blacks?

The fact that they did not tells of raveled issues that snarl the geography of race and ethnicity. In that tangle, racial discrimination and racial self-segregation, religious affiliation, social class, housing costs, and electoral boundary lines are jointly and simultaneously implicated. Ethnographers have long observed that the lines of racial and ethnic separation are not formed solely between majority and minority populations but within those populations themselves. Thus, one can still correctly speak of Italian, Greek, Polish, Ukrainian, and Jewish neighborhoods in New York, though none of these groups faces discriminatory walls and none of their enclaves is mono-ethnic. Even in a relatively open society the flocking urge remains powerful. It is likely that blacks did not judge Sunset Park's Puerto Ricans to be any more welcoming as co-tenants than were Sunset Park's older Europeans. One discerns similar spatial separations between blacks and Puerto Ricans elsewhere in New York. For example, the Lower East Side and South Williamsburg, both predominantly Hispanic, have relatively few blacks other than in nearby public housing projects. Conversely, Brownsville and Bedford-Stuyvesant are overwhelmingly black with relatively few Hispanics. A Puerto Rican–black checkerboard is likewise evident in much of the Bronx and Queens.

Sunset Park's demographic upheaval during the seventies was reflected in census turnover rates. Nearly one-half of the community's 1980 population had lived in a different place five years earlier, compared to less than 40 percent for New York City as a whole. Since there was virtually no net growth in Sunset Park's housing inventory, the entrants were replacing exiters, confirming the extraordinarily high rate of out-migration. Three-fourths of the new arrivals had come from other neighborhoods in Brooklyn—many, apparently, as

82. Like Sunset Park, none of these communities contains public housing projects, something that would virtually guarantee a substantial black population; it was usually public housing that brought a black presence even into tightly knit working-class ethnic neighborhoods such as Bath Beach and Red Hook in Brooklyn, Flushing and the Rockaways in Queens, and such blue-collar suburbs as Yonkers.

disclosed by other data from telephone and real estate directories, from other buildings in Sunset Park. But note (Table B–3) that 7 percent of the recent arrivals had come from abroad, a higher proportion than for New York as a whole. The New Immigration had begun to leave its mark on Sunset Park.

Compared to Sunset Park's aging indigenes, the ethnic newcomers—both Hispanics and Asian—were a youthful population arriving as, or soon forming, multi-child families. In 1980, consequently, the study area's age pyramid was wider at the base and narrower at the apex than that of other areas. Nearly one-third of Sunset Park's 1980 residents were 17 years of age or younger, compared to 25 percent for New York City and 28 percent for Brooklyn. By contrast, persons aged 65 and over constituted only 11 percent compared to 13.5 and 12.5 percent, respectively, for the City and Brooklyn. Within a relatively short span, Sunset Park's schools, which had lost enrollment, approached capacity and, later in the eighties, surpassed it.

Despite rising house prices and rents and the trickling in of yuppies and Asians, nothing in the 1980 census showed Sunset Park to be a gentrifying neighborhood. Quite the contrary. The decline in its real income, the growth in its poverty rate, and a shrinking, aging, white non-Hispanic base indicated that the opposite of gentrification—sometimes called "degentrification"—had occurred.

That finding is further confirmed by census data on occupation, employment, and educational attainment relative to nearby areas whose revival was already well advanced. Thus, only 10 percent of Sunset Park's jobholders reported themselves as managers and professionals (Table B–5). By contrast, managerial and professional classes accounted for nearly 36 percent of the work force in Brooklyn Heights—the nonpareil of Brooklyn's brownstoners—and for nearly 32 percent in Park Slope (a few notches below Brooklyn Heights on the social scale though much lower on the scale of house prices). Sunset Park in 1980 was, as it had been in its past, a neighborhood of industrial and service workers plus those in lower white-collar occupations. Factory operators and manual workers accounted for 26 percent and service occupations for another 15 percent. The administrative-support category, comprising mainly clerks, secretaries, and the like, made up another 27 percent.

The absence of yuppie traits is additionally attested to by the data on schooling. Of individuals 25 years of age and over, only 13.2 percent had graduated from college or carried some college credentials. For New York City as a whole, the comparable figure was nearly 30 percent and for fast-gentrifying Park Slope next door, 33.7 percent. Conversely, nearly 60 percent of that age group had not graduated from high school, a substantially higher proportion than for New York City and Brooklyn or Sunset Park's neighboring communities.

## The 1980 Housing Stock

Sunset Park's housing stock changed little in size or composition over the decade. A modest quantity of new construction and additions by conversion offset the demolitions and market withdrawals. Fewer than 700 dwelling units were constructed between 1970 and 1980 (Table B–7). (Even fewer had been built in the preceding decade; more than three-quarters of the study area's inventory had been put in place before 1939). A decade earlier, the 1970 census had reported a still higher proportion (91.4 percent) as pre-1939 inventory. Part of the decrease in the old housing stock was a result of fire or casualty, hopeless deterioration, or the razing by owners of uneconomic structures to lower tax and insurance costs. However, though hardly spared, Sunset Park did not suffer the frightful ravages of arson and vandalism of the Bronx. The greater part of removals was the result of the wholesale public taking to widen the Third Avenue roadway beneath the Gowanus Expressway, later expanded into a major arterial. Over Sunset Park's postwar life, relatively few removals were accounted for by the replacement of outmoded housing with higher-value uses, as was the case in active real estate markets elsewhere in New York and, even more so, in federal urban redevelopment areas.

In other words, Sunset Park was a community whose built environment had changed far less than had its social and demographic environment. Had some long-absent residents returned in 1980, they would have been struck at once by the radical transformation in the area's people. But the revenants would have been in no confusion about the neighborhood's identity nor be in doubt of their bearings. Of course, the names on many of the churches were different. And some of the houses were now clad in Permastone or aluminum siding, and most with a thick patina of age and neglect. Doubtless there would be outrage at the expressway and mourning for the conversion of the Greek-revival courthouse on Fourth Avenue into a shabby (if indispensable) community-service center, and for the loss of such cherished buildings as the handsome South Branch library.[83] But the

---

83. A 1905 gift of Andrew Carnegie, razed in 1970. It was one of the many splendid, handsome libraries the philanthropist had bestowed on older neighborhoods. To the young overachievers of Jewish Borough Park, the South Branch (or as they called it, the Fourth Avenue library) was a warmly appreciated enrichment of their own tacky and understocked storefront branch on Thirteenth Avenue. For the book-intoxicated, the long trek (well over a mile each way) was a flea-hop distance.

configuration of its streets and the types and layouts of structures would be instantly recognizable. If the language and complexions of the people on the stoops or the youth disporting in the Park were different, the stoops themselves and the contours of the Park would have been comfortably familiar.

The "people change" would have been much more evident in the multifamily inventory than in the serried rows of owner-occupied houses. To be sure, the ownership of the one- to four-family stock was already in flux, as was noted in the earlier discussion of the Section 235 program. But transfers across ethnic lines were not yet as frequent as they were to become in the years ahead. In 1980, the bulk of Sunset Park's owner-occupied dwelling units, which constituted about one-quarter of the neighborhood's total inventory, was still overwhelmingly in the hands of older residents. Though a portion (viz., 21 percent) of the lower-priced homes had passed into Hispanic ownership, three-quarters of all owner-occupied units were held by non-Hispanic whites (Table B–8). In 1980, after two decades of settlement, only one out of every seven Hispanic households was owner-occupied.

Sunset Park's Asians were better represented in the home owner sector than in the population at large, a testament to their penchant for saving and investment. In 1980, the Asian ownership rate was equal to that of whites. And, as will be shown later, their role in Sunset Park's real estate market went beyond home ownership; Asians were also conspicuous in the ranks of Sunset Park's real estate speculators, latecomers to that fraternity but quick learners.

Summing up, Sunset Park in early 1980 was a community still in the throes of its long twilight, with signs that presaged more of the same ahead. Though LMC and SPRC could be credited with arresting the decline and preventing matters from getting worse, theirs was an uphill struggle. SPRC's housing output, far more dependent on public subsidy than market forces, was relatively meager. As said before, organized community development is almost always hostage to those forces, the ultimate determinants of success or failure.

Sunset Park was restored by two external events—a resurgence of the City's economy and new floods of employed people looking for affordable housing. The combination powered a major surge in market demand. Owing to the stark drop in new construction and heavy losses in the supply of older housing, the surging demand was funneled into every neighborhood that possessed a habitable housing stock, resulting in a heady boom in some and varying degrees of uplift in virtually all, including Sunset Park.

# SUNSET PARK, BROOKLYN

**Housing for the middle class, early 1900s**

The old pond in what became Sunset Park

Freya, the first ambulance horse for the Norwegian Hospital

The housing of the laborers, 1911

Photos: Courtesy of Sunset Park Restoration Committee

**Fourth Avenue before the subway: the Grand Boulevard**

**Fourth Avenue:
the subway
comes, 1911**

**Bush Terminal:  the waterfront in its heyday**

A workday begins and ends at Bush Terminal

**Irving T. Bush: his entrepreneurial spirit commemorated, 1950**

The waterfront in 1989: an industry in ruin

Photos: Laslo Szekely

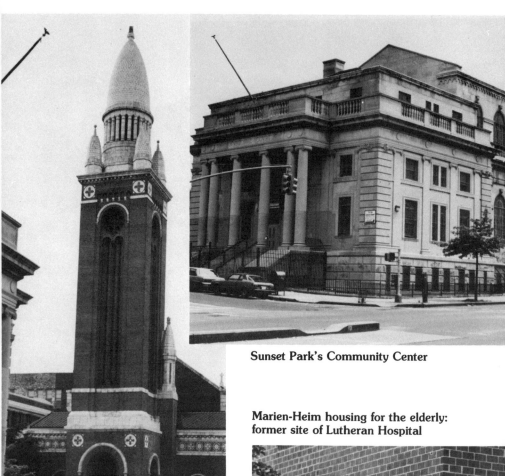

Sunset Park's Community Center

Marien-Heim housing for the elderly:
former site of Lutheran Hospital

St. Michael's and its
famous campanile

**Brooklyn Army Terminal, 1989: Cass Gilbert's atrium restored**

**Factory becomes a hospital: Lutheran Medical Center in 1989**

The Gowanus Expressway, 1989: it blights and splits the neighborhood

A vestige of the Norwegians: Scandinavian bread on Eighth Avenue, 1989

The brownstone belt, 1989

A new Chinatown is born: Eighth Avenue, 1989

The co-ops of Finntown, 1989

Photos: Laslo Szekely

A typical Hispanic street: frame houses and playful children

# CHAPTER 7

# Sunset Park Redux:
# The Post-1980 Years

By the mid-eighties Sunset Park was nestled securely in the curl of a rebounding wave. That fact was evidenced in any number of indicators: population growth, rising real income, retail activity, soaring real estate prices and rents, bountiful inflows of private mortgage capital. In 1987, a substantial majority (70 percent) of Sunset Park's residents rated it as a fair to excellent community.[84]

But notwithstanding its dramatic turnaround, Sunset Park's relative status was still well below that of the more highly favored communities on which it bordered—Park Slope, Windsor Terrace, Bay Ridge, and Borough Park. The rising tide of housing demand lifted every neighborhood but did not substantially close the distances between them.

Sunset Park's revival has been mixed and incomplete. Not every

---

84. Michael A. Stegman, *Housing and Vacancy Report, New York City, 1987*, p. 165, hereinafter referred to as the *1987 Housing Report*. It is the most recent of a series of triennial surveys mandated by the rent-control statutes and conducted by the U.S. Bureau of the Census. The 1987 sample was a little under 20,000 households. The sub-borough areas for which data were separately tabulated generally conform to community district lines. Hence, the data on Sunset Park taken from that source actually apply to Community District 7. The report is available at the New York City Department of Housing Preservation and Development.

segment in the community benefited. Many have been downright discomfited and some doubtless injured. The gains accrued mainly to those in the social and economic mainstream and, most strikingly, to those owning real estate or other proprietary interests. As late as 1987, at least one-quarter of its households were below the poverty level.[85] Residents who neither owned property nor enjoyed long leases or statutory tenancy, the circumstance of numerous store-keepers and thousands of tenants in uncontrolled shelter,[86] have been subject to steadily rising rents and an omnipresent threat of dislocation.

Nor have Sunset Park's infrastructure and physical environment improved nearly as much as its retail and housing sectors. Its public schools remain severely overcrowded, pedagogically weak, and decidedly uninviting to the middle class. Blight scars large parts of the Industrial Zone. A good many streets and avenues, especially in the vicinity of the Zone, but elsewhere as well, are dowdy and some worse than that. Though, as is later discussed, manufacturing jobs in the Industrial Zone are increasing, the waterfront economy per se is near death, even if some profess to hear a faint pulse returning.

It is not possible to date the precise turning point in Sunset Park's fortunes. As was noted in the last chapter, by the late seventies, even as Sunset Park was losing much of its older white middle class, a small stream of younger middle class and a larger stream of upwardly mobile immigrants began to trickle in. Some, mostly immigrants, were drawn there by local jobs, business opportunities, and relatives, and all by bargain house prices and rents.

At the turn of the decade, Sunset Park's housing market began to brighten as inflation brought prices and unregulated rents sharply up. It was noted, though, that since rehabilitation costs were simultaneously inflating, substantial write-downs were still necessary as late as 1980 for SPRC to sell restored houses on the less-attractive blocks, Sunset Park enjoyed anything but a runaway market. But soon thereafter the market took flight. In the next five years a quickening stream of buyers and renters poured in, bidding for dwellings at ever higher prices and rents.

Sunset Park's recovery was a lagged consequence of New York City's recovery. The strengthened demand for its housing was a spill-over from the incredibly booming housing markets of Manhattan and, more particularly, of West Brooklyn's home ownership neigh-

85. *1987 Housing Report*, p. 158.
86. An estimated 50 percent of all rental units. *Ibid.*, p. 162.

borhoods. As described in Chapter 4, by the late seventies, the City had begun a slow climb out of the economic and fiscal pit into which it had been cast in the early seventies. New York's recovery proceeded more slowly during the first years of the eighties, retarded by the deepest national recession since the thirties and a record spike in interest rates. After 1983, the winds of robust financial markets at its back, the velocity of New York's recovery accelerated. The City regained all the employment it had earlier lost. During those years, the prices of older free-market housing vaulted to unprecedented heights, carried there by a combination of growth in households, increased real income, steeply inflated construction costs, and limping new building.

In every viable neighborhood, the real value of nearly all standing structures dramatically appreciated, rising far more than the consumer price index. In due course, even barely standing structures in barely viable neighborhoods were swept into the market mainstream. The *1987 Housing Report* described a substantial improvement in housing quality and a surprisingly large addition of more than 40,000 units to the housing inventory, only one-third of them the product of new construction. The annual rate of loss, which had averaged nearly 45,000 units between 1977 and 1984, declined to 14,000 in 1984–1987.[87] The rate of abandonment and in rem takings fell steeply. So keen was investor interest in purchasing the City-owned stock of housing, that the Housing and Preservation Department was forced to curtail sales, to preserve a sufficient inventory to implement its ten-year housing program.

By the mid-eighties, the heightened Citywide demand for existing housing had rolled across every neighborhood. In 1983, Sunset Park's home ownership market cast off the last crutch of subsidy. Community restoration, once a receding prospect, had become an unmistakable reality. Middle-income buyers and renters, of heterogeneous social class and ethnicity, entered by the thousands. Home prices and unregulated rents rose in double-digit jumps, averaging more than 20 percent per year until 1988 when, as nearly everywhere in the metropolitan area, a flattening occurred and by 1989 an unmistakable retreat.

During the steep price ascent, anxieties were expressed, at least by some, about too much of a good thing. The apprehensions of the seventies of a chronic deficiency in housing demand gave way to apprehensions of an excess. The words "gentrification" and "dis-

87. *1987 Housing Report*, p. 202.

placement" resonated, sounded most often by the Hispanic community. Ironically, according to data soon presented, it was neither yuppies nor Asians but Hispanics (mainly Dominicans) who constituted the largest bloc of new entrants. To anticipate later findings, the post-1980 renewal of Sunset Park thus far is characterized more by a gradual broadening of its social and economic diversity than by any wrenching ethnic transformations.

As is true of both the City and Brooklyn, Sunset Park's population is again growing, albeit modestly. Some demographers and marketing forecasters, not yet sufficiently cognizant of the weight of New York's New Immigration, were caught by surprise. A number of local-area housing projections that were based on extrapolations of 1970–1980 trends fell short of actual gains in household formation. NYNEX projections of telephone demand within the service district that includes Sunset Park had persistently fallen short of actual installations.

According to the Department of City Planning, between 1980 and 1985 District 7's population, of which Sunset Park is the larger part, increased from 98,000 to 111,000, about 14 percent. Judging from more recent data for Brooklyn, the current level is surely higher. The count of Sunset Park's telephone listings continued to increase steadily through 1987; so has its subway ridership.

Sunset Park has plainly recaptured the esteem of all—housing consumers, merchants, real estate investors, the giant mortgage lenders and the smaller. What was once disinvestment became reinvestment, capped by a froth of speculation. Mortgage money for home purchase and improvement, so reluctantly granted in the sixties and seventies that it brought accusations of systematic discrimination by lenders, is freely proffered by fiercely competing mortgagees, institutional and noninstitutional. No one in Sunset Park spoke any longer of redlining, certainly not with respect to the non-rent-controlled stock.

Residential reinvestment in the community, however, has been channeled primarily into rehabilitation. Neither new construction nor co-op conversion is yet much in evidence. Between 1980 and 1985, only 500 additional new units were put in place, all with Section 8 subsidy; 368 were for the Marian Heim project, which was financed by a HUD Section 202 mortgage, rather than private capital.[88] Though builder interest mounted, private construction has remained spotty,

---

88. New York City, Department of City Planning, *Housing Database: Public and Publicly Aided Housing in New York City,* 1985, Table C1, R 103, p. 128. Section 202 provides mortgages for the aged and handicapped that pay virtually 100 percent of development costs. The loans came directly from HUD, bypassing the banks.

confined mainly to streets approaching Bay Ridge and Park Slope. The primary explanation is not a lack of available sites (though there is little vacant land) but of market economics. The handful of new units placed on the market even in the advanced stage of Sunset Park's revival have not been runaway sellouts. Thus, there is little incentive for builders to obtain sites by demolishing existing structures, as has been true in New York's stronger markets.

By contrast, private rehabilitation has occurred on a large scale, a response to the purchasing power of thousands of new, more affluent owners and renters. The exteriors and interiors of the one- to four-family housing stock have been extensively upgraded. It is a rare street without a nearly full façade of improved homes; even the frame houses in unprepossessing, mixed-industrial blocks boast new fronts and often elaborate ornamentation. The brownstone streets project a most pleasing appearance and, on some blocks, a touch of real elegance. The Sunset Park Restoration Committee, which repeatedly petitioned the New York City Landmarks Preservation Commission to designate a large irregular portion of Sunset Park as an historic district, achieved in 1988 an incomplete victory. It succeeded in placing the area containing nearly 4,000 homes on the national and state registers, though it has not yet persuaded the City Commission. It is the largest district thusfar inscribed on the national register.

As observed in property-transfer data, real-estate activity intensified throughout the study area, affecting low-grade as well as prime housing, and the poorer streets as well as the chic. Though still much below those of adjacent areas, Sunset Park's late-eighties house prices and unregulated rents were to its once-despairing older owners a thing of wonderment. Their balance-sheet wealth surpassed the dreams of working-class householders resigned to a lifetime of cumulating a substance solely from small savings. Between 1977 and 1987, prices of typical two- and three-family brick houses increased from a range of $35,000–$42,000 to $210,000–$275,000. Select houses boasting original architectural features coveted by brownstoners (e.g., high ceilings, ornamental moldings, colored glass, and fireplaces) were at a premium and occasionally sold for more than $300,000.

Over the same years, unregulated rental units in the smaller buildings increased from a range of $100–$150 to $550–$850 per month. Exceptional apartments—duplexes and those with access to a garden—could fetch $1,000. But since half of Sunset Park's rental inventory is under regulation,[89] average rent is still quite modest; in 1987

---

89. *1987 Housing Report*, p. 162.

median gross rent (higher than contract rent because it includes utilities and other charges) was $394. About one-fifth rented for less than $300.[90]

The dizzying escalation of house prices could not last forever. By 1987 the rate of increase fell off and by the middle of 1988 there was clear indication of a halt. Data culled from classified ads over the first half of 1988 indicated a mild reversal in asking prices and a pronounced tendency for offerings to linger longer on the market. Real estate brokers, though innately buoyant, grudgingly confirmed a stalled market, as did mortgage lending officers.[91] There was no evidence, however, of a break in the rental market; rents continued to rise without interruption in the smaller unregulated properties. Sooner or later, those increasing rents will drive property values higher. That suggests that sags in prices of the two- to four-family house markets are not likely to be deep.

Sunset Park's renascence has not, by a long measure, attained the breadth and height of its neighbors (Park Slope, Borough Park, Bay Ridge) or even its District 7 co-inhabitant, Windsor Terrace. Pockets of stagnation are still much in evidence. It says something, too, about the tentativeness of Sunset Park's recovery that sellers still frequently bait their ads with the tags of more esteemed markets nearby. It was not unusual for house offerings on the southerly blocks to be listed as "Bay Ridge area" and in the northern sections as "Park Slope vicinity." As late as 1987, Sunset Park's then-sole new private-housing development (at 33rd Street east of Fourth Avenue) was fancifully identified as "Villas at Park Slope"; its location is a good deal more than a stone's throw from Park Slope proper, certainly farther than the most exuberant realtor could throw one. More recently, a new low-rise co-op on 23rd Street proclaims itself as "Park Slope Heights" and a 14-story condominium tower on 64th Street as "Bay Royal Towers."

Nor, unlike its neighbors, has Sunset Park yet attained sufficient market strength to trigger a hectic co-op and condo conversion movement.[92] Listings of co-ops and condos in the classified ads average at

---

90. *Ibid.*, p. 160.

91. The tapering off of sales prices appears to be a pervasive phenomenon in the New York region, suburbs as well as the City, co-ops and condos as well as houses. It was seemingly engendered by the uncertainties of the October 19, 1987, stock market crash, perhaps also by a firming of mortgage interest rates.

92. Daniel McCarthy, *Brooklyn Housing Market Profile, 1986: Trends and Outlook* (New York: Municipal Research Institute, 1986). Most of the small volume of co-ops reported in this study for Community District 7 were in Windsor Terrace.

most an inch or two compared to three or four columns each for Park Slope and Bay Ridge. Aside from the original inventory of Finnish co-ops and the subsidized conversion of two subsidized "sweat equity" buildings during the seventies, only a scatter of additional transactions could be located before 1986; most of those were in small buildings (i.e., with fewer than six units) where the conversion was not impeded by statutory tenancy. Since then a few more conversions have occurred, and investors are closely scrutinizing vacant private or City-owned properties for additional opportunities.[93] But, given the relatively low quality of much of Sunset Park's multifamily inventory and the fact that a large proportion of its regulated units are occupied by low-income and welfare families, the conversion rate is likely to stay sluggish for a long time.

## SUNSET PARK'S NEW PEOPLE

It is time for a closer look at the proximate cause of Sunset Park's revival—an influx of new people—many of them yuppies but for the most part immigrants. In the years after 1980, Sunset Park's population turnover continued to proceed at an exceptionally high rate. Mobility did not slow much in comparison with 1980, when the census found that nearly 50 percent of Sunset Park's households had lived in a different dwelling five years earlier. According to 1987 survey data, 28 percent of Sunset Park's households had moved in during the preceding three years, one of the highest turnover rates in Brooklyn.[94]

### The Middle-Class Market

Sunset Park's brownstone belt has attracted a considerable yuppie market. Much of it is a spillover from Park Slope where attached houses of comparable size and quality sell for up to 50 percent more. Not all of Sunset Park's new middle class are really new; some had lived in the area before. Alice and Robert Walsh are examples of "the native's return," she a founder of the SPRC and he head of LMC's Office of Community Relations. So too are Victoria and Noel Fuestel, she a TV personality, born and reared in Sunset Park, he a prominent

---

93. In 1988, five additional subsidized properties containing 38 units were converted to low-income co-ops. In 1989, additional small clusters of coops and condos were built, none conspicuously successful. The aforementioned condominium tower was subsequently repossessed by the mortgage lender.
94. *1987 Housing Report*, p. 170.

real estate broker and promoter extraordinaire of the yuppie brownstone market. There are likewise intrafamily transfers within the older European stock, as retiring or deceased parents pass their homes on to grown children—young families who, a decade earlier, might well have elected the suburbs.

The arrival of baby boomers notwithstanding, Sunset Park displays few signs of transformation into a yuppie haven; their numbers, so far, are simply too thin. Indeed, during the first years of revival, and even now, the neighborhood has been the undisguised compromise of those priced out of Manhattan and other preferred locations. A vignette in the *New York Times* is illustrative:

> Daisy Edmondson and Stewart Alter, both magazine editors, left their small Greenwich Village apartment eight months ago because they had just had a baby and, what's more, their landlord had doubled the rent. After "systematically" canvassing neighborhoods just outside Manhattan for an affordable house to their liking, the couple finally bought a brownstone for $78,000 in the Sunset Park section of South Brooklyn. "It's a pretty poor area—there are no restaurants and the shopping is horrible."[95]

Though the SPRC and local realtors strive indefatigably to attract more of New York's younger middle class, they confront formidable obstacles. Foremost are the deficiencies in the area's public schools, sorely overcrowded, and burdened with the poor and educationally sub-par. Families with school-age children gravitate to more promising school areas, even if that means, as it usually does, higher housing budgets. In one way or another, occasionally contrived, many of Sunset Park's white (and, for that matter, ethnic) middle-class families manage to enroll their school-age children in academically superior and less crowded public schools, some within District 15 (which includes Park Slope) and others in magnet schools elsewhere.[96] Except for a few pre-school, Head Start, and day-care facilities (two of them now Chinese), with abbreviated educational curriculums, there are no private nonsectarian schools in Sunset Park. The parochial schools, increasingly of mixed ethnicity, are another option. But

---

95. *The New York Times,* January 22, 1984, Section 8, p. 1.
96. According to District 15 school officials, the tormenting trade-off between housing costs and school quality has caused many yuppie parents who strain to pay Park Slope's high housing costs to risk the local public schools. Increased white enrollment here has been sufficient to arouse the hope of a significant school revival. Sunset Park is not at that hopeful stage.

judging from their steadily shrinking capacity and enrollments, especially of whites, there is only limited middle-class recourse to that alternative. Those who can afford private schools send their children to Bay Ridge, Park Slope, or Brooklyn Heights.

As a consequence, Sunset Park's public schools remain overwhelmingly Hispanic—85 percent throughout the eighties (see Table 7–3). There is some prospect, however, of additional white enrollment if and when classroom capacity is expanded and pre-kindergarten programs spread. All things considered, future changes in the ethnic mix will be more likely due to enrollment by New Immigrants rather than yuppie children. More will be said about this later.

A second deterrent to the younger middle class is a lack of suitable shopping—goods and services attuned to their tastes. Because their numbers are below a critical mass, Sunset Park does not offer upscale shops or goods to match the tastes of baby boomers. The Fifth Avenue corridor, though a busy retail street, displayed even in the late eighties few marks of "boutiquification." There was no gelato, no nouvelle cuisine, no "white tablecloth" restaurant, no high-fashion clothing stores. On Eighth Avenue in the Fifties, a popular Chinese eating place, mimicking the realtor's strategem, calls itself the Bay Ridge Restaurant. The food shops on Eighth Avenue have improved, but mainly to accommodate the growing Chinese population. Some 1,200 Sunset Parkers are members of a food cooperative located in another community.

Thus far, The Gap and The Limited have yet to find in Sunset Park a profitable opportunity, let alone Benetton and Laura Ashley. For better merchandise and wider selections, Sunset Park's middle class looks to Bay Ridge and the shopping malls of Kings Plaza and the close-in suburbs. The Fulton Street Mall, anchored by Abraham & Straus, caters mainly to a nonaffluent minority clientele; massive redevelopment in downtown Brooklyn now in progress may give the mall a powerful economic boost. Manhattan, where most of Sunset Park's middle class works, is so far the favored option for shopping.

## The New Immigrants

To date, the dominant demographic force in Sunset Park's renewal has been not the yuppies but the New Immigrants. That is plain to any casual spectator who need not look beyond the people in the streets and on the subway stations and the merchandise and signage in the retail stores. But safe judgments depend on more than visual impressions; the researcher is obligated to supply supporting evidence. That is something easier said than done.[97]

The data vary in geographic coverage and reference dates, in methods of ethnic classification and quality. Fortunately, when taken together, the disparate sources proved mutually reinforcing and, generally, in agreement with data gleaned from interviews and site reconnaissance. Thus, it was possible to construct a rough but reliable framework of the numbers and proportions of the neighborhood's new ethnics as well as a map of internal distribution.

One of the more productive data sets bearing on Sunset Park's post-1980 ethnic shifts is *Cole's Dictionary*. *Cole's* is a "reverse" telephone book published annually in which the names of all listed telephone subscribers are arrayed by their street addresses; every building and street is included. Since family names offer good (though hardly conclusive) clues to ancestral lineage, it was possible to extract from *Cole's*, for any given year, a profile of Sunset Park's ethnic composition, in the aggregate and by census tract. Likewise, by tracing through successive directories all the name changes at given locations, it was possible to derive a sense of shifts in ethnicity over time. Complete tabulations of surnames for each of Sunset Park's census tracts was taken from both the 1981 and 1987 *Cole's*. These 100 percent tabulations were further updated through 1988 by complete tabulations from a subset of nine census tracts.[98] The names were classified into ten ethnic groups, as further described in Appendix A: Hispanic, Italian, Irish, Scandinavian, Polish, Chinese, Greek, Other Asian, Middle Eastern, Other European.

The telephone data yield convincing proof that the far-reaching ethnic transformations of Sunset Park, already evident in the 1970

---

97. Constructing a set of statistical measures of post-1980 ethnic shifts is an exercise in jigsaw-puzzle assembly, a jigsaw with key pieces missing and others that will not tightly lock in place. In that exertion, numerous data sources, varying in pertinence, coverage, and quality, were exploited. The principal ones, several earlier cited, were: *Cole's Directory*, the alien registration files by zip code compiled by the INS, Health Department birth records, school enrollments, a sample survey of the proprietors of retail establishments, the *Brooklyn Real Estate Register* (a compendium of past and current property transfers), and the Citywide housing surveys sponsored by the Department of Housing Preservation and Development that are conducted every three years.
98. *Cole's* dates its directories ahead of the actual calendar. Thus the 1988 directory is based on listings through October 1987, the 1987 directory through October 1986, and 1981 through October of 1980. The last date was close enough to the April 1, 1980, census to permit rough comparisons of selected data, as is commented on in Appendix A. Also discussed in that appendix are the ambiguities inherent in ethnic identification by surnames.

census and so strongly imprinted on the 1980 census, have continued. As shown in detail in Tables C–1 and C–2 and in the accompanying ethnic maps, the salient features of the post-1980 demographic transformation are:

- The clear predominance of Hispanics among the newcomers; Sunset Park is becoming ethnically more diverse but not less Latin.
- A steep increase in the number and proportion of Chinese and other Asians. That growth, however, ought not be exaggerated, as the media and some local spokesmen have been wont to do. The post-1980 gain is measured from a narrow base, so that the incidence of Asians in the Sunset Park community as a whole is still relatively light.
- An unabated diminution in the proportion of Sunset Park's households of European ancestry, despite the entry of yuppies who usually add to that ethnic category; it is further evidence of their limited numbers.
- An interpenetration of ethnicities. Every group is represented in every census tract; though newcomers of various ethnicities are drawn to co-ethnic agglomerations, they are spreading out into tributary enclaves. Ethnic settlement patterns are marked by both concentration and scatter.

Shifts in Sunset Park's ethnic composition between 1981 and 1987, as derived from telephone listings, are most conveniently grasped by looking at three related indicators. One refers to the geographic distribution of the ten classified ethnic groups, taken one at a time, and measured in absolute numbers; the second refers to shifts in relative shares, the details of which are presented in Appendix C. The third relates to interspersion, that is, ethnic distributions, jointly measured.

To begin with the two most prominent groups of newcomers—Hispanics and Chinese—the 1981 *Cole's* tabulations are strikingly parallel to the 1980 census maps presented in Appendix B. Hispanics continue to be distributed throughout Sunset Park, with the heaviest formations as before, between the waterfront and Fifth Avenue (cf. Map C–1).[99] In 1981, Hispanics were by far the largest (indeed, for

---

99. *Cole's* 1981 is consistent with the 1980 census in patterns of distribution, not in actual numbers or proportions. As discussed in Appendix A, Hispanics, Sunset Park's poorest ethnic group, are underrepresented among telephone subscribers.

some tracts virtually the sole) group of residents west of the expressway; they were only sparsely represented in the blocks east of Sixth Avenue.

By 1987, the frequency of Hispanics had increased in every tract (Map C–2). During the post-1980 era, the 1970–1980 intercensal changes, configurations reported earlier—higher densities in the enclaves and thicker satellite areas—were further accentuated.

As previously noted, Chinese residents had early on formed a nucleus in Sunset Park's southeast quadrant, that is, Tract 104 straddling Eighth Avenue between 56th and 60th streets, within walking distance of most Chinese garment establishments. The 1981 *Cole's Directory* confirmed Tract 104 to be the Chinese "center," with more spillovers into four adjacent tracts to the north and west (102, 122, 72, and 74, Map C–3). And a sprinkling of Chinese was present in every tract upland of the expressway.

By 1987, Chinese had increased in both nuclear and spillover areas (Map C–4). By then they occupied a cluster of eight census tracts extending from 65th Street to 48th Street. It is that cluster that has recently been dubbed New York's third Chinatown. A lesser but growing enclave was also observed in Tract 92 on the blocks just east of the Park.[100]

The small number (in 1981, fewer than 200 names) of non-Chinese Asians—Koreans, Indochinese, Pakistani, and East Indians—were similarly dispersed throughout the study area (Map C–5). But most non-Chinese Asians seem to have settled in areas of Chinese residence. A pocket of non-Chinese Asians was also found in Tract 72 near the Lutheran Medical Center, where many are employed. By 1987 the number of non-Chinese Asian telephone subscribers had doubled. Their residential distribution, however, was little changed (Map C–6).

Only a small number of Middle Easterners (mostly Jordanian, Egyptian, and Lebanese) have settled in Sunset Park (Map C–7). The primary settlement of Brooklyn's Middle Easterners remains downtown Brooklyn, clustered on Atlantic Avenue and its environs, where their retail shops predominate. Though distributed throughout Sunset Park, they have formed an enclave in and around Tract 98, where the mosque (Fatih Camh) is located, on Eighth Avenue near 59th

---

100. In accordance with Census Bureau practice, the Park, though devoid of inhabitants and dwellings, is designated as Tract 86. It appears as a white space on the maps displayed in Appendix C.

Street. There has been a small increase since 1981, in part due to some 400 immigrant arrivals between 1983 and 1987 (Map C–8).

As was amply documented by census data, Sunset Park's older European stock has been shrinking (absolutely and relatively) for several decades owing to exodus and death.[101] Though Europeans are overrepresented in Cole's telephone listings, that source agrees with the census with respect to the relative size of the various groups and their spatial distribution. Cole's 1981, as had the 1980 census, indicated Italians to be Sunset Park's largest European ethnic group plus the fact that they were most heavily settled in the northerly tracts abutting St. Michael's and St. Rocco's churches, 143, 145, 101, and 84 (Map C–9).

Cole's 1987 showed the traditional Italian tracts remained predominantly Italian (Map C–10). But a thinning out occurred in total numbers, particularly in the easterly tracts where Chinese were settling. As with every European group, the actual shrinkage of Italians because of death or exodus is doubtless greater than indicated in the net figures. As may be observed in the data on new telephone subscriptions, hundreds of Italians enter Sunset Park each year, of whom, judging from INS data, only a few are foreign immigrants. Most are native and doubtless well represented in the yuppie category. Except for Tract 22, few Italians (or, for that matter, any other Europeans) were located west of the Gowanus Expressway.

Irish, according to Cole's 1981, as in the 1980 census, were most frequent in the southerly tracts centered on Fifth Avenue and 59th Street, near the leading Irish church, Our Lady of Perpetual Help (Map C–11). There was also a solid Irish bloc in Tract 145 surrounding St. John's, on Fifth Avenue and 21st Street, Sunset Park's oldest Irish parish. In 1987, Irish surnames were scarcer, both in the total listings and among new subscribers (Map C–12).

As prefigured by successive censuses, Scandinavians, once the hallmark of Sunset Park, had grown rare. According to Cole's 1981, the bulk of those classified as Scandinavian were in tracts 102 and 104, nearest to Bay Ridge (Map C–13), which had replaced Sunset Park as Brooklyn's Scandinavian "capital." There was also a fair-sized number of Scandinavian names around the perimeter of the Park, where the early Finnish immigrants had settled and built their cooperatives.

---

101. A 1980 Health Department breakdown of deaths by ethnicity in Sunset Park's health areas indicates that three-quarters were Europeans, half of them the immigrants of earlier eras.

By 1987, Scandinavian names in most tracts had further declined, replaced by other ethnic names, conspicuously Chinese (Map C–14).

Greeks, a small but historical component of Sunset Park's ethnic mosaic, have also dwindled. Even the tracts surrounding their church—Kimisis Theotokou at Fifth Avenue and 18th Street—contained few Greek names. However, due to the substantial migration of prospering Greeks from Astoria and other settlements in New York to Bay Ridge, clusters of Greeks are found on the streets that border that community (Maps C–15 and C–16).

The early Polish immigrants, as stated in the historical summary, had formed a hamlet abutting on Our Lady of Czestochowa church on 24th Street east of Fourth Avenue, census tracts 101 and 145 (Map C–17). In 1987, that cohesive Polish community was still more or less intact (Map C–18), death and retirements offset by in-movements from other Polish sections of New York, plus, as discernible in INS data, a number of immigrants from the homeland. There is said to be, also, a sizable but unknown number of Polish illegals.

"Other Europeans" is a catchall for ethnicities not elsewhere assigned and constitutes the largest "ethnic" category. It comprises a miscellany of ancestral groups bearing English, Scottish, Slavic, German, Jewish, and other names. Included also are names of ostensibly European origin but whose particular ethnicity could not be determined. In 1981, they were widely dispersed throughout Sunset Park, predominantly in the tracts also occupied by Italians, Irish, and Scandinavians (Map C–19). By 1987, this heterogeneous category, unlike the individual European nationality groups, had increased in number (Map C–20), partly because it picked up yuppie entrants not elsewhere classified.

Next come the two supplementary measures—the shift in the relative proportions of the various groups and the extent of intermingling. That analysis confirms the dominant weight of Hispanics. It also indicates that it will be a long time before New York's third Chinatown attains the dimensions of the other two. A third finding is that, unlike other City areas (e.g., the Lower East Side and the Upper West Side) where large numbers were displaced by neighborhood renewal, Sunset Park's upgrading has not been at Hispanic expense, at least not in the aggregate. Quite the contrary. Between 1981 and 1987 the proportion of Hispanic residents increased. At both the earlier and later dates the number of new Hispanic subscribers was more than double that of the next largest ethnic group. As shown in the ethnic-distribution maps, Hispanic presence rose in nearly every tract

including those with the best housing.[102] The undiminished dominance of Sunset Park's Hispanics is additionally confirmed by INS,
school enrollment, and birth data. The finding is indisputable.

After 1980 Sunset Park's Hispanicity became, however, more
diverse. In moderate degree, Puerto Ricans who settled there in
the sixties and seventies were being replaced by Hispanics from
the Dominican Republic, Central and South America, and Mexico.
Though hard statistics are not available, the same trends are reflected
in INS and Health Department birth data, as well as the retail survey
later presented. The observation is likewise in accord with information obtained through interviews with community leaders.

Next examined are the measures of ethnic interspersion, that is,
the degree of turf-sharing. To simplify this analysis, the ten ethnic
categories were condensed to four—Hispanics, Asians, Italians, and
Other Europeans. In perusing Maps C–21 and C–22, what leaps to the
eye is Sunset Park's "rainbow." In varying proportions, every major ethnic group occupies a piece of every census tract. Note, too,
how modest is the Asian presence when measured against all residents. Even in their most concentrated tracts (104 and 106), Asians
were plainly a minority.

Further, one observes that in those tracts (104, 106, 108, 118, and
122) where Asians gained the most ground between 1981 and 1987,
the shrinkage of Europeans was more noticeable than the shrinkage
of Hispanics. In fact, in tracts 90, 92, and 94, the shares of both Asians
and Hispanics increased simultaneously. In other tracts, where there
was a net expansion of Hispanics, the only significant decline was of
Europeans.

In other words, the post-1980 demographic transformation of Sunset Park is far more a phenomenon of de-Europeanization than of de-
Hispanicization. One might be tempted to say that the Third World
displaced the First, were it not for the ambiguous word, displacement. The out-movement of older Europeans was seldom forced. It
was mainly due to deaths and retirement or to a voluntary sale at a
more or less satisfactory profit and, at the peak of the market, a good
deal better than that. The same was true of departing Puerto Ricans,
astute or fortunate enough to have become early home owners.

---

102. As discussed before, part of the Hispanic increase may be overstated since some
new listings doubtless reflect the acquisition by already resident Hispanic families of a
first telephone. But the overstatement factor cannot be substantial, since the increase in
total listings approximately matched the increase in population.

Sunset Park's post-1980 ethnic change is much more a process of traditional succession than of frictionful displacement.

After the ethnic tabulations for 1981 and 1987 had been completed, the 1988 *Cole's Directory* became available. Though a full updating of the statistics would have been desirable, time and resources permitted only a partial set of tabulations based on nine census tracts, about a third of the total.

The 1988 update, as discussed in Appendix C, contained few surprises and confirmed prior trends. There was a hint, however, that the turnover rate may have slowed. That would be consistent with the earlier observation that Sunset Park's housing market began, at that time, to show signs of moderating, as was the case in most of the metropolitan area.

### Post-1980 Ethnic Changes in School Enrollment

Sunset Park's post-1980 ethnic makeup is amply reflected in its public school rolls. A full breakdown of ethnicity and nationality is not available, though there may be one in future years.[103] What stands out in Table 7–1 is the continued overwhelming dominance of Hispanic children, far beyond the weight of Hispanics in the total population. Over the eight school years from 1980–1981 to 1987–1988, Hispanic enrollment in local elementary schools seesawed slightly around 85 percent and around two-thirds in the junior high schools, which are fed from other communities. It is no great exaggeration to say that Sunset Park's elementary schools had become by the eighties an Hispanic system, moderately pluralized by other races and ethnicities. Though the post-1980 Hispanic totals can no longer be split between Puerto Ricans and other Hispanics as was possible with pre-1980 school data, it is certain that, consistent with other data, the Puerto Rican share, though still predominant, has been gradually declining and the non-Puerto Rican share gradually rising.

The share of Asian children increased in the early eighties but stabilized in the mid-decade at 4.5 percent. On that point, Sunset Park's Chinese residents have recently established two private schools for young children from pre-kindergarten age to pre-teens, an explanation for the flattened enrollment in the public elementary schools. The larger one is Ming Yuen at Eighth Avenue and 64th Street, serving up to 300 children. The smaller one is Shih Shan at

---

103. Bogen, *op. cit.*, pp. 162–163.

SUNSET PARK REDUX: THE POST-1980 YEARS   **139**

**TABLE 7-1**
**Enrollment by Race and Ethnicity, Sunset Park's Public Schools, 1980–1988ᵃ**

Elementary Schools

| School Year | Asian | Hispanic | Black | White | TOTALᵇ |
|---|---|---|---|---|---|
| 1980–1981 | 3.3% | 84.4% | 1.9% | 10.4% | 6,296 |
| 1981–1982 | 3.7 | 84.6 | 1.7 | 9.9 | 6,495 |
| 1982–1983 | 3.5 | 85.7 | 1.9 | 8.9 | 6,435 |
| 1983–1984 | 4.7 | 84.4 | 1.6 | 9.3 | 6,476 |
| 1984–1985 | 4.5 | 84.8 | 1.8 | 8.8 | 6,756 |
| 1985–1986 | 4.4 | 85.5 | 1.5 | 8.6 | 6,509 |
| 1986–1987 | 4.4 | 86.0 | 1.7 | 7.8 | 6,455 |
| 1987–1988 | 4.5 | 85.0 | 2.3 | 8.2 | 6,300 |

Junior High Schools

| School Year | Asian | Hispanic | Black | White | TOTALᵇ |
|---|---|---|---|---|---|
| 1980–1981 | 3.5 | 63.7 | 9.4 | 23.2 | 4,025 |
| 1981–1982 | 4.1 | 64.9 | 9.3 | 21.6 | 4,020 |
| 1982–1983 | 5.9 | 64.0 | 8.5 | 20.6 | 3,758 |
| 1983–1984 | 6.4 | 66.8 | 7.1 | 19.6 | 3,762 |
| 1984–1985 | 7.4 | 66.4 | 7.4 | 18.6 | 3,793 |
| 1985–1986 | 9.1 | 67.9 | 6.6 | 15.9 | 3,995 |
| 1986–1987 | 9.1 | 70.0 | 7.3 | 14.0 | 3,769 |
| 1987–1988 | 11.8 | 69.0 | 6.8 | 12.3 | 3,369 |

Source: Board of Education of the City of New York.
ᵃ Data are based on five elementary schools (P.S. 1, 94, 169, 172, 314(140) and three junior high schools (J.H.S. 88, 136, 220), which serve most of the study area. Six schools are in School District 15 and two in School District 20.
ᵇ Inclusive of a small number of American Indians.

Eighth Avenue and 46th Street with 50 to 60 enrollees. For younger children the schools are substitutes for kindergarten and the lower grades of the public schools. Older children, at least from the more affluent households, go there after regular public school hours (and regular days in summer) partly to supplement their language and cultural education.[104] The more compelling attraction, however, is school doors that are open into late hours; children may stay there until seven o'clock at night, some until nine.

104. A high proportion, perhaps 30 percent, of Chinese youngsters in new-immigrant families take after-school jobs in restaurants and garment factories, averaging 20 hours per week. Cf. Betty Lee Sung, *The Adjustment of Chinese Immigrant Children in New York City* (New York: Center for Migration Studies, 1987), pp. 134–135.

**TABLE 7–2**
**Ethnic Enrollment by Individual Schools, Sunset Park, 1987–1988 School Year (Percent of Total Enrollment)**

| School | | Asian | Hispanic | Black | White |
|---|---|---|---|---|---|
| P.S. 1 | (309 47th Street) | 0.1 | 94.5 | 2.0 | 2.6 |
| P.S. 94 | (5010 Sixth Avenue) | 2.5 | 84.3 | 2.8 | 10.4 |
| P.S. 169 | (4305 Seventh Avenue) | 7.1 | 81.0 | 1.9 | 9.9 |
| P.S. 172 | (825 Fourth Avenue) | 3.5 | 76.3 | 1.5 | 20.2 |
| P.S. 314(140) | (Third Avenue at 60th) | 8.0 | 86.5 | 2.6 | 2.7 |
| J.H.S. 88 | (544 Seventh Avenue) | 2.8 | 60.4 | 17.4 | 19.4 |
| J.H.S. 136 | (4004 Fourth Avenue) | 2.3 | 86.5 | 2.6 | 2.7 |
| J.H.S. 220 | (Ninth Avenue at 48th) | 22.5 | 61.0 | 1.9 | 13.8 |

*Source:* New York City Board of Education.
*Note:* Details may not add to total because of rounding and the omission of a small number of American Indians.

The share of white children extended the decline that began in the sixties but appears to have stabilized at about 8 percent.[105] The ethnic distributions are substantially affected by each school's location (Table 7–2). Thus, the Asian share is as high as 8 percent at the two schools closest to the Chinese enclave (P.S. 314 at 60th Street and Third Avenue and P.S. 169 at Seventh Avenue and 43rd Street) and is next to zero at P.S. 1 (Third Avenue and 47th Street), the core of Hispanic settlement. Similarly, the white share is higher and the Hispanic share lower at P.S. 172, which is closer to Park Slope.

The ethnic configurations in the junior high schools are similar but not identical. Because these institutions draw older children from a wider area, the skewness in ethnic shares is less extreme. Post-1980, the Hispanic share rose from 63 to 69 percent. The white share, continuing its long descent, dropped by half over the eight years, from 23 to 12 percent. The Asian share rose sharply, from 3.5 to nearly 12 percent. One reason why Asians utilize Sunset Park's junior high schools more frequently than its elementary schools is the lesser need of older children for after-school care.

As in the elementary schools, there was considerable variability by location. Asian enrollment in J.H.S. 220, near the core of Chinese settlement, was more than 22 percent. In J.H.S. 136, located near the

105. That stability may owe something to the fact that the white category is enlarged by pupils of Hispanic ancestry who are no longer so counted. Thus, children of Puerto Rican heritage are classified as whites if both parents are mainland-born. That probability tends to increase with time as the generational line of mainlanders lengthens.

core of the Hispanic concentration, seven out of eight enrollees were Hispanic.

Post-1980 enrollment in Sunset Park's five Roman Catholic schools is parallel to the public school's pattern of declining white and rising ethnic enrollment (Table 7–3). In 1986–1987, St. Michael's, in the middle of the heaviest Hispanic concentration, had an 83 percent Hispanic enrollment, compared to 76 percent in 1981–1982; over the same years, whites declined from 15 to 9 percent. At St. Agatha's, whites by 1988 were also a minority. OLPH, serving a more affluent parish extending to much of Bay Ridge, had retained a slender white majority, 52 percent compared to 68 percent in 1982; Hispanics accounted for 40 percent and Asians for more than 7 percent, compared to 29 and 3 percent, respectively, in the earlier year. Only at Czestochowa, the small school that serves the Polish community, did whites predominate, enrollment sustained in part by new Polish immigrants.

In contrast to the public schools, every Catholic school is operating well below a capacity that is steadily reduced by the closure or conversion of classroom space. Thus St. Michael's now has a current capacity of 600 compared to 1,200 in 1974, but actually enrolls fewer than 300. Parochial schools were hit very hard by the mass exodus of parishioners during the sixties and seventies and the aging of those who remained.[106] The decline seems not yet to be at an end; total enrollment in most Catholic schools fell further in 1988 (Table 7–3). The shrinkage in Catholic enrollment is as much the result of supply as of demand factors, namely, a severely curtailed flow of teachers from the religious communities only partly offset by additions to the lay faculty. Tuition fees, far below those of most private schools, have steadily risen to pay the higher, though scarcely extravagant, salaries of lay teachers.

### Brooklyn's New Immigrants

Unmistakably, the New Immigrants are radically recasting Brooklyn's demography. Since 1980, the borough reversed a deep decline in population, regaining some 60,000 as new arrivals and rising births counterbalanced out-migrations and deaths. Brooklyn has become New York's primary immigrant destination, more so than Queens;

---

106. In 1966, all five parochial schools were at capacity, with enrollments three to four times higher than in 1988. Cf. New York City Department of City Planning, *Sunset Park*, January 1977, p. 64.

TABLE 7–3
Enrollment in Sunset Park's Catholic Schools, by Ethnicity in School Years 1981–1982 and 1986–1987, and Total 1987–1988

| School | Black | | Asian | | Hispanic | | White | | Total[a] | | Total[b] |
|---|---|---|---|---|---|---|---|---|---|---|---|
| | 1981–1982 | 1986–1987 | 1981–1982 | 1986–1987 | 1981–1982 | 1986–1987 | 1981–1982 | 1986–1987 | 1981–1982 | 1986–1987 | 1987–1988 |
| Our Lady of Perpetual Help | 3 | 6 | 23 | 44 | 247 | 249 | 576 | 318 | 849 | 609 | 594 |
| St. Michael | 9 | 12 | 14 | 11 | 261 | 239 | 55 | 27 | 341 | 289 | 295 |
| St. Agatha | 4 | 2 | 28 | 29 | 283 | 182 | 366 | 113 | 680 | 337 | 363 |
| Our Lady of Czestochowa | 3 | n.a. | n.a. | n.a. | 27 | 27 | 95 | 80 | 144 | 122 | 103 |
| St. John the Evangelist | 1 | 2 | 14 | 5 | 124 | 87 | 132 | 94 | 271 | 188 | 168 |

Source: The Roman Catholic Diocese of Brooklyn, courtesy of Reverend Peter Mahoney.
[a] Inclusive of a miniscule number of American Indians.
[b] Ethnic breakdown not available.

Manhattan is a distant third (Table 3–3). According to INS, more than 141,000 immigrants entered Brooklyn between 1983 and 1987. Interpolating an estimate for the unreported period between 1980 and 1982 and adding an allowance for the undocumented and others not included in the INS count, it is likely that the gross flow into Brooklyn since the 1980 census is well over 200,000, perhaps as high as 250,000, about three to four times Brooklyn's net growth from all sources. Despite Brooklyn's heightened attraction to the yuppie generation as a desirable alternative to Manhattan, that inflow alone would have left the borough with substantially fewer people than the already shrunken 1980 total.

The Caribbean—black and Hispanic—is the principal origin of Brooklyn's newcomers; Asia, however, is in second place and steadily narrowing the distance. Blacks, Hispanics, and Asians already contribute a decisive majority of Brooklyn's population; by the turn of the century, that majority will become an overwhelming one.[107] The racial mix of Brooklyn's subways, the Fulton Street Mall, and the beach at Coney Island are previsions of that future.

According to available data, Sunset Park has been sought out by more than an average share of Brooklyn's immigrant inflow; in 1980 the neighborhood accounted for about 4 percent of the borough's population but for 10 percent of its post-1980 foreign newcomers. Health Department birth data, INS registrations, and shifts in retail ownership attest that the bulk of Sunset Park's newcomers are immigrants of fairly recent origin, and community representatives indicate that most have entered the United States since the mid-seventies.

The ethnic mix of Sunset Park's new entrants, however, differs from Brooklyn's. The shares of Hispanics and Asians are moderately higher and the shares of West Indian and Haitian blacks strikingly lower, indeed altogether negligible. Because of the separatist tendencies earlier discussed, arriving Caribbean blacks seek out or are steered to sections of Brooklyn adjacent to the black concentrations of Bedford-Stuyvesant and East New York, like Crown Heights and East Flatbush. In 1988, Sunset Park was about as nonblack as it had been in 1980, as was most of southwest Brooklyn.

The New Immigrant share of Sunset Park's current population can only be approximated, by cumulating incomplete INS data. As shown in Table 7–4, at the end of 1980 more than 5,800 registered aliens lived in the two postal zones—11220 and 11232—that make up most of

107. Daniel McCarthy, *Brooklyn in Transition* (New York: Municipal Research Institute, 1986).

TABLE 7–4
Registered Aliens in Sunset Park, December 31, 1980,
Principal Ethnic Groups, by Country of Origin

| | Zip Code Area | | Total | Percent |
|---|---|---|---|---|
| | 11220 | 11232 | | |
| Asian | 1,623 | 44 | 1,667 | 28.4 |
| China (mainland and Taiwan) | 777 | — | 777 | 13.2 |
| Hong Kong | 397 | — | 397 | 6.8 |
| India | 222 | 44 | 266 | 4.5 |
| Philippines | 227 | — | 2,273.9 | 3.9 |
| Hispanic | 2,062 | 649 | 2,711 | 46.2 |
| Dominican Republic | 1,272 | 338 | 1,610 | 27.4 |
| Cuba | 187 | 84 | 271 | 4.6 |
| Ecuador | 603 | 184 | 787 | 13.4 |
| Peru | — | 43 | 43 | 0.7 |
| European | 1,048 | 369 | 1,417 | 24.1 |
| Finland | — | 64 | 64 | 1.1 |
| Greece | 471 | — | 471 | 8.0 |
| Italy | 363 | 216 | 579 | 9.9 |
| Norway | 214 | — | 214 | 3.6 |
| Poland | — | 89 | 89 | 1.5 |
| Others | — | 79 | 79 | 1.3 |
| Total | 4,733 | 1,141 | 5,874 | 100.00 |

Source: Demetrios G. Papademetriou, New Immigrants in Brooklyn and Queens (Staten Island, N.Y.: The Center for Migration Studies of New York, 1983), p. 64. The data are drawn from INS files that included current mailing addresses, then required of all registered aliens.

Sunset Park.[108] Between 1983 and 1987 (recall the lapse in data collection in 1981 and 1982), INS files show a total of nearly 7,000 additional

108. Among them, Hispanics accounted for 46 percent, more than half of them Dominicans and another quarter Ecuadorians. Disregarding the non-comparability in area boundaries, that was equal to less than 8 percent of Sunset Park's Hispanics; most of the latter were Puerto Ricans and therefore citizens. On the other hand, in 1980 Sunset Park's Chinese were almost entirely immigrants. Though less than 3 percent of Sunset Park's census count, Chinese constituted 20 percent of the legal aliens then living there. To put it differently, recent Chinese immigrants accounted for an overwhelming proportion of Sunset Park's Chinese people and, by all accounts, for most of those who settled there after 1980. Virtually all of today's Chinese residents in Sunset Park are New Immigrants and their children. Of 1980's registered aliens, 24 percent were of European origin, conspicuously Greek and Italian.

registered-alien entrants to Sunset Park. Since the number of arrivals in each of the three covered years fluctuated only mildly, the average was applied to the uncovered years, yielding a current total of
roughly 10,000 INS-registered newcomers reporting a Sunset Park
residence.

The files of the INS, however, exclude four categories of New
Immigrants. One comprises those who do not furnish a mailing address, no longer a legal requirement. The second are illegals, believed
by Sunset Park's community-watchers to constitute a significant proportion of the newcomers; they are largely Dominicans but include
substantial numbers of Chinese, Irish, Poles, and others. A third
comprises post-1965 naturalized foreign-born who are removed from
the INS register. And the fourth are the native-born children of both
legal and illegal immigrants; the latter, according to birth data later
discussed, contribute an annual average of 500 to Sunset Park's population or 4,000 since the 1980 census.

A reasonable estimate of Sunset Park's resident New Immigrants
by the end of 1988 is therefore on the order of 22,000. Thus, they
accounted for more than 20 percent of Sunset Park's total population,
and for much more than all the neighborhood's net population gain
since 1980 (estimated at about 14,000); the sizable difference between
the gross inflow and net change indicates that Sunset Park's native-
born population had substantially dwindled, a fact directly observed
in the Cole's tabulations. Like Brooklyn's, Sunset Park's demographic
destiny—the size and ethnic composition of its future population—is
being shaped by its New Immigrants.

As in pre-1980 years, the bulk of Sunset Park's post-1980 aliens
were Hispanic and Asian (Table 7–5). Registered Hispanics constituted 45 percent of the total inflow, about the same as before.
About half were Dominicans, probably more, were allowance made
for their undocumented. There was also a medley of other Hispanics.
From South America during those years came 11 percent, primarily
Colombians and Ecuadorians (the latter had a prior foothold in Sunset Park). From Central America came a little over 8 percent, notably
from El Salvador and Honduras. Cuba and Mexico were also sender
nations.

The pace of Asian entry to Sunset Park quickened after 1980,
reflecting regional and national trends. According to INS registrations, the Asian share climbed from 28 percent for the period ending
1980 to 35 percent in 1983–1987. Of Sunset Park's new Asians, nearly
two-thirds were Chinese, mostly from the mainland and Hong Kong;
the latter is a major way station for mainland émigrés. There was only

**TABLE 7-5**
**Registered Aliens in Sunset Park, by Country of Birth[a]**
**(Arrivals in Years 1983 to 1987[b])**

| | | | |
|---|---:|---|---:|
| Caribbean | 2,193 | Central America | 542 |
| Dominican Republic | 1,487 | El Salvador | 120 |
| Guyana | 490 | Guatemala | 97 |
| Haiti | 27 | Honduras | 126 |
| Jamaica | 61 | Mexico | 118 |
| Other Caribbean | 128 | Other Central America | 81 |
| Asia | 2,387 | Middle East | 443 |
| China[c] | 1,518 | Egypt | 78 |
| India | 278 | Israel | 55 |
| Kampuchea | 82 | Jordan | 188 |
| Korea | 59 | Lebanon | 34 |
| Pakistan | 35 | Yemen (Sanaa) | 27 |
| Philippines | 138 | Other Middle East | 61 |
| Vietnam | 199 | Europe | 486 |
| Other Asia | 88 | Greece | 72 |
| South America | 736 | Ireland | 28 |
| Colombia | 226 | Poland | 185 |
| Ecuador | 355 | Romania | 27 |
| Peru | 71 | Other | 100 |
| Other South America | 84 | Other and Nonreporting | 15 |
| Africa | 37 | Total, All Countries | 6,849 |

*Source:* New York City Department of City Planning, Population Division, based on INS data.
[a] ZIP code areas 11220 and 11232.
[b] Fiscal years ending September 30.
[c] Comprises mainland, Hong Kong, and Taiwan.

a handful of Taiwanese, who tend to favor Flushing. Asians other than Chinese included East Indians, Filipinos, Vietnamese, and Cambodians. Among the Middle Easterners (5.4 percent of the total), Jordan and Egypt figure prominently.

Relatively few of Sunset Park's post-1980 immigrants were from Europe. They accounted for little more than 7 percent. Even allowing for a goodly number of illegals, that represents a substantial decline from the pre-1980 levels of 24 percent. A similar decline is observable in national admissions. The inflow of Italians and Scandinavians dropped to such negligible numbers that they are relegated here to the residual category. Poles were most conspicuous.

**Birth Data**

Another data set that sheds light on the origins of Sunset Park's new ethnics are special Health Department tabulations of live births, by race and ethnicity of the babies and by place of birth of the mother. For the period 1965–1987, the tabulations cover four health areas that roughly approximate Sunset Park's boundaries.

The birth data confirm the dramatic impact of the New Immigrants on Sunset Park. Over the 22 years there was a steep progression in the proportion of newborn children whose mothers emigrated from countries other than Puerto Rico. Foreign-born mothers accounted for 12 percent of births in 1965, for 26 percent in 1975, and for 40 percent in 1987 (Table 7–6).

Not surprisingly, Hispanic births predominated, accounting for 67.7 percent of the total in 1980 (the first year for which ethnic classification was available) and for 64.2 percent in 1987. Both figures substantially exceed the Hispanic share in the aggregate population, reflecting a young age structure and high fertility.

The proportion of Puerto Rican babies steadily lessened, from 51 percent in 1980 to 35 percent in 1987. By contrast, Hispanic babies other than Puerto Rican rose over the same years from less than 17 percent to nearly 25 percent. The bulk of the latter were to mothers from the Dominican Republic and Central America; Mexico was a fast-rising third. Stated differently, the Puerto Rican share of Hispanic births declined from more than three-quarters in 1980 to less than two thirds in 1987. The diminished presence of Puerto Rican mothers was more pronounced than in the tabulations of Puerto Rican births, declining from a peak of 41.1 percent in 1970 to 17 percent in 1987. Plainly, more children identified as Puerto Rican were being born to native-born mothers.

The share of Asian births, less than 1 percent in 1965 and a little over 3 percent in 1975, soared to 10.2 percent in 1987.[109] The shares of Asian births were greater than their shares in the population. Though in lesser degree than Hispanics, they are, too, a relatively young and fertile people.

The share of white non-Hispanic births stabilized between 1980 and 1987 at about 19 percent, with minor oscillations in the in-between years. The total includes, however, some babies born to

---

109. The pre-1980 Asian figures were derived from the Health Department's tabulations by race. In those tabulations it was safely assumed that Asians account for most of the "Other Race" category.

**TABLE 7–6**
**Births by Race and Ethnicity and by Birthplace of Mother, Four Health Areas in Sunset Park, 1965–1987**

| | 1987 | | 1986 | | 1985 | | 1980 | | 1975 | | 1970 | | 1965 | |
|---|---|---|---|---|---|---|---|---|---|---|---|---|---|---|
| **Mother's Place of Birth** | 1,617 | 100.0% | 1,487 | 100.0% | 1,512 | 100.0% | 1,473 | 100.0% | 1,485 | 100.0% | 1,804 | 100.0% | 1,723 | 100.0% |
| Native | 684 | 42.3 | 646 | 43.4 | 692 | 45.8 | 573 | 38.9 | 522 | 35.2 | 716 | 39.7 | 956 | 55.5 |
| Puerto Rico | 285 | 17.6 | 297 | 20.1 | 293 | 19.4 | 473 | 32.1 | 566 | 38.1 | 741 | 41.1 | 553 | 32.1 |
| Foreign | 648 | 40.1 | 544 | 36.6 | 527 | 34.9 | 427 | 29.0 | 397 | 26.7 | 346 | 19.2 | 214 | 12.4 |
| **Foreign by Country** | 648 | 100.0 | 544 | 100.0 | 527 | 100.0 | 427 | 100.0 | n.a. | | n.a. | | n.a. | |
| Canada | 1 | 0.2 | 2 | 0.4 | 3 | 5.7 | 2 | 0.5 | | | | | | |
| Cuba | 5 | 0.8 | 6 | 1.1 | 4 | 0.8 | 4 | 0.9 | | | | | | |
| Mexico | 100 | 15.4 | 67 | 12.3 | 47 | 8.9 | 35 | 8.2 | | | | | | |
| Central America/Caribbean/South America | 227 | 35.0 | 216 | 39.7 | 210 | 39.8 | 182 | 42.6 | | | | | | |
| Europe | 32 | 4.9 | 39 | 7.2 | 35 | 6.6 | 38 | 8.9 | | | | | | |
| Africa | 8 | 1.2 | 4 | 0.7 | 4 | 0.8 | 3 | 0.7 | | | | | | |
| Asia | 152 | 23.5 | 119 | 21.9 | 120 | 22.8 | 97 | 22.7 | | | | | | |
| Not stated | 123 | 19.0 | 91 | 16.7 | 104 | 19.7 | 66 | 15.5 | | | | | | |
| **Baby's Race/Ethnicity** | 1,617 | 100.0 | 1,487 | 100.0 | 1,512 | 100.0 | 1,473 | 100.0 | 1,485 | 100.0 | 1,804 | 100.0 | 1,783 | 100.0 |
| White[a] | 316 | 19.5 | 314 | 21.1 | 334 | 22.1 | 283 | 19.2 | 1,321 | 89.0 | 1,733 | 96.1 | 1,674 | 97.2 |
| Black | 92 | 5.7 | 80 | 5.4 | 76 | 5.0 | 69 | 4.7 | 114 | 7.7 | 45 | 2.5 | 35 | 2.0 |
| Asian[b] | 165 | 10.2 | 134 | 9.0 | 135 | 8.9 | 116 | 7.9 | 50 | 3.4 | 26 | 1.4 | 14 | 0.8 |
| Puerto Rican | 635 | 39.3 | 601 | 40.4 | 616 | 40.7 | 750 | 51.0 | n.a. | | n.a. | | n.a. | |
| Other Hispanic | 403 | 24.9 | 345 | 23.2 | 336 | 22.2 | 246 | 16.7 | | | | | | |
| Not stated | 6 | 0.4 | 13 | 0.9 | 15 | 1.0 | 9 | 0.6 | | | | | | |

*Source:* New York City Department of Health, Special Tabulation, 1988. The health areas are 44, 47, 65, 66.

*Note:* Details may not add to totals because of rounding.

[a] Before 1980, Puerto Ricans and other Hispanics were included in the white category.
[b] The Other Races category of 1965–1975 is taken as Asian, only a modest overstatement. Asians have been separately classified since 1980.

parents of Hispanic ancestry who, themselves born on the mainland, chose to identify their children as Americans. Among whites, there was a sharp drop in births to European-born immigrants, from 8.9 percent in 1980 to 4.9 percent in 1987. That decrease was foreshadowed by parallel trends in both the *Cole's* and INS data and gives substance to the observation made earlier: the consistency across disparate and incomplete data sets adds immeasurable strength to the principal findings.

Black births, no more than 2.5 percent in 1965–1970, rose to 7.7 percent in 1975 and leveled off at about 5 percent thereafter. The higher level may have several explanations. One is in-movement of native-born blacks. Another is births to foreign-born black families. But most of it is more likely due to the construction of two large apartment buildings in Bay Ridge just outside of Sunset Park's southern perimeter but included in one of Sunset Park's health areas. It is known that these subsidized middle-income buildings, with more than 800 units, are occupied by a moderate percentage of black families, though no precise figure could be ascertained.

## Immigrants in Sunset Park's Economy

Thousands of Sunset Park's new foreigners have entered the local economy. They are employed in retailing, at the Lutheran Medical Center, in the Industrial Zone, and in the 40 or more Chinese-owned garment establishments.

Sunset Park's immigrant face is most directly observed on its retail streets—the store signage, the homeland products, the foreign-born proprietors. The ethnic succession of Sunset Park as a neighborhood is reflected in the ethnic succession in local retailing. The Scandinavian groceries, delicatessens, and travel agencies have mostly given way to the newcomers. So, too, have most of the Italian butchers and fruit and vegetable stores, the Greek restaurants and, to a lesser extent, the Irish bars. The latter seem an indestructible species. Even in such famously Third World neighborhoods as Flushing and Jackson Heights, a string of Donnellys, Shamrocks, Blarney Stones, and their ilk has managed to survive. Many of them, it is said, are the congregation points of undocumented Irish immigrants.

Professor Roger Waldinger and several of his students conducted a survey of Sunset Park's street-level businesses. They tallied more than 800 classified establishments (over a hundred others were vacant or defied categorization). All but the garment factories (and a few of undetermined activity) were engaged in the retail sale of neighborhood goods and services, manifestly weighted toward the ethnic composition of the immediate streets. Few people patronize Sunset Park's shops unless they live there. The stores offer the customary variety of food, housewares, clothing, travel services, personal care, coffee shops and small restaurants, and gas stations (Table 7–7).

The emphasis of the retail survey was on the changing ethnicity of Sunset Park's retailers. Of the 771 establishments whose owners' ethnicity could be identified, more than 60 percent were Hispanics, Middle Easterners, and Asians (Table 7–8). Along Eighth Avenue, a once-moribund street now springing back to life, three-fourths of the 240 stores from 39th to 65th streets are immigrant-owned, 60 by Chinese. Chinese banks, centered in Manhattan and Flushing, were actively combing Eighth Avenue for a branch to

**TABLE 7–7**
**Street-Level Businesses in Sunset Park, by Type, 1987**

| Type of Establishment | Number | Percent |
|---|---|---|
| Appliances: sales, repairs, and rental | 34 | 4.1 |
| Bakeries | 9 | 1.1 |
| Barber and beauty shops | 43 | 5.2 |
| Bars and liquor stores | 39 | 4.8 |
| Candy and ice cream | 8 | 1.0 |
| Car repair, service, and parts | 41 | 5.0 |
| Cleaners and laundry | 40 | 4.9 |
| Clothing, tailors, and shoe repair | 50 | 6.1 |
| Delicatessens | 13 | 1.6 |
| Drug stores and pharmacies | 14 | 1.7 |
| Groceries and supermarkets | 139 | 16.8 |
| Hardware stores | 13 | 1.6 |
| Home furnishings | 13 | 1.6 |
| Home repair and construction | 26 | 3.2 |
| Meat and fish | 20 | 2.4 |
| Newspaper and stationery | 32 | 3.9 |
| Real estate, travel, and insurance | 26 | 3.2 |
| Restaurants including fast food | 84 | 10.2 |
| Variety stores | 36 | 4.4 |
| Miscellaneous retail | 97 | 11.8 |
| Nonretail | 44 | 5.4 |
| Total Classified | 821 | 100.0 |

Source: Appendix E.
Note: Details may not add to total because of rounding.

**TABLE 7-8**
**Ethnic Composition of Sunset Park Store Owners, 1987**

|  | Number | Percent |
|---|---|---|
| Hispanic | 293 | 35.7 |
| Puerto Rican | 116 | 14.1 |
| Dominican | 99 | 12.1 |
| Cuban | 17 | 2.1 |
| Other | 61 | 7.4 |
| Asian | 127 | 15.5 |
| Chinese | 70 | 8.5 |
| Korean | 35 | 4.3 |
| Other | 22 | 2.7 |
| White | 317 | 38.5 |
| Foreign-born | | |
| Jewish | 58 | 7.0 |
| Italian | 56 | 6.8 |
| Greek | 29 | 3.5 |
| Irish | 13 | 1.6 |
| Other European | 52 | 6.4 |
| Native-born | 109 | 13.2 |
| Middle Eastern | 34 | 4.1 |
| Not identified | 50 | 6.1 |
| Total | 821 | 100.0 |

*Source:* Roger Waldinger, "Ethnic Business in Sunset Park,"
November 1987 (Appendix E).
*Note:* Details may not add to total because of rounding.

serve the burgeoning aggregation of Chinese firms and households. To celebrate its new vitality and ethnic heterogeneity, the Eighth Avenue Merchants' Association has sponsored an international street fair.

Within the defined retail categories, there is a slow but distinct tendency toward upgrading, as reported by realtors and as noted during the course of the study. The tiny grocery expands into a modest supermarket, its refrigerators more fully stocked with premium beers and its shelves with imported goods. The small Vietnamese take-out place that filled a once-vacant store on Eighth Avenue is now a waiter-served Chinese restaurant, though bare of décor and still without a liquor license. A barroom near the waterfront also expands into a restaurant to serve the resurrecting manufacturing district.

The nearest stylish restaurants, however, are in Bay Ridge and Park Slope.[110]

The dominant ethnicity—Hispanic—was divided roughly equally between Puerto Ricans and other Hispanics, mainly Dominicans and Central and South Americans. The latter are rapidly buying up the stores earlier acquired by Puerto Ricans. Among Asian owners, Chinese had primacy, followed by Koreans, East Asians, and a handful of Filipinos. Although nearly 40 percent of the proprietors were white, the majority of these were foreign-born, primarily European Jews, Italians, Greeks, and a scattering of other nationalities. Middle Easterners, too, have attained a degree of visibility.

Waldinger's team conducted face-to-face interviews with three groups of proprietors—whites, Hispanics, and Koreans—about 30 in each group. The same ethnic groups had been studied in immigrant areas elsewhere in New York and in other cities. They were interviewed for nearly an hour by a co-ethnic surveyor asking a wide range of questions comparable to those of prior studies of ethnic entrepreneurship.

Waldinger's study confirmed the findings of comparable surveys elsewhere.[111] Koreans were the newest entrants to the community's retail streets, more recent than the Hispanics, who in turn were more recent than the whites. The median year of immigration to the United States of Sunset Park's Koreans was 1980; they had been in business in Sunset Park for only 2.2 years. The corresponding figures for Hispanics were 1969 and 3.5 years. Within that group, Puerto Ricans, whose median year of entry was 1963, were being bought out by other Hispanics, with a median year of immigration in 1973. Whites, by contrast, had been in business for an average of 12.3 years; nearly 10 percent of their proprietorships were passed down by inheritance.

Other than the branches of some popular chains and franchises (e.g., Woolworth's, Lerner's, Key Foods, McDonald's, Burger King), the bulk of the stores are small and family-managed. Most had only two or three employees, predominantly co-ethnic. Korean and Hispanic establishments were quite literally "mom and pop" stores.

---

110. The dearth of good eating places in Sunset Park is said to be a hindrance in attracting not only yuppies but also new business to the Industrial Zone; plans are afoot to establish at least one restaurant in the Brooklyn Army Terminal now undergoing redevelopment, a subject later discussed.
111. Roger Waldinger, "Ethnic Business in Sunset Park," November 1987. Included here as Appendix E.

About 80 percent of the married Korean proprietors were aided by their wives, and the same was true of more than half of the Hispanics. Store hours were long. All groups reported a workday of approximately 11 hours and a workweek of at least 6 days. More than half of the Hispanic stores stay open on Sundays.

The nonretail establishments outside the Industrial Zone are predominantly garment factories, most of whose employees are Chinese female immigrants. Indeed, these establishments depend upon a continuing flow of foreigners since few second-generation Chinese females seek jobs at the sewing machine, except as occasional or after-school work.

Lutheran Medical Center, as does every metropolitan hospital nowadays, employs very large numbers of immigrants. LMC reports a major proportion of its 2,000-plus staff is foreign-born, distributed throughout professional and nonprofessional ranks. According to LMC's personnel files, many of these foreign employees live in Sunset Park, mostly within walking distance of the hospital, a finding confirmed in the analysis of telephone listings. LMC conducts English-language classes for the newcomers as well as job-development training. Many immigrants have progressed from entry-level jobs to semi-professional status, assisted by special training programs.

A substantial number of Sunset Park's residents, mostly Hispanics, are reported to be employed in Bush Terminal and other manufacturing establishments inside and outside the Industrial Zone. It was not possible, however, to obtain the figure or the proportion who are New Immigrants. The current status of the Zone is discussed later in the chapter.

### Immigrants in the Real Estate Market

New Immigrants are an acknowledged force in the City's real estate markets, active in the commercial streets and residential neighborhoods of every borough. Sunset Park is no exception. Several of the community's real estate firms are owned by New Immigrants, and many retain ethnic personnel specialized in home sales to co-ethnic newcomers. The fevered real estate activity of Chinese in Manhattan's Chinatown and Flushing has a counterpart in Sunset Park, notably alongside and adjacent to the Eighth Avenue axis.

To supplement anecdotal information from interviews with realtors and bank officers regarding the transfer of Sunset Park's housing into new hands, another data source was probed—the *Brooklyn Real*

*Estate Register.* From that compendium were tabulated the sales of Sunset Park's smaller residential properties during an 18-month span in 1986 and 1987. As set forth in Appendix A, the *Register* is a fecund data base for analyzing local real estate markets. For every type of property, it provides the raw material for cross-sectional and longitudinal analyses of turnover, prices, mortgage sources and flows, and debt-equity ratios.

Resources permitted only a skimming of that potential—the tracking of ethnic turnover. Since transfers of small properties are usually accompanied by buyers' names, the *Register* has prima facie value as an indicator of ethnic succession. Initial explorations indicated, however, that for such purposes it is less comprehensive than *Cole's* since it covers only owners. Nor, because of the considerable presence of absentee speculators, is it as unambiguous a test of residence. Judging from cross-checks with telephone directories, only about half the purchasers of the smaller residential properties appear to reside there.

Distinctions between resident and absentee ownership aside, ethnic classifications of the new owners of smaller residential properties (generally two- to four-family homes) show that the majority were Asians, Hispanics, and other non-Europeans (Table 7–9). The proportion of Chinese purchasers, 26.2 percent, was strikingly high, several times greater than their current weight in Sunset Park's population. They are also inveterate speculators and investors; the dividing line between the two roles is notoriously difficult to draw. Thus,

TABLE 7–9
**Purchases of Small Residential Properties in Sunset Park, by Ethnicity of Buyer, 1986 and 1987**

|  | *Number* | *Percent* |
| --- | --- | --- |
| Chinese | 63 | 26.2 |
| Other Asians | 4 | 1.7 |
| Hispanic | 50 | 20.8 |
| Middle Eastern | 13 | 5.4 |
| Irish | 10 | 4.2 |
| Italian | 22 | 9.2 |
| Other European | 78 | 32.5 |
| Total | 240 | 100.0 |

*Source: Brooklyn Real Estate Register,* Brooklyn, New York, Monthly Supplements from March 1986 through September 1987.

only about a third of those purchases were made by those who could be identified as resident home owners. But it is likely that proportion would be higher were the data tracked over more time, since a buyer's move-in is often long delayed. Moreover, because of the co-ethnicity factor, the speculative purchase by a nonresident Chinese investor often presages to a subsequent sale to a Chinese resident owner.

As several ethnic studies report (local informants, too), the new Chinese have a strong proclivity for home ownership. The high home ownership rate of Sunset Park's Chinese in 1980 was, as noted, equal to that of whites. The *1987 Housing Report* disclosed that for New York City as a whole, Asians had a home ownership rate substantially higher than that of any other ethnic group, only slightly below that of whites. In New York, the Asian home ownership rate rose steadily since 1980 and seems destined eventually to overtake the white rate.

Hispanic buyers were also plentiful in Sunset Park's real estate market, accounting for one out of five small-home transfers. That proportion, however, was less than the Hispanic share of Sunset Park's households and would be still lower were allowances made for the speculator component. The community's Hispanics, as was seen in the 1980 census tabulations of tenure, are overwhelmingly renters. Local realtors and bank officials report that the bulk of recent Hispanic buyers, as in the retail sector, are Dominicans and Central and South Americans. But they also report a moderate number of younger, middle-class Puerto Ricans.

Buyers with European surnames accounted for 46 percent of all residential purchases. Within that number were most of the yuppie brownstoners as well as considerable numbers of nonresident speculator-investors who, according to local realtors, are still the leaders of that fraternity.

Co-ethnicity in Sunset Park's housing market appears in various ways. As observed in the *Register*, a substantial proportion of the mortgage loans made to finance Chinese purchases was provided by Chinese banks. Though the loan windows of American banks are hardly closed to Asians, many are said to feel more comfortable dealing with their own institutions. One reason is language. Another, apparently, is access to satisfactory credit terms without an inordinate amount of verification and documentation. Asset pooling and cosigned loans across kinship lines are common transactional devices among Chinese purchasers, arrangements not always familiar or acceptable to American institutions. Also, Asians are no less guarded than other small businessmen about revealing actual incomes and assets.[112]

Chinese co-ethnicity was likewise observable in the rental of residential property. That was evidenced in a small sample of two- to four-family homes purchased between 1979 and 1985 and cross-referenced against the names of occupants listed in telephone directories. The exercise disclosed that Chinese ownership, whether resident or absentee, is followed within a few years by Chinese renters. Thus, the Cole's listings indicated that houses passing into Chinese ownership, which at the time of purchase contained only 3 Chinese families, were occupied in 1988 by 17. Nearly all the departed tenants had European surnames, further evidence of Sunset Park's de-Europeanization rather than de-Hispanicization.

## THE INDUSTRIAL ZONE: POST-1980

Sunset Park is no longer beholden, as it had been throughout much of its history, to the fate of its manufacturing belt and waterfront. That may be just as well since the Industrial Zone has lagged far behind the recovery of the community's residential and retail sectors. Plan after hopeful plan for the uplift of the waterfront has foundered.

It would be folly, however, to ignore the present and future of the Industrial Zone in any assessment of Sunset Park's status and prospects. On the negative side, the Zone generates heavy truck movements and other environmental nuisances. On the positive side, it remains, if much less so than in the past, a center of local employment and therefore a contributor to the demand for local housing and retail services. On the positive side also is its huge reserve of underutilized land; that reserve offers a significant potential in the years ahead for an accelerated growth of Sunset Park's population and housing inventory.

In any discussion of the Industrial Zone, it is essential to separate the nearly defunct maritime activities from the reawakening manufac-

---

112. The underreporting gap for small business people is substantial. According to its own analyses, the Census Bureau finds substantial underreporting among the self-employed of personal income when cross-checked with IRS returns. Income data from the IRS for the self-employed are also notoriously underreported. They explain in part a growing practice among U.S. mortgage lenders to forgo income verification provided that borrowers are willing to make a higher down payment and/or pay a premium interest rate.

turing activities. By the mid-eighties, the waterfront had become a potter's field, its wasting piers and rusting longshore railroad the gravestones of a once-vibrant economic sector. What is left of southwest Brooklyn's dockside employment is confined almost entirely to Red Hook and to the Port Authority piers below Brooklyn Heights.

To comprehend the waterfront's downfall is to unravel a tangle of unavoidable and avoidable causes. One strand consists of technological and economic innovations: the advent of airplanes; land transport in gargantuan trucks across a colossal intercontinental highway system; the triumph of the container over the cargo net and the baling hook. Giant jets captured nearly all the passengers and skimmed much of the high-value cargo. Trucks reduced the importance of the fixed rail system that had favored New York's port; they also preempted most of the coastal trade. World trade shifted from the Atlantic to the Pacific basin, a boon to Los Angeles and Seattle, a blow to Eastern ports.

These adversities, which all but wiped out New York City's longshore employment, were inevitable. But the coup de grace was self-inflicted—bewildering changes in local administration, misguided policies, and conflicts among fragmented jurisdictions. In the decade since the mid-seventies there was a succession of six commissioners of (what is now) the Department of Ports, International Trade and Terminals. Development affecting the City's waterways and waterfront is subject to federal, state, and municipal law. It is supervised by a dozen agencies with varying degrees of overlapping responsibility. And, when development affects navigable waters, as is the case with Sunset Park's piers, approval of the Army Corps of Engineers is required, compounding the complexities. Added to the traditional clashes over competing land uses—shipping versus industry versus housing versus recreation, each backed by resolute advocates—are the exacting federal and state environmental-impact statements to which large developments are subject.

The failures of the public sector were matched by the private—the inefficient practices of the railroads and shippers and the cost-raising rules of powerful and corrupt longshore unions. All added to the advantages of competing seaports and modes of transport.

Today, Brooklyn's piers account for less than 6 percent of the port's activity. Thirty years ago, 10,000 men shaped up every day at 50 working piers. At Sunset Park's last hiring hall (on 60th Street) 1,000 of the 2,000 remaining longshoremen "badge in" each day, engaging in the fiction of seeking a day's work. The gesture is pure theater; few, in fact, expect to find any. In a real sense, the hiring hall is a make-believe stage and the longshoremen performers in a set-piece play. The script is an extraordinary agreement hammered out years ago between the dock unions and maritime employers. By accepting the labor-saving containership, workers were compensated with a guaranteed lifetime annual income, irrespective of the actual demand for labor. The notorious no-show job arrangements of many monopolistic unions were in this instance neatly turned upside down into a show-no job contract.

In contrast with the waterfront, the manufacturing sector appears on a slow track to revival. But it is a laborious climb up a down escalator; New York's collapsing manufacturing sector witnessed a loss since 1950 of 500,000 jobs. Even during the recent decade of economic recovery the City lost 120,000 factory jobs, a 25 percent decline compared with less than 8 percent for the rest of the country.

Notwithstanding so unpromising a background, employment in the Industrial Zone has been on the rise. By 1988 there were 30,000 jobs, a substantial gain from a low of 18,000 in the seventies. The exodus of large firms, earlier discussed (Chapter 4), was offset by the entry of numerous small ones. Most of the new employment, however, is in low-wage light manufacturing and goods assembly, neither a source of the remunerative skilled and unionized jobs available in the Zone during its best years.

One sign of a better future is the quickening pace of occupancy in the Brooklyn Army Terminal. A second is the construction or renovation of smaller industrial buildings on several sites within the Zone. An example is the 10,000-square-foot plant erected for a Chinese fish processor, transplanted from Chinatown. Another plant of similar size was recently erected by a supplier of metal parts to the garment industry. One of Manhattan's largest printing corporations announced the move of a part of its operations to the Zone. Under way, too, was a larger venture, a 500,000-square-foot industrial center enfolding the site and buildings of the departed Monarch Wine Company. And, recent assemblages by real estate investors of vacant and underutilized parcels are harbingers of more industrial construction to come.

To a large extent, the Zone's manufacturing prospects rest on the promotional programs and financial packages of two economic development agencies—the Southwest Brooklyn Industrial Development Corporation (SWBIDC) and the Public Development Corporation (PDC). SWBIDC is the Zone's principal promoter, a quasi-public nonprofit organization financed mainly by municipal funds. SWBIDC's responsibilities include assistance in site assembly;

the marketing of industrial space; advocacy for adequate public services, especially security, and round-the-clock policing. Another selling tool is labor recruitment. Through its job-training and English-language classes SWBIDC reports placing 1,000 people per year, mostly Hispanic, including an indeterminate number of Sunset Park's poorer residents; some, it is purported, are reclaimed from the welfare rolls.

Allied with SWBIDC is PDC, City Hall's aggressive outreach to the private business sector. Like its counterpart, New York State's Urban Development Corporation, PDC possesses a kitbag of flexible powers and financial resources to acquire sites and to build, rebuild, and administer industrial facilities throughout the five boroughs. In Sunset Park, its most important venture by far is the reconstruction and modernization of the Brooklyn Army Terminal (BAT). By 1988, almost one million square feet, half of one of BAT's two 70-year-old structures, were near completion, paid for by an initial City allocation of $33 million. PDC is engaged in a vigorous marketing campaign to lease the rebuilt floors of the building. The key selling points are the extraordinary large expanses of unbroken floor areas, sturdy enough for the heaviest rolling truck, an efficient arrangement of loading docks and parking areas, tolerably good access to major arterials and, most tempting, a package of subsidies to reduce operating costs.[113]

Though it has tried long and hard, PDC has not yet succeeded in attracting an entire industry and is reconciled to firm-by-firm negotiation. As of mid-1988, 21 small firms had signed up for almost 600,000 square feet with a projected employment of 1,000 workers. The new tenants included printing and publishing establishments, manufacturers of ladies' belts and handbags, a sample card company, and others. PDC's executives are confident that the leasings will speed up as the building approaches move-in readiness and as amenities such as shops and restaurants are installed at the base of its handsome atrium. PDC will invest an additional $45 million to reconstruct the second half of the building. A roster of 4,000 workers is projected if

---

113. To meet market competition, BAT dangles a menu of inducements. One is concessional rents. In 1988, space was being offered at about $4 per square foot for the first half of a 10-year lease, rising slightly during the second half, plus $1 per square foot charge for a loading dock. These rents are sheltered from rising property taxes for 10 years. A critical lure for energy-dependent firms are discounts of one-half or more in electricity rates, though the discount is progressively phased out over an 11-year interval. A further incentive are grants and tax credits to offset the costs of relocating equipment and employees.

and when the full building is leased. High on PDC's list of prospects are the City's printing, jewelry, and garment trades.[114]

Bush Terminal, the industrial linchpin of Sunset Park, is also in a comeback and retains its role as the Zone's centerpiece. Though it has conveyed its piers and railroad to the City, it is still privately owned and in the hands of new investors. By 1988, its job rolls had slowly climbed back to 15,000 from a 12,000 trough at the start of the decade; to some extent, Bush competes with the BAT for the same customers. However, with a reported 20 percent vacancy rate, it still has much lost ground to recover.

All three corporations—SWBIDC, PDC, and Bush—target their promotional efforts on Manhattan's footloose manufacturing establishments which, displaced by skyrocketing prices and rents, tend to look to New Jersey and more distant places for relocation opportunities. All but one of BAT's recent tenants came from this affected group, the exception being a former New York firm lured back from New Jersey.

On present evidence, the reuse of the Zone's industrial sites is likely to expand further, albeit at a sluggish pace. But so extensive is the underutilized acreage, there is sure to be a surplus of land relative to any foreseeable industrial demand. It is a plausible speculation that in a not-too-distant future, City planners will relent and reclassify parts of the Zone's hopelessly irredeemable parcels for other uses. The most likely successor is new housing. More will be said about that in the concluding chapter, as well as about another redevelopment scheme that favors Sunset Park—a massive new office and financial center now under way in downtown Brooklyn. If brought to fruition, the downtown center will generate a white-collar economy, a modern-age replacement for west Brooklyn's fallen angel, its played-out waterfront economy.

### A Neglected Infrastructure

Sunset Park's infrastructure and physical environment have improved markedly less than its housing stock; the shortcomings have retarded its revival. The list of infirmities is a long one. Extensive stretches of land in and around the Industrial Zone and vacant junk-filled lots blemish the landscape. The quality of many of the commu-

---

114. PDC has also responsibility for the Brooklyn Meat Distribution Cooperative, the facility that once figured so dramatically in mobilizing the community (Chapter 6). Filling the space there proved a more stubborn problem than expected.

nity's streets and sidewalks is poor and, in spots, worse than that. Potholes and broken pavement abound and cave-ins are more than occasional. Sewer and water systems, among Brooklyn's oldest, experience frequent breakdowns with consequent flooding. One reason for these mishaps is the unstable subsoil in much of Sunset Park, owing to a high water table. That is so not only at the waterfront where surfaces and structures are built on landfill, but upland as well. The local histories disclose that, for the builders of the Fourth Avenue subway, excavation was a perpetual struggle with sandy or marshy subsurface and constant seepage.

The neighborhood's capital plant also suffers from neglect. Most of Sunset Park's schools are old and undermaintained, aggravating the serious crowding problem. The subway stations of its R and N lines are in an advanced state of squalor, a disfigurement likely to prevail for years to come. On the Transit Authority's capital-investment program, top priority has been accorded to the IRT lines rather than the BMT system, which is Sunset Park's lifeline. The decrepit subway cars have mostly been replaced or renovated. But the pace of track and other structural repairs seems glacial, resulting in frustrating delays and reroutings. In recent performance reports, the N and R trains were rated among the four poorest in the City, measured by malfunctions and late arrivals.[115]

The nemesis of Sunset Park's subways is no longer a want of users. After a prolonged decline, the number of riders is again on the rise. The recovery is Citywide and reflects in part the expanded job base. But in large part it reflects the masses of New Immigrants. The recovery of riders is most pronounced on lines that pass through immigrant settlements. Thus, the No. 7 line from Flushing to Times Square, which is flanked on both sides by dense concentrations of immigrants, accounts for only 6 percent of all City riders but for 60 percent of the post-1979 increment. Moreover, the increase in ridership since 1979 is entirely attributable to an increase in weekend traffic; despite a gain of 400,000 jobs, weekday traffic has actually declined. It is on weekends, of course, when the subway system reverts, so to speak, to an immigrant transportation system. To new immigrants, generally poorer and with fewer automobiles than others in the labor force, and often employed in restaurants, hotels, hospitals, and other places that are open seven days and nights, public transit is an all-purpose support system.

---

115. Kirk Johnson, "Survey Finds More Delays on Subway," the *New York Times*, July 22, 1988, p. B1.

In Sunset Park, the subway-rider upturn was first evident at the three southern stations, where the settlement of employed immigrants was heavy. Thus, from a low of less than 3.5 million in 1976–1978, paid ridership in the 53rd–59th–8th-Avenue cluster had by 1985–1987 climbed to over 3.8 million (Table 7–10). In the 25th–36th–45th-Street cluster, the recovery has been more tentative. But at no station has there yet been a return to 1970–1972 levels, when Sunset Park had fewer automobiles, let alone to the peaks just before and after World War II, the golden age of New York's public transit.

Sunset Park is encircled by tourist attractions—Prospect Park, Greenwood Cemetery, the Verrazano Bridge, the cross-bay vistas. But the neighborhood's interior offers few inviting walkways. The Restoration Committee's walking tours are prudently limited to the brownstone belt, the Park, and a handful of historic buildings. Except for a look at three of those buildings—BAT, the New York State Arsenal, and the Auction House (where stands the life-size statue of Irving Bush)—the waterfront is no place for a pierside stroll except by those who relish the contemplation of a ruin. Third Avenue, densely trafficked and darkened by the elevated expressway, is a hodgepodge of marginal retail and industrial buildings, likely to remain so indefinitely. Nor is Fourth Avenue, though still graced with several churches and buildings of architectural and historical interest—the relics of a larger ensemble—most people's idea for a Sunday promenade. Fifth Avenue is a street for quotidian marketing, not window-shopping. In short, urban walkers are more likely to admire Sunset Park as a diorama of New York's immigrant saga than as a compelling spectacle.

**TABLE 7–10**
**Subway Ridership, Principal Stations in Sunset Park, 1970–1987 (in Thousands)**

|  | Northern Stations | Southern Stations |
|---|---|---|
| *Three-year Averages* | *25th, 36th,* *45th Streets* | *53rd, 59th Streets,* *8th Avenue* |
| 1970–1972 | 4,135.3 | 4,301.4 |
| 1973–1975 | 3,611.5 | 3,771.1 |
| 1976–1978 | 3,328.2 | 3,486.1 |
| 1979–1981 | 3,441.2 | 3,637.5 |
| 1982–1984 | 3,259.1 | 3,732.8 |
| 1985–1987 | 3,363.8 | 3,867.5 |

*Source:* New York City Transit Authority.

Community Board 7 has perseveringly petitioned the City's capital budgeters for funds to remedy Sunset Park's most urgent physical and structural lacks. It is under no illusion that it can do much to speed the schedule of subway improvement; the Transit Authority appears well armored against local political pressures. Of the priorities that lie in the board's range of influence, the highest is relief for its overcrowded schools. For many years it has pleaded for new elementary schools or, as a stopgap, additional classrooms at existing school sites.[116] The board's second capital-budget priority is street improvements and the renewal of the aging water and sewer system.

Come what may, much time will pass before Sunset Park restores an infrastructure impaired by decades of neglect. City Hall's response to the community's capital-budget requests has been anything but galvanic. The excuse, at first, was the 1975 fiscal crisis and its unhappy sequels. Later, its finances restored, the City stepped up capital plan allocations to District 7, but well short of meeting the jurisdiction's priority list.[117] Though some street improvements are now in progress, the translation of budget allocations into brick and mortar stretches into interminable years. The reasons for delay are political as much as administrative. A public budget is both more and less than a financial statement of objectively determined policies and programs. It is also a scorecard of points to be won and lost in the intriguing game of electoral politics, endlessly played by fluid coalitions of officials and interest groups. The feuding and horse-trading of mayors and borough presidents are stellar constants in cross-river governance. Other than for undisputed emergencies, budget funds granted, denied, or deferred represent deposits into, and withdrawals from, a "favor bank." Relations between City Hall and Court Street have been anything but cordial, and the strains worsened through most of the eighties. During the eighties, few of Borough President Howard Golden's entreaties that fell within Mayor Koch's discretion to affirm or reject were granted, other than those, such as business-decentralization subsidies, that served some mutual interest. No one can now foretell how charter revision will affect the political balance. One may be confident, however, that new and untested arrangements are likely further to stall the administrative procedures.

---

116. Community Board 7, Brooklyn, New York, "Fiscal Year 1987 Statement of Needs," August 18, 1987.
117. Cf. *Community District Needs, Fiscal Year 1988, Brooklyn*, New York Department of City Planning, pp. 115–137.

Political rewards and punishments aside, the City's capital plan is not a statement of commitments but of hopes and promises, eternally postponable. Nearly eternal, too, is the implementation process, even for those items that have advanced from the Capital Plan to the Capital Budget, itself a long-drawn passage. Though the Board of Education is searching for school sites to add 1,200 seats, it can easily take ten years until an approved new school opens its doors. Sunset Park's Community Board therefore musters much of its energies on the here and now, namely, the City's annual expense budget. It doggedly petitions for additional public services such as police, health, welfare, and sanitation.

## Social Problems

On top of the agenda, by a wide margin, is a reinforced 72nd Police Precinct, with emphasis on aggressive measures against drug-related crime. In truth, scored against the crime rates of all 75 of New York's police precincts, Sunset Park stands well above average, with a 1987 rank of 61 on a scale where 75 is first. The current ranking is a considerable improvement over the ranking of 46 recorded earlier in the eighties. Indeed, other than drug offenses, the incidence of crime had drifted down. As shown in Table 7–11, total index crimes declined from 8,152 in 1981 to 5,507 in 1987, though most of the gain was realized before 1985.[118] During the same years, crimes against persons decreased from 1,510 to 1,329 and crimes against property from 6,642 to 4,178.

All contemporary discussions of crime begin and end with drugs. It has become the *summmum malum* of the urban predicament. The drug market nourishes every heinous felony perpetrated by crazed addicts, vengeful dealers, and warring gangs. It is an incubus that suffocates the entire criminal justice system—police, courts, and prisons—with no relief in sight. And not the criminal justice system alone. Drug abuse is also crushing New York's social service system. Drugs are supplanting alcohol as a trigger mechanism in the abuse of women and children, in the dissolution of family and the abdication of parenthood. It fills the foster homes and swells the ranks of the homeless. The drug needle has been implicated as the principal transmitter of AIDS to the heterosexual population, a premature death sentence for unwary women and a tragic new mode of infanticide.

---

118. Index crimes are the seven categories registered in the FBI's national data system: murder, rape, robbery, assault, burglary, larceny, and motor vehicle theft.

**TABLE 7–11**
**Index Crimes Reported in 1981–1987, 72nd Precinct (Community District 7)**

|  | 1981 | 1982 | 1983 | 1984 | 1985 | 1986 | 1987 |
|---|---|---|---|---|---|---|---|
|  | No. (Rank) | No. (Rank) | No. (Rank) | No. (Rank) | No. (Rank) | No. (Rank) | No. (Rank) |
| Murder | 27(27) | 18(34) | 11(49) | 16(33) | 25(21) | 14(45) | 12(45) |
| Rape | 29(55) | 27(55) | 32(46) | 26(53) | 31(46) | 28(48) | 36(40) |
| Robbery | 970(52) | 923(50) | 920(49) | 724(51) | 790(46) | 676(54) | 580(56) |
| Assault | 484(40) | 447(43) | 412(45) | 589(35) | 527(40) | 608(40) | 710(37) |
| Total Person Crime | 1510(50) | 1415(48) | 1275(46) | 1355(43) | 1373(42) | 1326(46) | 1329(46) |
| Burglary | 3245(24) | 2429(30) | 1977(30) | 1597(35) | 1656(32) | 1457(44) | 1243(53) |
| Larceny | 2073(53) | 2280(50) | 2243(46) | 2172(49) | 1811(61) | 1937(60) | 1975(62) |
| Motor Vehicle Theft | 1329(34) | 1180(35) | 1124(33) | 983(35) | 770(42) | 876(43) | 960(42) |
| Total Property Crime | 6642(46) | 5889(49) | 5344(46) | 4752(49) | 4237(54) | 4270(56) | 4178(59) |
| Total Crimes | 8152(46) | 7304(48) | 6619(46) | 6107(50) | 5610(55) | 5596(59) | 5507(61) |

*Source:* Information Services, Department of City Planning, City of New York.

165

Sunset Park, as in varying degree are most New York neighbor-hoods, is permeated by a drug scourge. In a typical year, over 1,200 drug arrests are made in the 72nd Precinct. Sunset Park's police, veterans of a moderately successful engagement with marijuana and heroin, are now in what seems like a hopeless battle with crack, cocaine's pernicious derivative. Crack is the matrix of a mushrooming subeconomy and subculture. The market for crack—processing, sell-ing, and possession—has exploded in its dimensions and, more fear-fully, in its firepower.

Drugs are Topic A at community board meetings. The board exerts itself to strengthen the precinct's narcotics squad but is guardful of any expedient that would reassign officers from other patrols. Of course, every neighborhood routinely demands more police, some with desperate urgency, as in the Red Hook area to Sunset Park's north where the public housing project has become a branch of the drug industry and, periodically, a free-fire zone. Though City Hall is committed to a heavy reinforcement of the City's narcotics squads, Sunset Park, given its not unfavorable crime statistics, is not likely to get top priority. Neither, in the face of current budget strains and a thinned-out police force, will most other residential areas. Thus, in the competition among neighborhoods, Sunset Park will not be, rela-tively speaking, disadvantaged.

Side by side with Sunset Park's drug problem, and in many re-spects its correlate, are two other unsolved social problems—an ex-cess of chronic poverty and its correlate, the rundown condition of much of the multifamily housing stock.

The rehabilitation of deteriorated rent-regulated multifamily houses has proved a wearying struggle. From the early eighties on, once the health of the market for one- to four-family houses seemed assured, SPRC diverted its capacities to the stricken multifamily sector. But, preoccupied with an entrepreneurial as much as with a restorative agenda, SPRC's accomplishments were meager. To sus-tain itself, it turned to two income-producing activities. One was as property manager for both City and privately owned buildings. The other was as a general partner in tax-shelter syndications. Since most of SPRC's operating budget depended on earnings from such real-estate pursuits, its attention, understandably, turned to buildings promising the most rewards, not necessarily to those in grimmest circumstance.

In 1986 and 1987, SPRC was mortally wounded by two blows. It was named a party in litigation stemming from alleged misarrange-ments in certain of its tax-shelter partnerships. As a result, it lost several management contracts and much of its syndication earnings. Aggravating that injury was the embezzlement of a nearly half-million-dollar bank account; there has been no recovery to date. These traumas undermined SPRC's viability. All but in name it is dead, another closed chapter in the community's annals.

Even had SPRC survived, the rehabilitation of Sunset Park's multifamily stock, for reasons economic and political, would have presented intimidating obstacles.[119] The restoration of a rent-regulated inventory occupied by poverty-stricken, often socially disorganized, tenants is wholly dependent on an uninterrupted flow of public subsidies, subject to the resources and rules of a multiplicity of government agencies. Itself socially divided, the Sunset Park community has not been avid to batter down the ramparts. In any event, federal Section 8, the most effective subsidy for the poorest tenants in the worst buildings, has been all but eliminated. Its replacement—housing vouchers (a rent-assistance subsidy resembling Section 8)—is much less effective.

These handicaps notwithstanding, slow progress is evident. Each year, by stitching together a variety of public aids, more buildings are restored without displacing existing occupants.[120] And private-investor interest in the ownership and renovation of Sunset Park's multifamily properties, as almost everywhere in New York, has been rekindled. In Sunset Park that interest is keenest with respect to the buildings less encumbered by rent regulation (i.e., properties with fewer than six units), and those that can be delivered fully or partially vacant. As the more advantageous opportunities disappear, sooner or later even the large occupied properties will be gathered into the rescue net, drawn there by the City's comprehensive rehabilitation programs. Yet it is difficult to conjure up a picture in the immediate years ahead wherein Sunset Park's larger rental properties will have

---

119. And not just in Sunset Park. That is likewise the experience of virtually all community development organizations. Thus, to look just at Brooklyn, the home ownership blocks of Flatbush are in full bloom. But the multifamily buildings on many of Flatbush's avenues, occupied by large numbers of poor families and heavily dependent on public intervention, are only slowly and incompletely being restored. Comparable conditions prevail in Crown Heights, Bedford-Stuyvesant, East Flatbush, and even such booming neighborhoods as Borough Park.

120. The exemplar in such programs is the Community Preservation Corporation (CPC), a consortium of leading banks and insurance companies. CPC, blending public aid with private capital, had by 1988 restored more than 20,000 low- and moderate-income apartments. Once concentrated in Washington Heights and Harlem, CPC has moved heavily into Brooklyn. Sunset Park is likely to be a target area.

advanced to the flourishing state of its free-market inventory. That is a general belief in community development everywhere. It is the reason why grass-roots organizations commonly favor home ownership or its variants—co-ops and condos—in their renewal plans even in the most severely distressed places such as Brownsville and the South Bronx. In Sunset Park, too. It was earlier observed that several of the rehabilitated projects characterized by tenant participation emerged as low-income co-ops, and most recently, a building for artists.

What exacerbates the multifamily housing problem is that these buildings are, predominantly, the habitats of Sunset Park's large poor population. In 1985, 27.5 percent of District 7's residents were on public assistance, slightly higher than the 26 percent rate in 1980 and substantially above the 18.2 percent for the City as a whole. And, were separate data available, poverty in Sunset Park proper would be surely greater than District 7's; recall its 30 percent rate as reported in 1980 census data when a separation was possible.[121]

Apart from some poverty among the elderly, Sunset Park's poor are overwhelmingly Hispanic, especially Puerto Rican. The community's Hispanics are patently dividing into a two-class structure. One comprises chronically dependent families who are the principal tenantry of the rent-regulated multifamily units, subsidized and unsubsidized. The other tier comprises upwardly mobile working and middle-income families who live in the two- to five-family houses as owners and market-rent tenants, or in the refurbished apartment buildings. As observed earlier, telephone listings indicate that Hispanics are settling in considerable numbers on Sunset Park's better residential streets.

Despite the disquiet over gentrification, wholesale push-outs are less apparent in Sunset Park than in other recovering neighborhoods. That is attested to not only by the perpetuation of poverty but also by the overwhelmingly Hispanic school enrollment and the minuscule rate of co-op conversion. As repeatedly noted, the Hispanic population, if not its Puerto Rican component, continues to grow. The most significant shrinkage is in the older European stock, few of whose departures have been forced.

---

121. The City of New York, "Community District Needs," August 1986, p. 115. There is uncertain evidence of a decline two years later. The *1987 Housing Report* indicated for District 7 a 25 percent poverty rate (compared to 26.1 percent in 1980) and a 14.5 percent public assistance rate. Both figures, however, are based on an extremely small sample subject to a high sampling error.

Indeed, many Puerto Rican out-movers have been voluntary, including those who sold price-appreciated homes for impressive capital gains; some, it is said, have returned to the commonwealth, considerably more affluent than when they left. The risk of displacement is highest in the unregulated rental units in the smaller properties. The majority of renter families, however, is in larger buildings where statutory tenants are protected by rent control and rent stabilization or else they live in subsidized, means-tested apartments. Unless and until Sunset Park is beset by a large-scale co-op conversion movement (a contingency not now in sight), its extensive multifamily stock will continue to provide accommodation to many thousands of poor.

It must also be said that not everyone in Sunset Park is opposed to gentrification. Many ardently welcome it. The sentiments hostile to the poverty designation of the sixties and the Neighborhood Strategy Area designation of the seventies (discussed in Chapter 6) have not evaporated. If anything, they have been bolstered by many of the new middle class and brownstoners who yearn for Sunset Park to evolve into a closer substitute for Park Slope, in the manner that Park Slope evolved into a closer substitute for Carroll Gardens and Brooklyn Heights. That vision has, in large measure, animated the Sunset Park's Restoration Committee campaign for historic designation, now partly won. In the spring of 1988, following several unsuccessful attempts, a large irregular swath of Sunset Park, covering parts or all of the blocks between Fourth and Seventh avenues, 39th to 65th streets, was placed on both the national and New York State registers of historic places. However, a designation by the New York City Landmarks Preservation Commission does not appear imminent. City landmarking would have far more significance than does the federal and state's. It would impose not only more severe restrictions on demolition but also rigorous controls on the architectural design of new construction and structural alterations, on signage and accoutrements, and on "street furniture" (e.g., light standards, gardens, street paving material, and the like).

Arrayed against the votaries of Yuppieville is the low-income coalition—UPROSE (Sunset Park's federation of Puerto Rican organizations)—plus a handful of religious leaders and middle-class liberals. That coalition resists direct or indirect steps that would shrink the low-income base and other actions deemed inimical to the poor. Its influence, however, has palpably weakened as new people entered and as many one-time supporters of the coalition graduated into the middle class or left the community. It is noteworthy that on the community board's current capital-budget agenda the request for housing funds is confined to "new construction of small homes," rather than for any further expansion of the subsidized multifamily inventory.

Between the extremes—those who strive for Sunset Park as Park Slope South and those who would preserve it as an inviolate habitat for the community's poor and near-poor—is a broad band of those at neither battlement. They include many middle-class Hispanics whose sympathies appear torn between ethnicity and class. Among the nonengaged are also the new Asians, who keep a low public profile. As much research demonstrates, though they seek and acquire naturalization earlier and more frequently than do other immigrants, the political participation of Chinese-Americans is as yet restrained. Their firmest attachments are to job, family, and intra-ethnic affairs. In Sunset Park their urges are to enlarge the existing Chinese community—more kinsmen, more customers, more hands for the factories. Since there is so little new construction, the newcomers can be accommodated mainly by the departures of others. Many of Sunset Park's Asians are also store proprietors, no less fearful of crime than other businesses. It strains credulity to believe that the community's Asians would lament a dwindling of Sunset Park's welfare dependents whence spring so much drug abuse and so many youthful criminals.

In truth, the term "community," so profusely strewn throughout the study, is a superficial courtesy title. In actuality, Sunset Park is a loose conglomeration of numerous communities, differentiated by race, ethnicity, religion, social class, and values. The boundary lines conferred on Sunset Park in the mid-sixties gave it geographic, not cultural, cohesion. Locational propinquities do not imply other propinquities. That was always so. The great European migrations, Sunset Park's raison d'être, also formed self-demarcated enclaves, distanced by nationality, language, occupation, and culture. In the main, each enclave fraternized with its own kind, gravitated toward its own streets and shops, and worshipped at its own churches.

Though due to adventitious causes, the demise of SPRC, which was the spearhead of Sunset Park's renewal and a champion of its poor, symbolized the end of the once-fervent community-development movement. It had given Sunset Park a semblance of unity because common purposes derives from common threats. A base of solidarity was cemented by adverse government intrusions, by the frightening fall of real estate prices, by empty stores and churches, by rising crime and an impaired quality of life. Nothing banks the fires of protest so much as complacency. As fears of depopulation and disinvestment dissipated, so did much of the fervor.

Sunset Park's present property owners, including its middle-class ethnics, are confident that its housing market, if no longer in ascent, is agreeably secure.

It is no wrench with its past to suggest that Sunset Park is not likely ever to be anything but a community of communities. The brownstoners constitute one. Themselves heterogeneous, they are bound together primarily by block associations, by the quest for landmarking, and by an abiding interest in the status score of their housing. In size they are overshadowed by the Hispanics, themselves divided by nationality and economic class into subcommunities. And both groupings are distinct from the emergent Chinese, who are separately joined by the affinities of language, kinship, occupation, and the imperatives of ethnic defense.

Sunset Park's collective voice today is not a community-development organization but its community board, one of the 59 officially designated by the City as a grass-roots planning and administrative agency. But the board must attend to the preoccupations of numerous "communities" with names that betell their special interests: the Restoration Committee; UPROSE, which represents most of the Puerto Rican community; the Community Relations Office of LMC, concerned with issues that jointly affect hospital and community; the Fifth Avenue and Eighth Avenue merchants associations; the Southwest Brooklyn Industrial Development Corporation; and numerous block associations. Each has a vision of a better Sunset Park. But the visions are not all congruent.

The several interests coalesce around what remains of shared concerns, especially the noncontroversial. Although turnout at district board meetings varies with season, weather, and agenda, the assembly on an average evening is more likely to be agitated by the presence of too many trucks and too few traffic lights than by philosophical debates over whither Sunset Park. The nettlesome issues on the agenda are, as noted, drugs, overcrowded schools, and crumbling streets, rather than the visceral agitations that churned the sixties and seventies, the specter of a neighborhood headed for some urban Gehenna. Sunset Park's relative quietude may be as persuasive an index as any of its return to "normalcy."

The question, Whither Sunset Park? is perhaps best left to those not immersed in day-to-day affairs or engrossed by self-interest. It is the question that occupies the next, and concluding, chapter.

# CHAPTER 8

# Whither Sunset Park?

As earlier said, Sunset Park is a speck in a vast social and economic universe. Its decline and its recovery were the consequences of events over which it had small control. Easy mortgage credit and new broad highways lured its people away. Its Industrial Zone was struck low by economic trends upon which its residents gazed as mere spectators. By the same token, its revival was the boon of a thunderingly prosperous Manhattan and of an imperfectly understood immigration law enacted a generation ago by a Congress with other perspectives in view.

Sunset Park will have no more control in shaping its future. That is not to say that a self-aware community is a helpless pawn, utterly foreclosed from action. A community may elect a pro- or antidevelopment role, to press for either prohibitive or permissive zoning rules, to seek or oppose the protective mantle of historic preservation. It may or may not organize community development corporations or civilian police patrols or civic associations to attend to local amenities. Those choices matter. But, in the end, the part of its destiny that a neighborhood can influence through discretionary acts is minuscule in comparison with the immensity of forces beyond its reach. Those forces comprise both the unforeseeable imponderables—cultural change—and the foreseeable ponderables—the demographic and economic trends that lend themselves, at least in principle, to informed projection.

Among the imponderables is how the community's political complexion will change. Since the residents and leaders of tomorrow's Sunset Park will not altogether be those of today, that change will determine the nature even of its residual discretionary choices. Significant long-term shifts have occurred in Sunset Park's political credo over the course of its history. Its European descendants were a bulwark of the New Deal coalition. Until World War II, the precincts that now compose Sunset Park were solid cogs in Brooklyn's Democratic machine, ruled by an Irish political ascendancy. Later, the Irish clubhouses, their constituencies dwindling, were surrendered to a predominantly Italian leadership. But as early as the thirties, strains of political and populist conservatism had begun to surface, including traces of the Christian Front and Father Coughlin.

By the sixties, Sunset Park's politics were increasingly blue-collar conservative, the onset of the Irish and Italian crossover to Republican Party affiliation, to a political coloration more akin to Bay Ridge and Staten Island than to the rest of Brooklyn. (It is owing mainly to astutely drawn electoral boundary lines that Sunset Park is now represented by a Democratic congressman, rather than, as is Bay Ridge–Staten Island, by a Republican.)

Sunset Park's politics will surely change again as the newer ethnics enter the electoral arena in greater number, as inevitably they will, though some less rapidly and completely than others. And a generation of younger, educated professionals, many with a keen interest in local governance, is already injecting itself into the political culture.

Less predictable still is the future character of a community's values, its prevailing system of beliefs. Those imponderables are influenced not just by the changing mix of individuals who will live in a community but by the changes in the individuals themselves. Personal mores and ethical codes do not remain fixed any more than do political creeds; indeed, the latter is an expression of the former. Sunset Park would be today a much different community had there not been three decades of ethnic succession—no out-migration, no Hispanics, no Asians—no one there but the descendants of the historical European migration. There still would be more divorces and broken families, shallower religious observance, and a good deal more permissiveness. The magazines on its newsstands would still reveal more flesh than the pious Scandinavian Lutherans of an older immigration might have glimpsed in the bedrooms of a married lifetime. The resolute opposition to mortgage debt of the Finnish cooperators would still appear, in this hedonistic age of guiltless if not reckless borrowing, wondrously quaint, akin to the stamped tin ceilings of the brownstones. Physically, too, Sunset Park would now be what it is whatever its ethnic mix. It was not the Puerto Ricans who built the expressway or brought the trucks or who were responsible for collapsed subway service and deteriorated public services.

The least knowable imponderable concerns the ultimate consequences of the drug scourge. Drugs are no respecter of ethnicity, race, age, sex, or social class; no moral code will long remain intact in the grip of a runaway drug culture. In recent years, not a few Italian and Irish youth (some Asian, too)—the offspring of South Brooklyn's strong-family traditions and comparative affluence—have succumbed to the aberrant behavior stereotypically associated with youth of welfare-dependent and minority families. In former days, the transgressions of Sunset Park's street gangs were less randomly destructive, usually held in check by group codes that frowned on drug use. Such constraints, apparently, no longer prevail. In the age of crack, nothing prevails save the next fix and the one after that.

It is certain that Sunset Park's ethos 50 years from now will be as different as its 1938 was from its 1988. But no one is wise enough to write the script. Hence, it is more rewarding to cling to the comfortable ponderables—the conventional exercise of projecting demographic and economic trends to a date not as distant as a half-century, say the year 2000. How are these trends likely to affect Sunset Park? To perform that exercise, it is conventional to fall back on two assumptions. One is that Sunset Park's destiny will be bound up with New York City's destiny. The second is that the recent trends possess sufficient inertial force and stability to justify their extrapolation to the turn of the century, not so many years away.

## RECENT TRENDS PROJECTED

In speculating about New York's tomorrow, one must repeat the caveats about the lopsided imbalance between self-determination and external forces. Cities, like neighborhoods, are not self-navigating vessels, though they have more freedom to maneuver. Because of its size, wealth, and legal powers, New York has more steerage way than most. But not an awful lot. It, too, is carried by the winds and currents of the global economic and political universe. Thus, it requires some sense, perhaps only notional, of where region, nation, and globe are headed. In other words, to sketch a scenario of what lies in store for Sunset Park is to sketch a scenario of what lies in store for New York. That, in turn, implies a scenario of what is likely to happen on a hierarchy of higher stages.

To economize on so daunting a forecasting task, it is convenient to resort to the 1987 report of the Commission on the Year 2000, *New York Ascendant*. The report (introduced in Chapter 4) was widely acclaimed for its breadth, competence, and nonpartisanship. It set forth plausible prognostications of where New York was pointed and how it might look at the turn of the twenty-first century. In formulating the projections, the commission's research team panoramically scanned the international, national, and regional scene before narrowing its focus to the five boroughs. Examined were a host of exogenous and endogenous factors that impinge on the City's principal sectors: economy, population, schools, transportation, housing, poverty, crime, and others.

The commission's overall verdict was shadowed optimism. It prophesied a bright economic future for New York but one dimmed by lingering infirmities in infrastructure, housing, and environment and darkened by drugs, crime, and an underclass. On the sunny side, the commission projected a highly productive City with hundreds of thousands of additional jobs and higher average levels of real income. A robust demand was foreseen for all the City's specialties, its financial and business service sectors, its sumptuary markets, its health-care and medical sectors, its prestigious academic centers, its cultural institutions, and its performing and visual arts. That buoyant scenario would yield opportunities for all—yuppies and immigrants, those at the peak of their careers and those starting out, providing the aspirants brought or acquired a sufficiency of educational qualifications.

The commission's long-term projections were indirectly ratified by the actions of the private sector, most convincingly by those with a vital financial stake in correctly gauging the City's long-term future. Moody's and Standard & Poor's progressively up-rated the $15 billion of outstanding City bonds, most not maturing until well into the twenty-first century. The long-term optimists also included a multitude of international financial giants—Japanese, Canadian, and European—whose investment radars are beamed on a distant horizon. It is said of Japanese firms what the Victorians said of canny Scottish insurance and pension funds: Their investment calendar is not the year nor the decade, but eternity. The overseas billions wagered on New York office buildings were at such extraordinarily high price-earnings ratios, they could be warranted only by the prospect of substantial asset-appreciation in some far-off future.

Of course, multiple endorsements by knowledgeable investors are no guarantee of the outcome. All the optimists—commissions, bond raters, foreign investors—might easily prove wrong. The gods of uncertainty are notoriously capricious and take delight in tweaking the noses of confident seers.[122] Still, the long-term projections represent the best judgments of professional analysts employing the best available data and command respect for their basic contours, if not for their every detail.

The commission's optimism derived from the premise that New York would remain the hub of the world's expansionary financial and business service sectors. Periodic business cycles aside, that growth was deemed to be unlimited by time or geography. Even the relatively undeveloped resource-based economies such as the Soviet Union, China, and Latin America have been actively creating sophisticated banking, financial, and trading systems. The momentum of global growth assured the commission of further gains for New York, conceding a sharing with rival financial capitals, notably Tokyo and London. In short, the Sunset Parks of New York—the communities that make up the five boroughs—would be uplifted by a basically thriving economy. As pertinent to Sunset Park's future was the commission's strong urging that more of Manhattan's gains be diverted to the outer boroughs, back-office white-collar jobs in particular, as well as a maximum of Manhattan's weakening industrial sector.

That recommendation was a preachment to the converted. For more than two decades, City policy had been committed to decentralizing its employment base, at first manufacturing and government agencies and later finance. A dramatic expression of that policy is the comprehensive redevelopment plan for downtown Brooklyn, now in execution. If fulfilled, that plan would bring in 10 million square feet of office, retail, hotel, and educational space and a base of 35,000 to 40,000 jobs, most of them incremental to Brooklyn.[123] In a real sense, the downtown Brooklyn plan represents the modern era's substitute for the Brooklyn maritime economy of times past.

---

122. The stock market collapse of October 19, 1987, occurred a few months after the commission issued its report. Black Monday did not materially affect the City's basic economy, which resumed its healthy growth. By early 1989, however, that growth had halted.
123. Downtown Brooklyn's development program includes Pierrepont Plaza (already completed), Metrotech, Atlantic Terminal, and Renaissance and Livingston plazas. Morgan Stanley, Goldman Sachs, and other investment houses are already committed to Pierrepont Plaza, and Brooklyn Union Gas, the Securities Industry Automation Corporation, and Chase Manhattan to Metrotech. The other ventures have also attracted major builders and potential occupants, but are subject to many uncertainties.

Sunset Park, just a few miles and subway stops south of downtown, is sure to feel the radiating effects of that redevelopment. The projected new jobs are, in the main, at salaries more in line with Sunset Park's housing prices and rents than with the expensive neighborhoods closer to downtown Brooklyn. Thus, Sunset Park's housing and retail sectors would be strengthened not only by a favorable Citywide economic climate and by the improving fortunes of its Industrial Zone but also by a major uplift of Brooklyn's economy.

Sunset Park's housing and retail sectors would further be strengthened by prevailing demographic trends. The commission peered at New York's future population. It foresaw a post-1980 gain of a half-million people, an aggregate of over 7,500,000 by the year 2000. That increment comprises young careerists who, as during the post-1977 revival, would be drawn to the City's dynamic financial, business, service, and cultural sectors. But the larger component of population growth would come from foreign immigration. The commission spoke of 750,000 to 1,250,000 new admissions between 1985 and 2000, both figures well in excess of the projected net gain in total population; in other words, without new immigrants, City population would go down, not up. Viewed in 1989, the commission's population—based on older data—seemed unduly conservative. Even more so were its immigration projections. They presupposed an average inflow of only 50,000 to 80,000 foreigners per year. Even the higher estimate is well below the legal inflow of recent years, and substantially more so when realistic allowance is made for the undocumented, about whom the commission said little. Since pending legislation, certain to broaden the incoming stream, had not yet been formulated at the time, the commission gave it no weight.

Because future levels of immigration are so critical to Sunset Park's demographic future, one should examine the bases of the competing estimates. As indicated in Chapter 3, the factors that point to a stable or rising level of immigration overbalance those that point to the low level set forth in the commission's report. Indeed, the one justification for a conservative forecast is the presumption that, post-amnesty, illegal immigration would significantly diminish. Employers, exposed to severe penalties, would no longer risk hiring the new or residual undocumented, hence the latter would lack motive for illicit sojourn or entry. That presumption is dubious; a recent Rand-Urban Institute study indicates only a modest reduction in unauthorized entry. Illegal entrants are inordinately resourceful in uncovering job opportunities. And small firms—the bulk of the City's employers—are less inhibited than large firms in providing them. Moreover, because illegal flows to

New York have not been as inundating as in California and the Southwest, much of INS's limited enforcement manpower has tended to be deployed there.

Whatever the drop in illegal entry, it is sure to be offset by countervailing factors, the rules that govern legal entry. One factor is the power of family-unification provisions, which is further magnified by amnesty. As illegals are turned into legal residents, the volume of claims against the various admission categories is swelled through the workings of the immigration multipliers. Those family members who are brought in by the newly legalized sooner or later exert claims for *their* relatives. It is that process that forges the so-called "chain of migration," which figures so prominently in ethnographic literature and public policy.

Nor is there any likelihood of an imminent shortage in the pool from which the migration chain draws. In 1986, even prior to amnesty, nearly 2 million prequalified foreigners were waiting their turn for entry; in 1980, the number was only about 1 million.[124] In recent times, the queue has steadily grown longer, notwithstanding a rising level of legal admissions. As more names are called from the head of the line, even more grasp a number for a place at the tail.

Also pointing to higher admission levels is new legislation, already passed or in the pipeline. Bills introduced in the 100th Congress sought to expand admissions by formulas likely to increase New York's intake. Various amendments before the Senate and House would raise the quotas for those with special employment skills and English-language competence. The gesture was intended, in part, to favor Irish applicants who are disadvantaged by present family-reunification preferences (because they no longer have very many nuclear-family relatives in the U.S.). But it would simultaneously favor India, Pakistan, and other nations with substantial numbers of educated and/or English-speaking people. One amendment that was enacted in the closing days of the 100th Congress would add some 50,000 special visas to a special lottery pool. Other amendments, if enacted, could raise U.S. admissions by 100,000 per year, some believe more. New York would likely get more than a due share of the increment. The City has been a preferred destination for several of the sending countries likely to be benefited.

It is now a near-certainty, too, that the Soviet Union will progressively widen its emigration gates; under Gorbachev, visas have risen

---

124. "Using National Recording Systems for the Measurement and Analysis of Immigration to the United States," *Immigration and Migration Review*, Vol. xxi, No. 4, p. 1230.

to more than 4,000 per month, the highest level since the seventies, another plus factor for New York, judging from prior destination choices.[125] In 1988, an estimated 6,500 came to the City compared to 750 in 1986; more than 15,000 are projected for 1989. There will also be refugees other than from the Soviet Union. The recent actions of other nations, such as Malaysia, Thailand, and Hong Kong, to erect walls against Indo-Chinese are likely to divert many more to the U.S. In 1988, as Thailand became restive over its overcrowded settlements, the U.S. was persuaded to accept 15 percent more refugees than it had in 1987, in turn a level higher than in 1986; the refugee quota for Indo-Chinese was raised in 1988 to 25,000, triple the 1987 level. That, too, will add to the New York admission flow. Though New York has not in the past been a major gateway for displaced Indo-Chinese, the small enclaves now here are attaining the threshold levels that generally stimulate further growth.

Nor is New York's appeal to New Immigrants confined to new admissions. On net balance, the entry here of foreign-born is augmented by internal migration as well as external. The Northeast has attracted immigrants from regions in the U.S. afflicted by weakened economies. The robust New York metropolitan job market—which saw more jobs chasing people than people chasing jobs—proved an irresistible lure to admittees seeking wage and salary employment.[126] The commission projected payroll jobs to grow by an average of 20,000 a year; the actual rate of increase until 1989 was more than twice that. Though total employment gains have subsided, there is still an acute demand in such immigration-dominated industries as health care and services. And the structure of the City's economy still lends itself to uncounted opportunities for those bent on self-employment.

Weighing all the factors, it is reasonable to conclude that the average level of foreign entries to New York might easily reach 100,000 and, eventually, perhaps 110,000, per year, substantially more than

---

125. Local immigration agencies estimate that half of the Soviet émigrés who enter the United States settle in New York. That proportion, however, will fall if Soviet émigrés are denied refugee status. That denial was imposed by the State Department in 1989, causing the bulk of Soviet émigré Jews to opt for Israel, which proffers unlimited access.

126. In 1986, the Port Authority foresaw an impending labor shortage, the result of a demographic hollow in the 16- to 24-year-old cohort. Cf. "A Forecast of Employment, Population and Labor Force in the New York–New Jersey Metropolitan Region in 1995." Two years later, as noted in Chapter 4, the Authority restated its concerns in even stronger terms, cf. the Port Authority of New York and New Jersey, "Challenges and Opportunity for the Coming Decade," September 1988.

the commission's estimates; by 1987, legal admissions alone had crossed the 91,000 mark, and by 1988, 93,000. Such levels would significantly alter the commission's projections of the size and composition of New York's future population. Barring an unforeseen acceleration in current rates of out-migration, total population by the turn of the century would reach 8 million rather than 7.5 million. What raises that probability are the high birthrates of the principal immigrant groups, especially from the Caribbean. The bulk of New York's rising birth levels since 1980 is accounted for by children of foreign-born mothers. The proportion of foreign-born could, by the year 2000, easily surpass the 1910 peak of 40 percent. So sizable a cumulation of newcomers would heavily impact every City neighborhood, especially receiving areas like Sunset Park.

## SUNSET PARK IN THE YEAR 2000

Assuming the validity of the commission's projections, these things might be said about Sunset Park in the year 2000.

• It would contain a considerably larger population, with a preponderance of first- and second-generation immigrants.

• That population would be more prosperous and fully employed; more would be working at white-collar jobs.

• Its poverty rate as officially measured would be reduced at the same time that its underclass problems—drugs, crime, and chronic dependency—are likely to deepen.

• Its housing market would remain healthy, experiencing, for the first time in many decades, a measurable inventory expansion.

• Many deficiencies in its infrastructure will have been eased—almost surely the school plant, sewers, and paving. But others, like the expressway and mixed land use, are built in and unlikely ever to be cured.

• Sunset Park's public identity as a distinct neighborhood would be even more firmly established and its standing higher. But it would lag behind its neighbors with their higher-quality housing stock and greater cachet; their standings, too, will have risen.

This fast-forward picture of Sunset Park is a statement of probabilities, not certainties; many events, good or bad, could derail the projections in either direction. Amid all the uncertainties, however, two projections merit more confidence than do the others—Sunset Park's future demographics and the status of its housing market.

In recent years, Sunset Park's population has increased at a faster rate than the City's, between 1980 and 1985, nearly 4 percent compared to less than 2 percent. Should New York attain 8 million people at century's end—a gain of 13 percent over 1980—and should something like that differential persist, Sunset Park would register a gain of 20 percent or more. That would bring the area's total population to something approaching 100,000.[127] So substantial an increment is conceivable even with only a modest volume of housing construction, no more than could be achieved by infill on the scattered sites now occupied by old garages, warehouses, gas stations, and low-value dwellings. The rest of the increment is likely to be accommodated within the larger households characteristic of immigrants who by then would constitute a majority.

And a multitude of New Immigrants there is sure to be. The best evidence indicates that Brooklyn will continue to draw each year the largest share of New York's 100,000-plus and that Sunset Park would draw at least a disproportionate share of that share. That would mean a cumulative influx into Sunset Park of perhaps 25,000 by the turn of the century, more than the net increase projected for Sunset Park's total population.

Given the magnetism of ethnic affinity, the composition of future arrivals would probably resemble that of the recent past. Asians, Dominicans, Central and South Americans would continue to find Sunset Park an even more congenial setting than before. Were there to be some deviation from past patterns, the chances are it would be toward higher proportions of Asians, especially Chinese. One reason was already noted—the rate of Asian entry into both nation and City has been substantially rising and is likely to increase still more. Political and economic uncertainties in Hong Kong, South Korea, and India, as well as continued distress in Indo-China, reinforce that flow. The vigor and structure of New York's economy have attractions that compensate for the great distances between New York and the Asian continent that have historically favored the West Coast. Likewise, Asian family-reunification multipliers—higher than most—assure that admission privileges will be subscribed to the last person (if not

---

127. Within the Eighth Avenue boundary line. For the 27 full census tracts that extend to Ninth Avenue (on which the 1980 profile was based), the projected figure would approach 110,000.

illegally oversubscribed). Chinese, more so than other ethnic groups, extend the chain of immigration by bringing in parents as well as spouses and children. The entry of a parent touches off a series of linkages to more distant relatives: to his parents, an immigrant's brother is a son—a top preference not subject to the quota ceiling. That son can then bring in *his* wife, also as a non-quota priority, whose preference would otherwise have been low.

The rate of Chinese entry into Sunset Park would also be enhanced by the burgeoning local economy: The number of Chinese garment shops is likely to expand as the resident labor force grows and as space rents in Chinatown and lower Manhattan mount. The earlier-cited move of a Chinatown fish processor to the Industrial Zone may be a sign that Chinese firms other than apparel will also be drawn to Sunset Park. And each increment in the Chinese population brings with it at least a proportionate increase in local retail and service establishments. The growth in Chinese population and Chinese business is a reciprocal that feeds on itself.

Though ethnic organizations are not noted for unduly modest estimates of client populations, the Chinese-American Planning Council, which envisaged a total of 1 million Chinese in New York by the year 2000, with 250,000 in Brooklyn, seems likely to prove right. The Council expects Sunset Park's Chinese population to double during the same years. That, too, for the reasons just suggested, seems plausible; it would bring the share to about 15 percent of Sunset Park's turn-of-the-century total. The pace of Chinese entry would doubtless be hastened had they readier access to Sunset Park's rent-regulated apartments. However, the turnover in such units, which account for about half of Sunset Park's rental inventory, is at an all-time low.[128]

---

128. Whatever the ultimate level of Sunset Park's Chinese population, a related question concerns their distribution within the community. As noted earlier, the new Chinese settlers tend to spill out in nearly every direction from their first landing places. By 1987, a westerly extension along the streets of the upper Fifties was clearly noticeable as was a northward extension past the Fifties into the upper Forties. A movement south to Bay Ridge was likewise evident. The one exception was the east, where stands Borough Park. Expansion routes toward Ninth Avenue and beyond would collide with the Jewish Hasidic and Orthodox communities, who overtly favor coreligionists as purchasers and renters. With their numbers exploding and their incomes rising, religious Jews are willing to pay extraordinary premiums for group contiguity. Indeed, there is more chance that Borough Park's Jews will drift into parts of Sunset Park than that Chinese will drift into Borough Park. Already, the Jewish community has begun to settle quite close to Sunset Park's Eighth Avenue boundary in the upper Fifties, building there a sizable new condominium. The most advantageous opportunities for in-

Given a prospect of 15,000, and probably more, Chinese residents, the commonly held expectation that Sunset Park will evolve into New York's third Chinatown is plausible. Nonetheless, one ought not overlook the fact that Chinese move out of, as well as move into, ethnic enclaves. Indeed, many of Sunset Park's newer and assimilated Chinese are exiters from Manhattan and Flushing; between 1975 and 1980, 22 percent of the City's Asians moved to the suburbs.[129] Chinese exercise many locational options, far more than blacks, and more so even than religious Jews. As recent research shows, Chinese and other Asians are characterized by a distinct tendency toward diffusion as well as concentration. Since the more affluent among them are prepared to own as well as rent, the residential choices of Asians are extensive, not much different from those of whites with equal income. At the same time, nonaffluent Asians are less deterred by low-status neighborhoods, even those inferior to Sunset Park; recall that most of the first 32 private unsubsidized two-family houses built in Bedford-Stuyvesant went to Asians. Because Asians are free to pick from a wide range of sites at various economic and social levels, Sunset Park represents only one among many competing choices. At some point, an increasing fraction of Sunset Park's more prosperous and assimilated Chinese residents will also move out, a partial offset to those coming in.

Despite the large gains projected for Sunset Park's Chinese population, ethnic primacy in the year 2000 would still belong to Hispanics. The Caribbean remains New York's "Mexico" and there is more reason for believing the flow from the Hispanic Caribbean Basin will increase than it will decrease. The best available evidence suggests that, despite U.S. efforts to improve the Caribbean's local economies, the Basin will continue to generate a labor force much in excess of expected job growth.[130] The pressures to emigrate are likely to be undiminished.

---

coming Chinese will therefore lie in every direction but east, with the less prosperous seeking the cheaper dwellings to the north and west, and the better off the brownstone belt and Bay Ridge.

129. Nathan Glazer, "The New New Yorkers," in Peter D. Salins (ed.), *New York Unbound* (New York: Basil Blackwell, Inc., 1988), p. 65. In 1987, more than one-third of the New York region's Asians (exclusive of Indians and Pakistani) lived outside the five boroughs. Cf. "Outlook: The Growing Asian Presence in the Tri-State Region," a study conducted by the Regional Plan Association on behalf of the Chinese-American Planning Council and the United Way of Tri-State, 1989, p. 4.

130. Thomas J. Espenshade, "Projected Imbalances Between Labor Supply and Labor Demand in the Caribbean Basin: Implications for Future Migrations to the United States" (Washington, D.C.: The Urban Institute), June 1988.

Moreover, as in the past, upwardly mobile Hispanic New Yorkers will find Sunset Park's low density a pleasing alternative to the drug-saturated warrens of public housing and Washington Heights. For these reasons, Sunset Park is not likely to be much less Latino as it goes into the next century than it was in 1980 or 1988. Because it is likely that Sunset Park's unregulated rents will rise further and because the income gap between Puerto Ricans and other Hispanics seems persistent,[131] there will be additional transfers from Puerto Rican to non-Puerto Rican occupants. But Puerto Rican exits are not likely to be much faster than the low turnover rate in rent-regulated and subsidized buildings.

A second confident projection is that the demand for Sunset Park's housing, despite the recent retreat, will retain basic strength. As far as one can see, housing pressures generated by economic and demographic factors will not be much relieved by a significant easing of the housing shortage. It would take a reckless housing market analyst to forecast a significant reversal in the City's depressed residential-building rates. Even the generally optimistic Commission on the Year 2000 was not so bold. Though the commission proposed the reduction or elimination of existing impediments to a higher building rate—for example, more permissive zoning standards, a re-mapping of underutilized industrial zones, and some relaxation of rent controls—it did not project a private-housing boom. Rather, it placed its emphasis on the efficacy of the City's comprehensive 10-year housing program, 250,000 units, dependent almost entirely on subsidy. Even assuming the City's program target will be achieved, a close review of its components indicates that not all of that output will lead to an equivalent net increase in the housing supply; further, only a moderate portion of that increase, averaging 6,000 per year, would be new construction. Moreover, much of any step-up in subsidized production is likely to be offset by further declines in unsubsidized construction. As long as the cost of developing a new unit in New York continues to rise faster than household income—a near-certain prospect—the effective demand for unsubsidized new housing will remain narrow and usually oversupplied. Indeed, the inexorable rise in per-unit production costs is also a heavy drag on the City's programs since it raises each year the per-unit burden of public subsidy. Federal and state governments, given their fiscal constraints, cannot

---

131. In 1986 as in 1980, there was a wide disparity between the two groups; non-Puerto Rican Hispanics had a median household income 60 percent higher than that of Puerto Ricans. Cf. *1987 Housing Report*, p. 84b.

be counted on to shoulder those costs, which means that the City itself, now under budgetary pressure, might well undershoot its declared targets.

A régime of sluggish housing production in the face of sizable increases in population and households therefore suggests that Sunset Park's relatively inexpensive housing stock will retain a competitive advantage. As of 1987, less than 2 percent of the area's apartment units rented for more than $750 per month; in the Park Slope–Carroll Gardens area the figure was 22.3 percent.[132] Sunset Park therefore will continue to feed from a pool of housing demanders constantly replenished by new immigrants and white-collar workers (including those in any new downtown Brooklyn) for whom west Brooklyn is an ever more popular and convenient alternative.

This leads to the conclusion that Sunset Park will ascend slowly but steadily to higher middle-class status, though without overtaking its neighbors. The key word is slowly; it was noted that as late as 1987, after years of recovery, the area was hardly affluent.[133] More and more it will be the relatively better-off—both immigrants and native-born—to whom the area will be affordable. The exceptions will be poorer immigrants who double up and those fortunate enough to gain access to Sunset Park's subsidized or rent-regulated apartments. But such favored opportunities are not overabundant, and decrease year by year as the last-remaining protected residents in the smaller properties vacate and as additional co-op conversions occur. Thus, all things considered, Sunset Park's economic status is likely to edge closer to the City's norm, though it will remain in any foreseeable future a socioeconomic valley between Park Slope and Bay Ridge.

## A REDEVELOPED WATERFRONT?

These previsions of Sunset Park's year 2000 are, on the whole, mechanical extrapolations of recent trends. Are there no wild cards, something beyond projecting "more of the same"? One is conceivable—a comprehensive redevelopment of Sunset Park's waterfront.

---

132. *1987 Housing Report*, p. 160.
133. Median household income in District 7, even by 1986, was 25 percent below the Citywide average (*1987 Housing Report*, p. 94b). The figure for Sunset Park per se, exclusive of Windsor Terrace, would have been still lower.

Were that to happen, it would significantly accelerate the community's growth and substantially raise its relative status.

Infill sites notwithstanding, Sunset Park does not possess a wealth of developable residential building land. The sole potential site for large-scale new housing is its Industrial Zone, especially at the defunct waterfront. Though now forbiddingly zoned against residential use, the prospect of a policy shift cannot be peremptorily dismissed, and indeed is probable. There are formidable pressures, stemming from both planning and economic considerations, that could lead to imaginative and productive uses of discarded waterfront areas.

From an urban planner's viewpoint (sharply etched by the Commission on the Year 2000), New York's hundreds of miles of riparian land is at once its most neglected resource and its most exciting opportunity. Owing to the dead hand of the past, the City's millions have too long been denied access to the waterfront as a locus for recreation and residence.

From the economic standpoint, it is axiomatic that urban waterfront sites everywhere command a substantial premium for residential use. Such premiums now reach extraordinary heights. It is not uncommon for apartments with waterfront vistas to yield twice the prices or rents of apartments in the same building not so favored and for waterfront sites to sell at prices several times those of interior sites. Such market premiums have stimulated a headlong rush to erect new residential buildings at or near every accessible beachfront, river, or lake. Outside New York, the trend manifests itself at the waterfronts of most older industrial cities—Hoboken, Jersey City, Baltimore, Boston, Portland (Maine), Toledo, Seattle, and San Francisco, to cull only a few from an infinite list of examples. Closer to home, New York's Planning Commission has year after year, albeit grudgingly, surrendered maritime to other uses in Manhattan, where the last of its once-active piers has by now been de-mapped. In industrial Brooklyn, too, the residential reuse of waterfront areas has been approved at Gravesend Bay, Fulton Landing, and a small strip of Williamsburg. The pressures in Williamsburg are mounting; private developers have a pending application for a change to residential zoning for a six-block site. Recently, the New York–New Jersey Port Authority, whose mandate, after all, is commerce and transportation, not housing, has proposed two waterfront redevelopments, in Hunters Point, Queens, and in Brooklyn Heights. At the latter site (which has more relevance for Sunset Park's future) six piers would be replaced with up to 2,800 units of new housing to be set amid

20 acres of parks and recreation. Planning Commission staff has affirmatively supported the Hunters Point plan and has offered no opposition, indeed, even a cautious endorsement, for the Brooklyn Heights plan.[134]

The superb vistas of the bay and Manhattan skyline that Sunset Park's waterfront dwellers would enjoy have inestimable market potential. Sites in the area have in the past attracted numerous proposals for residential redevelopment, every one rejected. Ultimately, the rejections will likely give way to consent. In a sense, to hark back to an earlier episode in Sunset Park's history, the transplant of the Lutheran Medical Center to the American Machine and Foundry property in the core of the Industrial Zone (described in Chapter 6) was an unplanned precedent for what could become planned policy. To be sure, that transaction occurred at a particular time and under particular circumstances, a mutually advantageous political bargain. Yet, in the event, it represented also an intrusion by an activity, patently incompatible with industrial use, into one of the City's most vigilantly guarded industrial zones. Moreover, experience proved the transplant efficacious and the presumption of incompatibility erroneous. Though now financially strained by the cost-containment policies from which every hospital suffers, LMC has been successful at its new location, more than such industrially conforming uses as the wholesale meat market.

Public policies are not eternal absolutes. A zoning policy, once beneficially compromised by expediency could again be beneficially compromised, this time by rationality. The City cannot justify leaving productive sites forever sterile.

A comprehensive rezoning of the waterfront for large-scale residential use could have substantial consequences for Sunset Park's future. Much would depend on the scale of the project and its socioeconomic character. In the opinion of those familiar with waterfront issues, City officials could be persuaded to relinquish up to 50 acres for housing and related uses, though it might proceed to do so in stages. Depending on permissible densities, building heights, and site configurations, a development of such dimension could add between 2,500 and 4,000 new units, considerably more than were built in Sunset Park over the past half-century. That new stock would accommodate some 6,000 to 10,000 people, a substantial increment to the population increase earlier projected.

---

134. David W. Dunlap, "Brooklyn's Waterfront: Two Visions of a Compelling Vista," the *New York Times*, August 19, 1988, pp. B1-2.

The new housing's impact would depend not only on scale but on the programmed mix—the proportion of town houses, apartment towers, rentals, condos, co-ops, subsidized and unsubsidized units. Also, depending on scale and economic levels, the redevelopment would alter the local retail economy and possibly its ethnic composition. By adding critical mass, it would justify an enriched range of merchandise and services and thus further enhance Sunset Park's residential attractions.

The consequences for Sunset Park's ethnic structure are indeterminate. Were one to judge from "Towers on the Bay," the two large Mitchell-Lama (subsidized middle-income) cooperatives built in 1973 immediately south of Sunset Park, white and black occupancy could be higher, and the Hispanic and Asian occupancy lower, relative to the pattern of Sunset Park's current inflows.[135]

A redeveloped waterfront would be a powerful booster toward a higher-status Sunset Park. But the community could edge into that future even with an untouched waterfront. The contingencies point to a neighborhood whose economic diversity will continue to broaden as its ethnic diversity already has. Its middle class will gradually expand and its poverty class gradually diminish, resulting in a balance closer to west Brooklyn's norm.

Some will condemn that evolution, construing it as another neighborhood "lost" to gentrification. But it must once again be emphasized that the operative word is gradual. Unlike degentrification, which can occur at incendiary speed, the reverse process of gentrification in a jurisdiction like New York is rarely, if ever, sweeping. Because of the City's comprehensive system of tenant protection—rent-regulated and means-tested housing accounts, it was noted, for more than half the inventory—any changeover from a predominantly nonaffluent to a predominantly affluent economic mix will take decades and is never complete. Even Yorkville and Green-

---

135. The Towers, however, were occupied before there were many Asians in Brooklyn or an Hispanic middle class. According to *Cole's* listings, only a small number of Asians and Hispanics were occupants of the more than 800 apartments. Nor, according to the data on new telephone subscriptions, was there much tendency for the Asian and Hispanic occupancy to increase; turnover in these desirable projects is slow and not always based on first-come, first-served. More than 90 percent of the tenants bore European names. Judging from visual observation, they included a number of blacks, who, according to state housing officials, accounted for between 5 and 10 percent in 1980. The presence of blacks is also evident in Health Department birth data. As was earlier noted, since the Towers opened, the annual number of black births in its health area almost doubled.

wich Village, possibly the most dramatic examples of neighborhoods that bounded from nonaffluence to affluence, contain to this day thousands of low- and moderate-income rental units, regulated by one law or another. Nor has the blooming of Carroll Gardens extinguished the social and economic heterogeneity of the Red Hook peninsula. Black and Hispanic poor in the two large public housing projects continue to live close to the nonaffluent in rent-regulated units, and all close to the middle class and affluent in the co-ops and brownstones.

The consensus of urban planners is that diversification is the *summum bonum* of neighborhood development. But no one has yet put forward the ideal model of diversification. There does not exist a compelling analysis of the traits to be diversified, in what proportions, and in what spatial configurations (each census tract, each block, each block front, each building?). Income is merely one aspect of neighborhood diversity and hardly exhausts its essence. The Lower East Side, where the gentrification controversy resonates at its highest pitch, remains, after a decade and more of market revival, one of the most heterogenous abodes in the entire New York metropolitan area. It is an anomalous mosaic not only of poverty and affluence but of race and ethnicity, age and occupation, and every characteristic connoted by the term, life-style. Lawyers and MBA's are matched by penurious artists and both by squatters, Hell's Angels, and resident drug merchants. Along with youthful escapees from Scarsdale's conformities are graduate and undergraduate students from nearby Cooper Union, Manhattan Community College, New York University, and the New School. Their neighbors are Ukrainians, Polish, and Asian immigrants, elderly Jews, and thousands of Puerto Ricans. One suspects that a decade from now, and probably two or three, the Lower East Side will still be a socioeconomic motley defying description, however changed the weights of particular subgroups.

Given recent trends in Sunset Park, it would be caricature to accuse the bulk of its recent middle-income entrants of being perpetrators of gentrification. They are in the main Hispanics and Asians born and reared in poverty, most of whom would not think themselves even now as remotely affluent. Sunset Park's middle-income newcomers are more likely to be Third World than white and more likely to be wage-earners and civil servants than lawyers or architects or Wall Street wizards. In their number are the toiling families who own the small bodegas, and the Chinese second chef whose wife stitches garments. They eke out the monthly rent (sometimes with the help of a boarder or two) in a house that the frugal among them yearn one day to buy. Ambitious and hardworking they mostly are; gentry they are not by the stereotypes that word conveys.

Sunset Park in year 2000 will not be Yuppieville. At its newsstands, foreign-language papers and New York's tabloids and comic books are likely to sell as briskly as *House and Garden*, the *New York Times*, or the *Wall Street Journal*. Nor will it be, despite the concentrations of Hispanics and Asians, an ethnic ghetto. There is too much pluralism for that. It will simply be another of New York's typical "backbone" neighborhoods, neither excessively rich nor poor, inviting but not trendy.

Thus, Sunset Park will be, though in different guises, what historically it had been, a neighborhood sustained by those who journeyed to America for a second chance, who in seeking to advance themselves also advance neighborhood, city, and nation. In the sixties and seventies Sunset Park came very close to losing that historic character. In a genuine sense, it was rescued, not so much by housing subsidies and community action as by a 1965 act of Congress that reopened the nation's gates to a renewed flow of aspirants. They brought a clash of cultures and burdens for the schools and an accelerant to crime and drugs. But, by and large, they also brought their labor and productivity and a faith that their tomorrows will be brighter than their todays, as much as their todays are from their yesterdays. Who, cognizant of the urban hemorrhages of the last generation, would believe that New York would now be better off had Congress not passed that monumental act?

# APPENDIX A

# Data Sources and Data Gaps

The richest data trove for any study of neighborhoods is, of course, the decennial census—the published and unpublished tabulations by block and tract. Those tabulations, however, are less comprehensive in coverage and considerably more prone to error than are the aggregates for city, state, and metropolitan areas. Worse yet is early obsolescence. So swift can be the course of neighborhood change and so sudden the turning points that any study launched in 1987, as was this one, soon enough learns that 1980 census data are coated with rust. Although in broad outline the anatomy of today's Sunset Park can be sketched from that source, the factors making for the current comeback are not there discoverable, or only superficially so. For that story, one must await the 1990 censuses of population and housing, realizing that the small-area tabulations may not be fully available until 1992. Even then, the analysis would be confined to end-point comparisons of a ten-year interval, without allowing a grasp of the year-to-year dynamics.

As stated at the opening of this volume, the most valuable data base for understanding those dynamics—the pathways and processes by which a neighborhood changes—would be a series of annual or biannual household surveys. They would be designed to link with the decennial census tabulations, though more heavily skewed toward ethnographic inquiries. Needless to say, any survey questionnaire containing a sufficiency of "comparability" items plus a sup-

**193**

plement of ethnic and nationality items would be necessarily of considerable length. Moreover, sample size would have to be sufficient to assure reliable results for each principal ethnic group and neighborhood subarea. In short, a proper survey instrument would impose exceptionally high costs. Telephone interviews might substantially reduce such costs. But the telephone is seldom suitable for protracted interviews. Because of language and related difficulties, telephone surveys tend also to yield data of lesser quality than is obtainable from face-to-face interviews where trained interviewers can detect the nuances of response and decide when to press, defer, amplify, or omit a particular question. Further, an examination of Sunset Park's telephone listings indicates that some 20 percent of resident households do not possess a telephone, listed or unlisted. Those without telephones are not, of course, randomly distributed. As later noted, Hispanic names tend to be underrepresented and European names tend to be overrepresented.

Another problem for any privately sponsored household survey is that, without the legitimacy of an official census and the publicity that precedes it, there is risk of unduly low response rates and of unduly high response errors. Even households willing to cooperate will not always be eager to divulge sensitive information to prying strangers or give accurate answers concerning family income, nature of employment, or the actual number of people who share a dwelling unit. That reluctance runs deeper in immigrant neighborhoods where there are often substantial numbers of undocumented persons, off-the-books workers, and undeclared sources of money—in short, the precise neighborhoods in which ethnographers have the keenest interest.[136] Some immigrant groups are less forthcoming than others. "The Chinese people," states one experienced researcher, "are suspicious of outsiders, but they are careful not to offend. Consequently,

---

136. For a recent and illuminating survey of undocumented immigrants by researchers who were positioned to earn their confidence, see Papademetriou and DiMarzio, *op. cit.* [footnote 61]. The survey was conducted through the auspices of Catholic Charities, whose officers had both contacts and rapport with the respondents, nearly all of them from the Caribbean and most of them Hispanic. Though no claim is made concerning the "scientific" representativeness of the sample of more than 700 respondents, among a number of informative findings is that, other traits equal, the undocumented do not differ much from the documented, an observation also made by Muller, *op. cit.* [footnote 20]. Another is that given households typically commingle documented, undocumented, and U.S.-born citizens; that is, the legal and illegal are intertwined, not separate, categories.

they will provide 'putoff' information contrary to fact, or they will provide favorable information but nothing adverse. They are concerned about 'face' and are prone to bury their heads in the sand. Social science research is something foreign to their experiences. Hence, for them the unfamiliar is cause for suspicion."[137]

Census data, of course, do not escape the pitfalls of the guarded or refused response or, worse yet, the false. Census Bureau staff acknowledge, for instance, a systematic downward bias in self-reported income even where receipts, such as welfare and Social Security, are regular and on the record. There are sizable disparities between the sums that government agencies report as paid out and those reported on census forms. There are likewise substantial disparities in census reports on employment, ancestry, and race when measured against other data sets. Because of its relatively inexperienced interviewers and mailed returns, the decennial census is more vulnerable to error than are its Current Population Surveys; the latter, however, are useless for neighborhood studies. However much social scientists, for want of better alternatives, must rely on the census data, their aura of officialness is no guarantee of their quality and reliability. Ironically, virtually all the lawsuits instituted against the Census Bureau are for failures in counting population, something the bureau does best, and none for inaccuracies in reporting income, race, and ancestry, something at which it is admittedly bad.

These hesitations notwithstanding, opportunities to experiment with the efficacy of a variety of survey instruments would have been welcomed had resources permitted. All that could be managed was, as reported in the text, one face-to-face survey of selected groups of retail merchants to ascertain current ethnic patterns in local enterprise.

Another research loss was the inability to station in Sunset Park a skilled participant-observer. Site visits and individual interviews, no matter how frequent, are no substitute for direct, round-the-clock monitoring of local events and issues. Given the constraints of memory and interview time, the interviewees conveyed much of value. But one could detect, on occasion, a reluctance to share with outsiders more than was necessary and a tendency to gloss over frictions arising from personalities and conflicts. Trained participant-observers are positioned to cultivate a wide range of sources and to validate and cross-validate information. They build a base of trust that can yield

---

137. Sung, *op. cit.* [footnote 16].

candid views on delicate matters such as interethnic tensions, local power struggles, and the incidence of illegal aliens.

So much for the regrets. If short of the ideal, the inquiry nevertheless succeeded in assembling and exploiting productive secondary data obtained from a variety of public and private sources. Set forth next is a summary of those sources, a list that grew longer as the research trail and contacts widened.

First was a voluminous collection of local chronicles that served as the basis for the historical summary. The sources include A. N. Rygg, *Norwegians in New York, 1825–1925* (Brooklyn: The Norwegian News Company, 1941); Erling N. Rolfsrud, *The Borrowed Sister* (Augsburg: Augsburg Publishing House, 1953); Katri Ekman, Corinne Olli, John B. Olli (eds.), *A History of Finnish American Organizations in Greater New York, 1891–1976* (New York Mills, Minnesota: Parta Printers, Inc., 1976); Christen T. Jonassen, "Cultural Variables in the Ecology of an Ethnic Group," *American Sociological Review*, Vol. 14, February 1949, pp. 32–41; David Ment and Mary Donovan, *The People of Brooklyn: A History of Two Neighborhoods* (Brooklyn: The Brooklyn Cultural and Educational Alliance, 1980); Elliot Willensky, *When Brooklyn Was the World* (New York: Harmony Books, 1986); David W. McCullogh, *Brooklyn and How It Got That Way* (New York: Dial Press, 1983); Margaret Latimer, *Brooklyn Almanac: Illustrations/Facts/Figures* (Brooklyn: The Brooklyn Cultural and Educational Alliance, 1983); Nanette Rainone (ed.), *The Brooklyn Neighborhood Book* (Brooklyn: The Fund for the Borough of Brooklyn, Inc., 1985); Robert J. Walsh and Alice Walsh, *Sunset Park: A Time Remembered* (Brooklyn: Sunset Park Restoration Committee, 1980); Alan P. Kahn and Jack May, *The Tracks of New York: Brooklyn's Elevated Railroads* (New York: The Electric Railroads Association, 1975); Joseph Cunningham and Leonard de Hart, *Rapid Transit to Brooklyn* (New York: The Electric Railroads Association, 1977).

Historical inquiry is open-ended. It comes to closure, not by exhaustion of material, but by the press of other priorities; much of pertinence to Sunset Park's past is contained, one may surmise, in libraries under unrevealing headings, and much else is tucked away in distant places. For example, a fertile source of insights on Sunset Park's early development would surely be the archives of the *Norske Tidende*, the principal newspaper of Brooklyn's Norwegian immigrants. It constitutes a contemporary record of issues and events related to Scandinavian settlement, a nice approximation to synchronous research. Like diaries and letters, the ethnic press is a contemporary portrayal of the mind-sets and reactions of actual people to actual issues and events. Alas, those files are stored at the Norwegian-American Historical Society at St. Olaf's College in Northfield, Minnesota. The cost of a prolonged visit and translations would not be trivial. Another, but less pinpointed, source would be the files of the *Brooklyn Daily Eagle* and other Brooklyn newspapers of general circulation. But that temptation, too, had to be forgone since the index for the early years is incomplete. From the *New York Times,* however, was retrieved a 15-year printout of articles referring to Sunset Park. Local neighborhood institutions, particularly the Lutheran Medical Center and the Sunset Park Redevelopment Committee, shared reports on past and present local urban renewal and community development programs.

The statistical data were culled from a wide variety of public sources. Public agencies, primarily the Department of City Planning (supplemented by university libraries) provided an array of selective census data, applicable to the tracts that approximate today's Sunset Park. These data cover the decade years 1940 to 1980; the characteristics and level of detail diminish progressively as one goes back in time. Tract data permit the assemblage of a data set for Sunset Park, exclusive of Windsor Terrace, the co-occupant of Community District 7.[138] Tract data also permit analyses of Sunset Park's subareas. The Planning Department was likewise the source of selected data on Sunset Park's land use and housing programs. Another Planning Department data base, though only partly explored, is MISLAND (Management Information System, Land Use). This geocoded computerized file provides (reasonably) up-to-date information, by census tract and sometimes by block, on structures, vacancies, property transfers, sales prices, tax arrears, and other features.

From the Immigration and Naturalization Service came data on recent immigrant arrivals in Sunset Park's two main postal zones by country of origin. The Board of Education and School District 15 provided data on public school enrollment by ethnicity and the Roman Catholic Diocese of Brooklyn a time series on local parochial school enrollment by ethnicity. Annual data on local crime rates by type of crime were obtained from the Office of Information Services at the Department of City Planning. The Health Department provided a special tabulation of data on live births by ethnicity of child and nativity of mother for the four health areas roughly congruent with

---

138. Though not perfectly; several tracts extend to Ninth rather than to Eighth Avenue, Sunset Park's official eastern boundary. A rough estimate, based on block totals, was made for the overage in the 1980 population and household aggregates. But it was not feasible to derive similar estimates for other characteristics.

Sunset Park. The Transit Authority furnished a time series on the number of riders using Sunset Park's principal subway stations. From Community Board 7 listings were obtained covering proposed street, utility, subway, and other public improvements.

The most productive source of fresh data—a keystone of the study—were *Cole's* directories for 1981, 1987, and 1988. The directories are compendia of telephone listings in which the names of listed subscribers are tabulated by street address and year of installation. Though subject to ambiguities and errors, described below, these data were an invaluable guide to tracking post-1980 shifts in the principal ethnic groups, both for the entire community and for each census tract. From another private source—the *Brooklyn Real Estate Register*—were derived useful data on property purchases by name of buyers, thus permitting categorization by ethnicity. The *Register* also tabulated sales prices, mortgage loans by amount and by lender; these privately compiled property-transfer data are similar, in several respects, to those in the Planning Department's MISLAND file. Unfortunately, owing to confidentiality rules, that part of the MISLAND file is restricted to public agencies. Data on recent prices and rents, covering all of 1987 and 1988 and part of 1989, were also culled from the classified ads in the Sunday *Times*.

Professor Roger Waldinger of City University's Sociology Department and his students conducted a census of Sunset Park's street-level retail establishments, with ethnicity of proprietors denoted where ascertainable. From that list some 80 establishments—Hispanic, Korean, and white—were selected for extended interviews (Appendix E).

Finally, as noted, interviews were conducted with a host of individuals having particular knowledge of various events and issues affecting Sunset Park. Included were community leaders, realtors, bankers, and public officials; their names and affiliations appear in Appendix D.

### *Cole's Directory:* A Current Indicator of Changing Ethnicity

The *Cole's Directory* for Brooklyn is a "reverse" telephone book that systematically and sequentially arrays building addresses for every street in that borough.[139] Attached to these addresses are the names

---

139. In the New York metropolitan area, a separate directory is published for each borough and for Westchester, Nassau, and Suffolk counties. Altogether, *Cole's* covers 150 locales in the U.S. and Canada. The directory may be leased (not purchased) from the company, Cole Publications, 901 West Bond Street, Lincoln, Nebraska 68521–9989. For casual research, copies are usually available in the larger libraries.

of every listed telephone subscriber. It is the mirror image of Nynex's regular telephone book. There, knowing a subscriber's name enables one to ascertain from the alphabetic listing an address as well as a listed number. *Cole's* allows one to go the other way, from any street address to the occupants' names and telephone numbers. The coverage is comprehensive and includes every address in Sunset Park— nonresidential as well as residential, even buildings without listed phones. Like Nynex, *Cole's* publishes a new compendium every year. Changes in listed names at given addresses can therefore be tracked over time. Thus, the directories are an exploitable source for many (but not all) types of studies of the ethnic mix in defined geographical areas at any point in time as well as over time. Though the directories are widely consulted by private marketing and investigatory firms and by various government and planning agencies, *Cole's* staff is not aware that they have previously been used as a data base for ethnic research.

*Cole's* contains additional information of potential value for neighborhood research, particularly studies of turnover. It identifies by coded symbols new listings, that is, subscribers whose names appear for the first time. For continuing subscribers (i.e., those still at a given address), *Cole's* provides the year in which the telephone was first installed. Further, *Cole's* recapitulates by census tract the total number of phones, unlisted as well as listed, about which more later. *Cole's* records and codes similar data for business establishments. But these data have less relevance for ethnic studies, since many of the phones are listed under a business rather than personal name. The directory also summarizes selected 1980 census data by tract, such as number and type of residential structures.

For the Sunset Park study, a considerable research effort was invested in tabulating and analyzing *Cole's* data. That investment was justified by two premises. One was that the changing names of telephone subscribers in Sunset Park's 27 whole and fractional census tracts (comprising 100 blocks, 400 block fronts, and 15,000 to 18,000 listings) would serve as a tolerably reliable guide to shifts in ethnic composition, for Sunset Park in its entirety and for each subneighborhood. The second premise was that, given what was known about the community, these compositional shifts could be mainly accounted for by inflows of foreign immigrants. It would thus supplement other data sets, themselves incomplete, in comprehending the impact of the New Immigration on neighborhood change.

Both premises are beset with difficulties. In a society characterized by a substantial degree of out-marriage and by no small amount of legal or self-adopted name changes, the linkage between surname and ethnicity can be no more than a rough approximation to the underlying actuality. To be sure, a presumption that subscribers named Toy Shing Wong, Ananda Chavraty, Juan Perez, Giuseppe Varghese, and Stanislaus Kalinski are, respectively, of Chinese, Indian, Hispanic, Italian, and Polish ancestry is not open to much doubt. The further presumption that the first two names refer to New Wave immigrants is also reasonable. But whether or not the other three are recent immigrants, one can only say, perhaps. In other words, Cole's can be used to measure ethnic change, not the nature of that change. For the latter one must resort to other data for confirmation. Fortunately, as indicated in the text, there was a gratifying measure of consistency among all the data sources.

The relevance of Cole's to ethnic-succession studies is subject to an important qualification: The more ethnically distinct the new entrants are from older residents, the more dependable will be the results. The Cole's data base is most promising for neighborhoods like Sunset Park where Asians and Hispanics with readily recognizable names are the predominant newcomers. Cole's would serve less well, and possibly not at all, in neighborhoods where European and West Indian entrants predominate and are grafted onto a resident base of similarly named people. Thus, East European Jewish immigrants now settling in Borough Park or West Indian blacks in Bedford-Stuyvesant or Jamaica and parts of Flatbush would be next to undetectable. In these cases, the names of foreigners could be differentiated from those of older residents only by such weak clues as "alien" first names or distinctive spellings of surnames—for example, in Borough Park, Heschel and Chaya Fainshtain versus the American Harry and Eva Feinstein. For new black entrants (other than Haitians) into long-settled black areas, even such weak clues are lacking.

For all census tracts in 1981 and 1987, and for a sample of census tracts in 1988, every residential telephone subscriber listed by Cole's was assigned an ethnic designation.[140] Ten separate ethnic classes were established, each a category for which there was a good likelihood that, with reasonable accuracy, a particular name could be associated with a particular ethnicity. The categories were: Chinese, Other Asians, Hispanics, Middle Easterners, Irish, Italian, Scandinavian, Polish, Greek, plus a catchall, Other Europeans.

---

140. With more resources, the data for each intervening year between 1981 and 1987 could likewise have been tabulated. A future test of the accuracy of Cole's data awaits the next census. One could match the 1980–1990 ethnic shifts as derived from Cole's against the 1980–1990 changes in census reports of ancestry, nativity, and prior residence.

In the vast majority of cases, ethnic designations required no great pondering; they were self-evident to the research team, who, in addition to name-wise New Yorkers, included a Chinese, East Asian, and Hispanic. Also, the Census Bureau made available internal documents that catalogue the most common surnames of Hispanics and several categories of Asians. In doubtful cases, individuals were assigned to the residual categories of "Other Asian" or "Other European." Thus, Andersen was assigned to the Scandinavian class, Anderson to the "Other European." First names were also a telltale. A Botero or Abarco, who might be either Hispanic or Italian, were classified as one or the other depending on whether the first name was, say, Rocco or Raúl. Happily, the number of ambiguous cases susceptible to gross misclassification, such as the Lee Young who might be of either Chinese or European heritage, the Dolores Martin who might be either Hispanic or European, were few.

Ethnic classification by name, of course, merely skims the surface of ethnicity. It suffers from all the perplexities that confound ethnic classifications of every kind, including those published by the Census Bureau. These quandaries involve the fundamental meanings of ethnicity—the nuanced, complex interrelations between ancestry, ethnic self-identification, legal nationality (country of birth), and cultural affinity. A native of the Philippines bearing an Hispanic name might be part Chinese and part Malaysian by ancestry, "American" by culture, and Filipino by self-ascription. Likewise, a person of East Indian heritage might be a third-generation Guyanese or Kenyan. (That individual would have been categorized an Asian in the *Cole's* tabulations but as a Caribbean or African immigrant in the INS data set. However, as attested by other data sources, there were few of these equivocal categories in Sunset Park.)

Another difficulty concerns the assimilated of European heritage where, with varying degrees of frequency, intermarriage and Americanized names blur ethnic identification. A Richard Rosetti could well be the scion not just of Italian progenitors but also of a tangled mix of Irish, Polish, or Scandinavian. A Peter Deming might have been born Panyottis Demetrios and a Thomas Kale might be Stanislaus Kalinski's brother. Though the "mainstreaming" of names is a prominent theme in American ethnic history, one is less surprised by its occurrence than by the extent to which original surnames persist. Moreover, because of the rebirth of ethnic pride in recent decades, there seems to be a diminished tendency to mask ancestral identifiers. Even TV and radio personalities, once fastidious bearers of unexceptionally Anglo-Saxon names, now virtually flaunt their ethnic origins. For all that, free use was made of the "Other European" category in which, among others, all mainstream (i.e., Anglo-Saxon) names were assigned; the data for Europeans in the aggregate are therefore more reliable than are those for any particular class of Europeans.

Another limitation of *Cole's* for studies of immigration is that in an area like Sunset Park with a large population of new and old Hispanics, names cannot be classified by place of birth. Thus Juan Perez might be a Puerto Rican and, whether a new arrival from the commonwealth or born in the United States, not legally an immigrant. Alternatively, he might be a New Wave immigrant from the Dominican Republic or Peru, El Salvador, Ecuador, or elsewhere in Latin America. Thus, the finding that Dominicans and other Latinos were replacing Puerto Ricans was based on sources other than *Cole's*. In future years, local school records will carry an identifier for nationality information that is now available only for the school system as a whole and only for those enrolled in special language programs. Such identifiers, inscribed on each pupil's bio-file, should prove a fruitful new data source for studies of year-to-year changes in local immigration flows.

Last is a problem that affects all telephone-based research, namely, incomplete coverage. The names published in *Cole's* include only those with listed telephones. According to the Census Bureau, some 7 percent of U.S. households do not have a phone at all, listed or unlisted, and the percentage may be three times as high for households of low income. Nynex's research staff indicates that in the telephone-service district encompassing Sunset Park, upward of 90 percent of households have listed or unlisted telephones. There is evidence, however, that the proportion was considerably lower in Sunset Park proper, at least in 1980 when local census data were available as a check.[141]

Sunset Park's households without phones are primarily Hispanic. Their underrepresentation shows up in a comparison of the 1981 *Cole's Directory* with 1980 census data. That comparison check discloses that *Cole's* listings tend not only to underreport Hispanics but to overreport Europeans. Hispanics, who accounted for 36 percent of all households, accounted for 21 percent of all listed residential telephone subscribers. The gap would no doubt be narrowed were business telephones also included, since many Hispanics in retailing or services live in the back or on top of their stores. Nevertheless, some

---

141. According to *Cole's* count of listed and unlisted phones in the census tracts contained in Sunset Park, approximately 15 to 16 percent of all phones in both 1981 and 1987 were unlisted, the proportion ranging by tract from 10 percent up to 25 percent in the heavily Hispanic tracts.

fraction of the increase in Hispanic listings between 1981 and 1987 is doubtless due not to new entrants but to the fact that an already resident Hispanic family had acquired its first telephone. That source of error, however, could not have been very significant. The 1981–1987 increase in total telephone listings was close to the increase in total population for Community District 7 as estimated both by the Department of City Planning and by the *1987 Housing Report*. Apparently, the *Cole's* total of subscribers was raised more by growth in the population than by belated subscriptions.

As noted, the ethnic patterns assembled from *Cole's* were consistent with those derived from independent sources, namely, the 1980 census ancestry tabulations, INS data, Health Department data on ethnicity of newborn children and place of birth of mothers, and interviews with local informants. They were also consistent with plain shoe-leather observation. Thus, for all its shortcomings, *Cole's* was deemed to be a useful guide in determining the extent to which, after 1980, Asians and Hispanics were replacing Sunset Park's older European stock in each census tract, block, and block front. It was exceedingly helpful in filling in the portrait of Sunset Park's changing ethnic face, if not every feature and wrinkle.

### The Brooklyn Real Estate Register: Property Transfers by Ethnicity

The *Brooklyn Real Estate Register* is a commercially produced listing of real estate sales and mortgage loans. The data are stored in a central computerized file and kept up to date by mailed monthly supplements.[142] The details of each transaction are derived from official deed and mortgage recordings; additional information is solicited from trade sources. The *Register* is regularly consulted by real estate investors, appraisers and brokers, banks and other mortgage lenders, and insurance companies. Similar compendia are available for every borough in New York.

The monthly supplements provide the following for each property sold: address; purchaser's name and address; sales price; amount and type of mortgage; mortgage lender's name and address; building classification.[143] The last is available in fine detail, namely, by type of property and by such structural descriptions as number of stories,

---

142. The *Register* and supplements are obtainable by lease, not purchase. They are published by the *Real Estate Register*, 502 Gravesend Neck Road, Brooklyn, New York 11223.
143. Buyers' names are reported only in the monthly supplements for the most recent

number of units, type of exterior (brick, frame, etc.), whether attached, semi-attached, or detached, walkup or elevator. Like *Cole's,* the *Register's* tabulations are arranged by street and building address and thus have potential value for various kinds of neighborhood-based research studies.

Since names of buyers are recorded, it was presumed that the *Register* could offer prima facie clues to the ethnicity of Sunset Park's more recent home owners. The exploration was confined to the new owners of smaller residential properties, that is, structures with one to four units. From the eight monthly supplements published between August 1986 and March 1987, the names of all bona fide purchasers of such properties were extracted, a total of 240.[144] The buyers' names were then cross-checked against the *Cole's Directory* of comparable date. The cross-check indicated that fewer than 30 percent of the buyers were listed as residents. In some cases, however, a resident-owner's telephone installation will not occur until well after legal title has passed. Also, because of existing leases or pre-occupancy remodeling, buyers and sellers sometimes arrange for deferred possession. To allow for a longer interval between acquisition and occupancy, a second check was conducted, matching data from the oldest available supplement (August 1986) with the Nynex telephone book of 1988. That match yielded a higher proportion of resident owners, but still under 50 percent. It appears that a majority of the buyers even of smaller properties were absentee owners. Thus the *Register* is a better source for determining the ethnicities of real estate investors rather than of settlers per se.

Such data, however, are not without significance for those with an interest in the role of immigrants in the local economy. To probe that question, buyers' names were assigned to the same ten ethnic categories employed in the analyses of *Cole's* data base. These data revealed that, for the time period and type of property covered, Chinese, Other Asians, Hispanics, and Middle Easterners constituted a majority of all purchasers. Clearly, the New Immigrants had become a dominant component of Sunset Park's residential real estate market.

---

two years. However, back-number supplements carrying name identifiers may be consulted by subscribers at the *Register's* office.

144. For this exercise, all so-called nominal sales were winnowed out. These involve property transfers for which no or only token amounts are listed in the price or mortgage columns. Such transactions are usually intrafamily exchanges; others serve to correct or modify property title. Nominal recordings account for about 30 percent of all transactions. Also eliminated were transfers of larger apartment buildings, which are generally held in corporate names.

But, as noted in the text, the ethnic distribution of purchasers did not parallel the ethnic distribution of residents. One striking difference was a pronounced presence of Chinese purchasers, a finding consistent with what is known about their propensity for both home ownership and for speculation. Much of the "overrepresentation" was no doubt motivated by the prospect of later resales to co-ethnics seeking resident home ownership. Thus, in considerable degree, the activity of Chinese speculators is a leading indicator of subsequent Chinese settlement.

It was Europeans, however, who constituted the largest single class of purchasers, reflecting in part the presence of yuppie brownstoners (whose names were typically assigned to that ethnic group). But the larger number seemed to be outside investors and speculators; many of their addresses were ascertained to be those of Brooklyn and Manhattan real estate offices. By contrast, many Hispanic and Chinese purchasers were already residents of Sunset Park, though living at addresses other than the purchased property.

Another line of inquiry that invites further research is the relationship between ethnicity of new owners and ethnicity of subsequent renters. As noted in Chapter 7, the rental units within properties acquired in 1981 by Chinese investors were, by 1987, almost all occupied by other Chinese. At the time of acquisition, the renter-occupants were almost all European. It appears, and realtors confirm, that Chinese owners tend to give preference to Chinese apartment seekers, often kinsmen or friends. Thus, as was observed during prior waves of immigration, co-ethnicity exists within residential real estate markets as well as in other types of business enterprise.

All things considered, the *Register* is a more productive data base for studies of housing market dynamics than for ethnic succession; it was frequently consulted to validate price data obtained from real estate brokers and classified ads. Although neither time nor resources permitted, it would be entirely feasible to design a research program that drew from the *Register*'s compilations the following:

- Flows and sources of mortgage money, with emphasis on the changing proportions of institutional compared to noninstitutional loans, as well as debt-to-equity ratios. Such data could be disaggregated by block and census tract.

- For any given year, the average prices of each type of home sold (e.g., one-family frame, three-family brick); those figures could be obtained for Sunset Park as a whole and, less dependably, for each subneighborhood (block and census tract).

- Since the *Register*'s central files go back 35 years or more, it is also possible to construct an annual time series of changes in average selling prices of each class of residential structures. Moreover, several subsets of "same houses" (i.e., houses of comparable type and location) could be extracted and their price trends ascertained over time. That exercise could yield, at least in principle, what is so rarely available to housing-market analysts, an approximation to a "true" price index.

# APPENDIX B
# The 1980 Census Profile

**TABLE B–1**
Selected Characteristics, Puerto Ricans and Other Hispanics,
New York City, 1980

|  | Puerto Ricans | Other Hispanics |
|---|---|---|
| Family income, 1979 dollars | 8,913 | 12,400 |
| Female-headed households | 43.5% | 32.2% |
| Not in the labor force |  |  |
| Male | 34.1 | 23.3 |
| Female | 66.2 | 48.8 |
| With public assistance | 38.9 | 19.6 |

*Source:* Evelyn S. Mann and Joseph J. Salvo, "Characteristics of New Hispanic Immigrants to New York City: A Comparison of Puerto Rican and Non-Puerto Rican Hispanics" (New York: Department of City Planning, May 1984). The data are from the Public Use Microdata File, a 5 percent sampling of the 1980 census.

**TABLE B-2**
**Population by Selected Ancestry, Sunset Park, 1980**

|  | Number | Percent |
|---|---|---|
| Hispanic | 42,964 | 49.6 |
| Puerto Rican | 35,073 | 40.4 |
| Other Hispanic | 7,891 | 9.1 |
| Italian | 9,148 | 10.6 |
| Irish | 5,401 | 6.2 |
| Other West European | 5,441 | 6.3 |
| Polish | 2,605 | 3.0 |
| East Central European | 1,774 | 2.0 |
| Asian | 2,413 | 2.8 |
| Other ancestries and unreported | 16,942 | 19.5 |
| Total | 86,688 | 100.0 |

*Source:* 1980 Census of Population.

**TABLE B-3**
**Population by Residence in 1975, Sunset Park, 1980**

|  | Number | Percent |
|---|---|---|
| Same house | 40,437 | 51.0 |
| Different house, same county | 28,680 | 36.1 |
| Different county, same state | 3,328 | 4.2 |
| Different state | 1,436 | 1.8 |
| Abroad | 5,411 | 6.9 |
| Total reporting | 79,292 | 100.0 |

*Source:* 1980 Census of Population.

**TABLE B-4**
**Population by Age, Sunset Park, 1980**

|  | Number | Percent |
|---|---|---|
| 0 through 17 years | 27,870 | 32.1 |
| 18 through 29 years | 17,520 | 20.2 |
| 30 through 44 years | 15,863 | 18.3 |
| 45 through 64 years | 15,867 | 18.3 |
| 65 years and over | 9,568 | 11.0 |
| Total reporting | 86,688 | 100.0 |

*Source:* 1980 Census of Population.
*Note:* Details may not add to total because of rounding.

**TABLE B–5**
**Distribution by Occupation, Sunset Park, 1980**

|  | Number | Percent |
|---|---|---|
| Private sector managers | 1,793 | 6.5 |
| Professional | 988 | 3.6 |
| Sales occupations | 1,826 | 6.5 |
| Administrative support occupations | 7,589 | 27.4 |
| Service occupations | 4,184 | 15.1 |
| Health technicians, therapists, nurses | 448 | 1.6 |
| Precision production, craft, repairs | 3,598 | 13.1 |
| Operators and manual occupations | 7,306 | 26.3 |
| Total reporting | 27,732 | 100.0 |

*Source:* 1980 Census of Population.
*Note:* Details may not add to total because of rounding.


**TABLE B–6**
**Education by Age, Population 25 Years or Older, Sunset Park, 1980**

|  | Number | Percent |
|---|---|---|
| 25 and over, not high school graduate | 28,669 | 59.7 |
| 25 and over, high school graduate | 12,993 | 27.1 |
| 25 and over, some college | 3,597 | 7.5 |
| 25 and over, college graduate or more | 2,733 | 5.7 |
| Total reporting | 47,992 | 100.0 |

*Source:* 1980 Census of Population.


**TABLE B–7**
**Dwelling Units by Year Structure Built, Sunset Park, 1980**

|  | 1970–1980 | 1960–1969 | 1950–1959 | 1940–1949 | 1939 or earlier | Total |
|---|---|---|---|---|---|---|
| Number reporting | 693 | 582 | 1,449 | 4,153 | 22,363 | 29,240 |
| Percent | 2.4 | 2.0 | 5.0 | 14.2 | 76.5 | 100.0 |

*Source:* 1980 Census of Population and Housing.
*Note:* Details may not add to total because of rounding.

**TABLE B–8**
**Tenure by Race and Hispanic Origin, Sunset Park, 1980**

| | Renters | | Owners | | Total | | Owners as Percent of Ethnic Group |
|---|---|---|---|---|---|---|---|
| | *Number* | *Percent* | *Number* | *Percent* | *Number* | *Percent* | |
| Whites | 13,490 | 54.7 | 5,805 | 73.9 | 19,295 | 59.3 | 30.1 |
| Blacks | 503 | 2.0 | 112 | 1.4 | 615 | 1.9 | 18.2 |
| Asians | 668 | 2.7 | 289 | 3.7 | 957 | 2.9 | 30.2 |
| Hispanics | 10,009 | 40.6 | 1,648 | 21.0 | 11,657 | 35.8 | 14.1 |
| Total | 24,670 | 100.0 | 7,854 | 100.0 | 32,524 | 100.0 | 24.2 |

*Source:* 1980 Census of Population and Housing.
*Note:* Details may not add to total because of rounding.

**Map B-1**
**Sunset Park, Median Household Income, by Census Tract, 1980; All Households.**

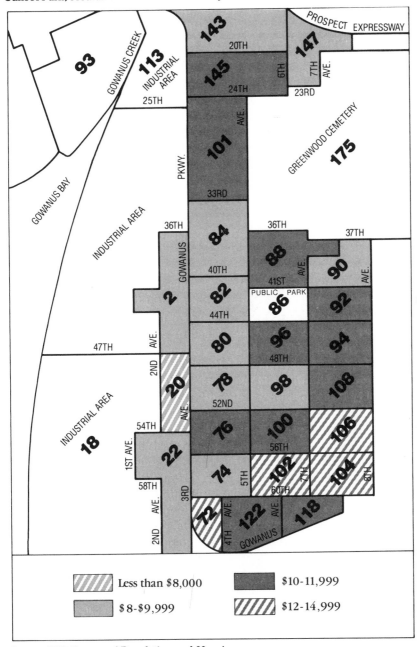

Less than $8,000

$8-$9,999

$10-11,999

$12-14,999

*Source:* 1980 Census of Population and Housing.

**Map B–2**
**Sunset Park, Median Household Income, by Census Tract, 1980;**
**Owner Households.**

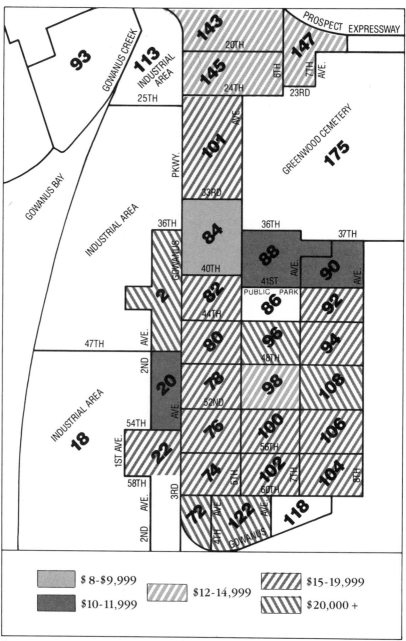

*Source:* 1980 Census of Population and Housing.

**Map B–3**
**Sunset Park, Median Household Income, by Census Tract, 1980;**
**Rental Households.**

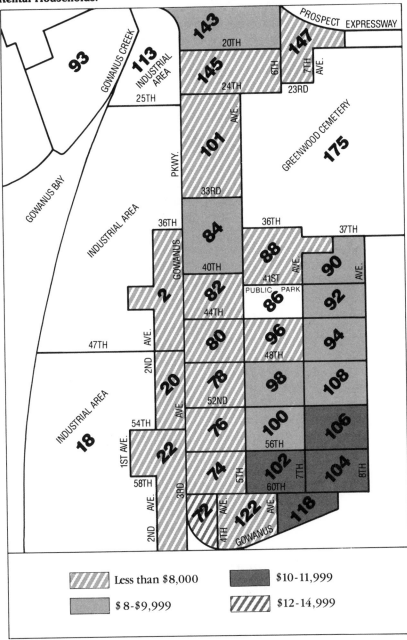

Less than $8,000

$ 8-$9,999

$10-11,999

$12-14,999

*Source:* 1980 Census of Population and Housing.

**Map B–4**
**Sunset Park, Ethnic Distribution, by Census Tract, 1980; Hispanic Households.**

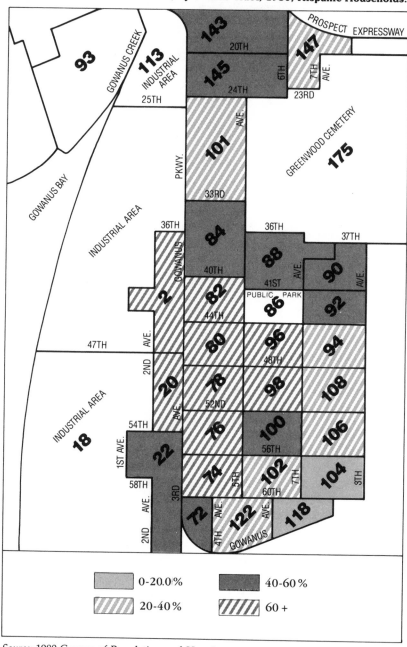

Source: 1980 Census of Population and Housing.

**Map B–5**
**Sunset Park, Ethnic Distribution, by Census Tract, 1980; Italian Households.**

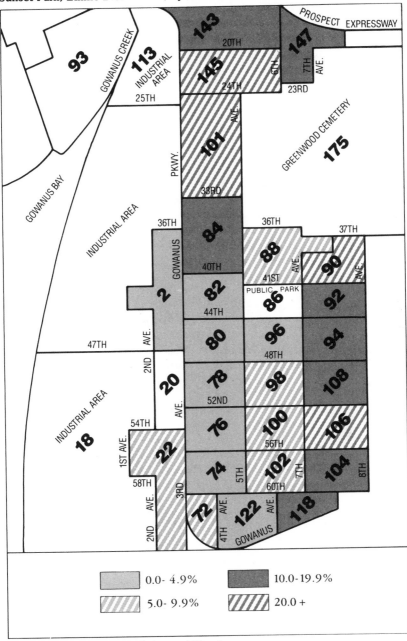

| | |
|---|---|
| 0.0- 4.9% | 10.0-19.9% |
| 5.0- 9.9% | 20.0 + |

*Source:* 1980 Census of Population and Housing.

**Map B-6**
**Sunset Park, Ethnic Distribution, by Census Tract, 1980; Irish Households.**

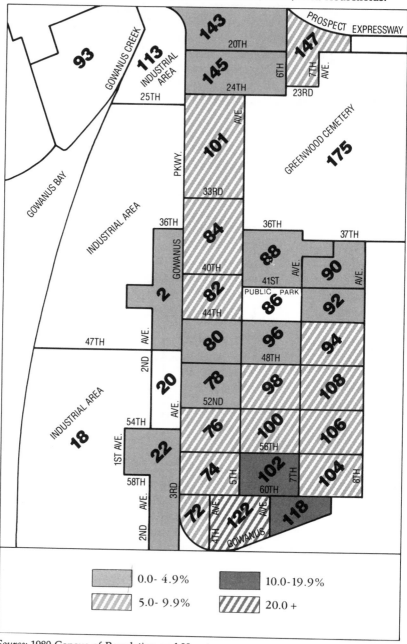

| | |
|---|---|
| 0.0- 4.9% | 10.0-19.9% |
| 5.0- 9.9% | 20.0 + |

*Source:* 1980 Census of Population and Housing.

**Map B–7**
**Sunset Park, Ethnic Distribution, by Census Tract, 1980; Chinese Households.**

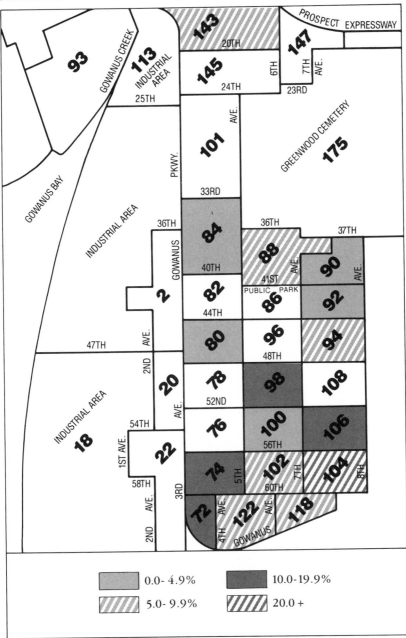

| | |
|---|---|
| 0.0- 4.9% | 10.0-19.9% |
| 5.0- 9.9% | 20.0 + |

*Source:* 1980 Census of Population and Housing.

217

# APPENDIX   C
# Post-1980 Ethnic Patterns

As derived from the *Cole's* directories, the changing weights, post-1980, of Sunset Park's principal ethnic groups in percentage terms are as follows:

- Between 1981 and 1987, the proportion of Hispanics increased from 20.8 to 28.5 percent (remembering that both the starting and ending figures underrepresent the actual proportions of Hispanic households). In each of the two years Hispanics accounted for more than 40 percent of all new subscriptions. Hispanics are distributed in every census tract, even those strongly favored by Chinese (Maps C–1, C–2). As will be further discussed, the dominant ethnic pattern of Sunset Park is heterogeneity not homogeneity, turf that is shared, not exclusively preempted.

- In 1981, Chinese accounted for 2.9 percent of all listed phones, a figure approximately equal to their share in Sunset Park's 1980 census count. By 1987, their share had climbed to 6.8 percent (Maps C–3, C–4). Among new subscribers in the same years, the respective percentages were 4.1 and 10.2, indicating an accelerating rate of entry. Chinese plus other Asians accounted in 1987 for less than 10 percent of Sunset Park's total listed subscribers and for less than 15 percent of all new subscribers.[145] The bulk of Asian listings occur

---

145. No doubt Filipinos with Spanish names who properly belong in the Asian count

in prior-established colonies, and increasing numbers are now present in virtually every tract, with the greatest concentration in tracts 98, 100, 102, 104, 106, and 122 (Maps C–5, C–6). But Asians were also dispersed throughout adjacent tracts in the west and as far north as the Prospect Expressway. To date, except for the environs of Lutheran Medical Center, they have confined themselves to areas east of the Gowanus Expressway.

• Middle Eastern residents, notwithstanding a 4 percent share of retail proprietorships and the appearance of local Islamic institutions, are still very lightly represented. They accounted for a minuscule 1.4 percent of subscribers in 1981, and 2 percent in 1987 (Maps C–7, C–8).

• Sunset Park's European base continued to shrink, absolutely and relatively. The share of Italian subscribers, 18 percent in 1981, dwindled to 15.3 percent in 1987 (Maps C–9, C–10). Irish names declined from 7.6 to 6.3 percent (Maps C–11, C–12), and Scandinavian names even more sharply, from 7.5 to 3.7 percent (Maps C–13, C–14). Greeks (Maps C–15, C–16) and Poles (Maps C–17, C–18) declined to a lesser degree, owing in part to the entry of hundreds of new immigrants, as indicated in the INS data shown later.

• The category "Other Europeans" decreased from 33.8 percent in 1981 to 29.9 percent in 1987 (Maps C–19, C–20).

• The decline of Europeans in total listings is paralleled in the declining figures on new subscribers (Table C–1); where the shares of Italian, Irish, and Other Europeans all fell. The "New Subscribers" column also indicates that a substantial majority was composed of Hispanics, Asians, and Middle Easterners rather than Europeans. Given that a portion of European-named subscribers are also New Immigrants, it is again made clear that it is they, not yuppies, who are the bulk of Sunset Park's new entrants.

The 1988 sample extended the 1981–1987 pattern of change (Table C–2):

• The Hispanic share continued to rise (Maps C–21 and C–22). The proportion of total listings increased over the year from 21.2 to 24.4 percent. However, judging from new listings, the upward trend

---

were placed in the Hispanic category, thus understating the former and overstating the latter. But both the 1980 census and post-1980 INS data show their numbers to be quite small.

**Ethnic Distribution of Total and New Listed Telephone Subscribers, Sunset Park, 1981 and 1987**

| | All Listed Subscribers | | | | New Subscribers | | | |
|---|---|---|---|---|---|---|---|---|
| | 1981 | | 1987 | | 1981 | | 1987 | |
| | Number | Percent | Number | Percent | Number | Percent | Number | Percent |
| Hispanic | 2,928 | 20.8 | 4,277 | 28.5 | 1,094 | 42.0 | 1,404 | 42.0 |
| Italian | 2,534 | 18.0 | 2,296 | 15.3 | 308 | 11.9 | 335 | 10.0 |
| Irish | 1,085 | 7.6 | 945 | 6.3 | 117 | 4.5 | 114 | 3.4 |
| Scandinavian | 1,051 | 7.5 | 547 | 3.7 | 80 | 3.1 | 32 | 0.9 |
| Polish | 557 | 4.0 | 502 | 3.3 | 51 | 1.9 | 76 | 2.3 |
| Chinese | 414 | 2.9 | 1,017 | 6.8 | 106 | 4.1 | 341 | 10.2 |
| Greek | 354 | 2.5 | 222 | 1.5 | 57 | 2.2 | 51 | 1.5 |
| Other Asian | 213 | 1.6 | 414 | 2.7 | 70 | 2.7 | 133 | 4.0 |
| Middle Eastern | 199 | 1.4 | 305 | 2.0 | 70 | 2.7 | 97 | 2.9 |
| Other European | 4,761 | 33.8 | 4,484 | 29.9 | 639 | 24.7 | 749 | 22.5 |
| Total | 14,098 | 100.0 | 15,009 | 100.0 | 2,592 | 100.0 | 3,332 | 100.0 |

*Source: Cole's* directories for Brooklyn, 1981 and 1987.
*Note:* Percentages may not add to total because of rounding.

**TABLE C–2**
**1988 Distribution of Telephone Listings, by Ethnic Surnames, Total and New, in Selected Census Tracts, Sunset Park (in Percent)**

| | All Listings | | New Listings | |
|---|---|---|---|---|
| | 1988 | 1987 | 1988 | 1987 |
| Hispanic | 24.4% | 21.2% | 30.7% | 32.8% |
| Italian | 15.7 | 16.6 | 11.0 | 11.5 |
| Chinese | 7.7 | 7.4 | 12.0 | 11.7 |
| Irish | 6.9 | 6.1 | 4.9 | 3.4 |
| Polish | 3.5 | 4.2 | 2.7 | 3.1 |
| Other Asian | 3.5 | 3.7 | 6.7 | 5.9 |
| Scandinavian | 3.3 | 3.3 | 0.7 | 1.5 |
| Middle Eastern | 2.5 | 2.6 | 4.1 | 4.2 |
| Greek | 1.9 | 2.2 | 2.0 | 1.9 |
| Other European | 30.5 | 32.7 | 25.2 | 24.8 |
| Total | 100.0 | 100.0 | 100.0 | 100.0 |

*Source:* Cole's directories for Brooklyn, 1987 and 1988. The tracts are 72, 94, 98, 108, 118, 122, 143, 145, 147.
*Note:* Details may not add to total because of rounding.

seemed to be leveling off; the share of new subscribers in the nine tracts, 32.8 percent in 1987, was only 30.7 percent in 1988.

- The share of Chinese and other Asians likewise continued to rise, also at a lower rate. In the sample tracts where Asians accounted for 4.6 percent in 1981 and 11.1 percent in 1987, their share increased to only 11.4 percent in 1988. The corresponding shares of new telephone listings, which had doubled between 1981 and 1987, rose only slightly, from 17.6 to 18.7 percent.

- Further shrinkage of the European stock was likewise evident. In these tracts, the share of Italians, Poles, and Other Europeans all declined, the last from 32.7 percent in 1987 to 30.5 percent in 1988. It is not clear whether the upturn in new listings of Other Europeans, 25.2 percent compared to 24.8 percent a year earlier, was a statistical aberration or reflected increased yuppie interest in Sunset Park. There was a distinct rise in the Irish-name category. It is generally acknowledged that illegal Irish immigration has increased significantly, with many thousands settling in the traditional Irish neighborhoods of Inwood, the North Bronx, and Woodside. According to informants, there has also been some settlement in Sunset Park.

**Map C–1**
**Hispanic Names; Telephone Listings, 1981.**

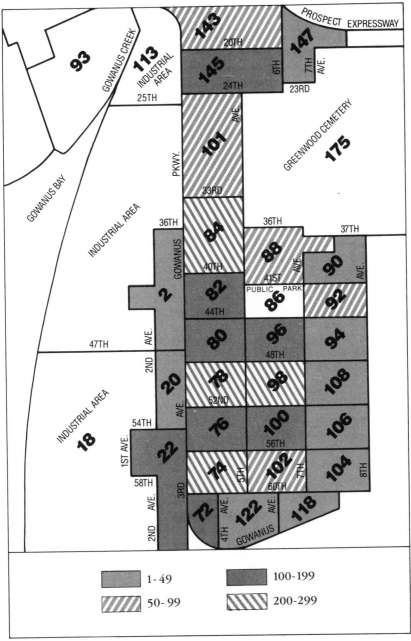

| | |
|---|---|
| ▨ 1- 49 | ▨ 100-199 |
| ▨ 50- 99 | ▨ 200-299 |

*Source:* Cole's Directory, Brooklyn, 1981.

**Map C–2**
**Hispanic Names; Telephone Listings, 1987.**

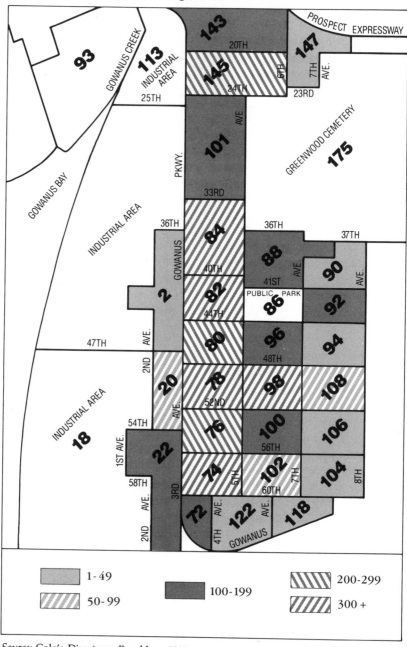

*Source:* Cole's Directory, Brooklyn, 1987.

**Map C–3**
**Chinese Names; Telephone Listings. 1981.**

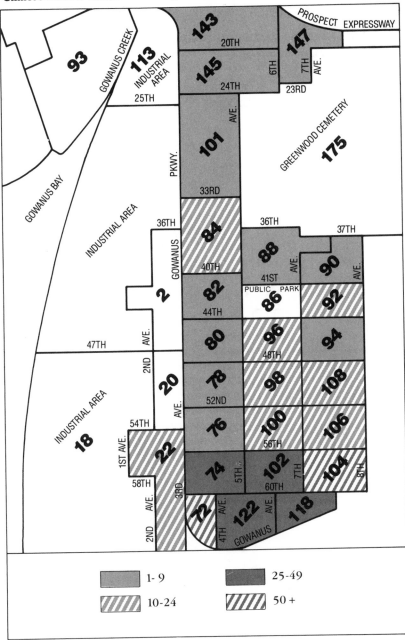

*Source:* Cole's Directory, Brooklyn, 1981.

**Map C–4**
**Chinese Names; Telephone Listings, 1987.**

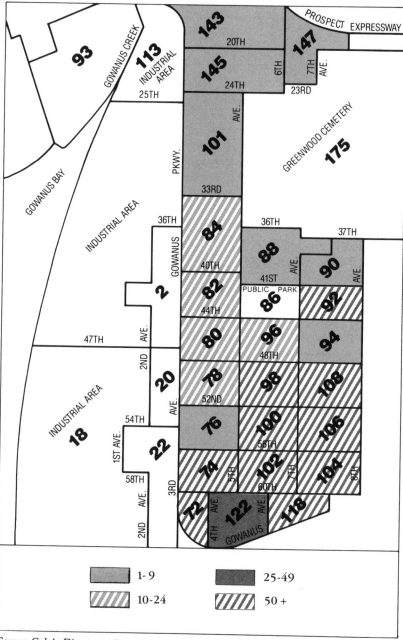

*Source:* Cole's Directory, Brooklyn, 1987.

**Map C–5**
**Other Asian Names; Telephone Listings, 1981.**

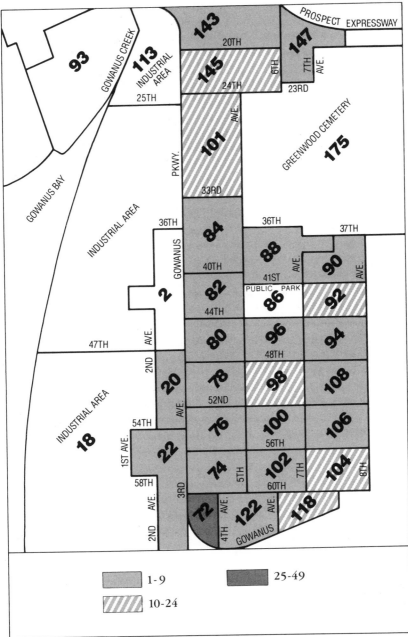

Source: Cole's Directory, Brooklyn, 1981.

**Map C–6**
**Other Asian Names; Telephone Listings, 1987.**

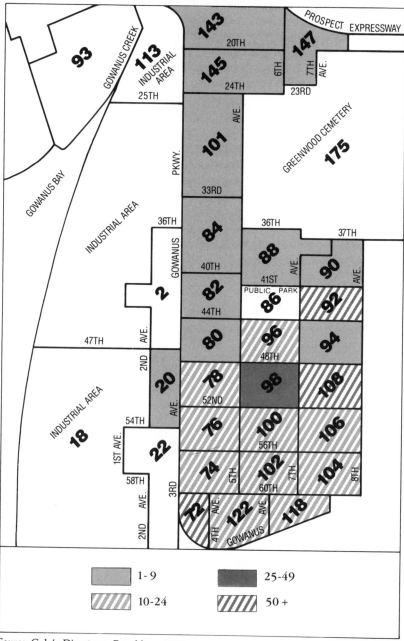

| | 1-9 | | 25-49 |
|---|---|---|---|
| | 10-24 | | 50 + |

*Source:* Cole's Directory, Brooklyn, 1987.

**Map C–7**
**Middle Eastern Names; Telephone Listings, 1981.**

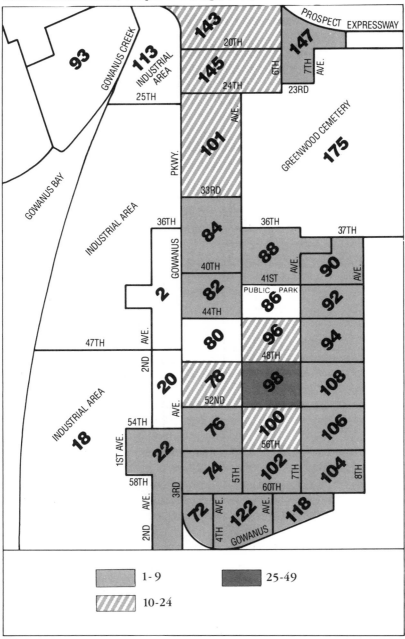

1-9

10-24

25-49

*Source:* Cole's Directory, Brooklyn, 1981.

# Map C–8
## Middle Eastern Names: Telephone Listings, 1987.

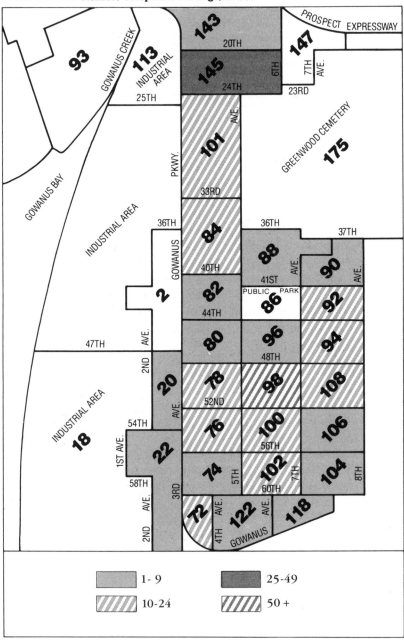

Legend:
- 1- 9
- 10-24
- 25-49
- 50 +

Source: Cole's Directory, Brooklyn, 1987.

**Map C–9**
**Italian Names; Telephone Listings, 1981.**

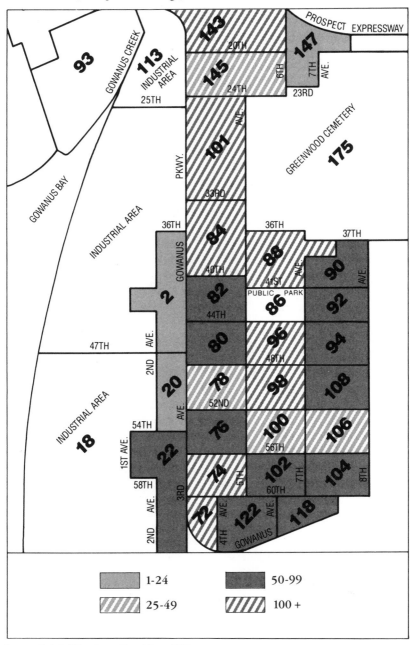

*Source:* Cole's Directory, Brooklyn, 1981.

**Map C–10**
**Italian Names; Telephone Listings, 1987.**

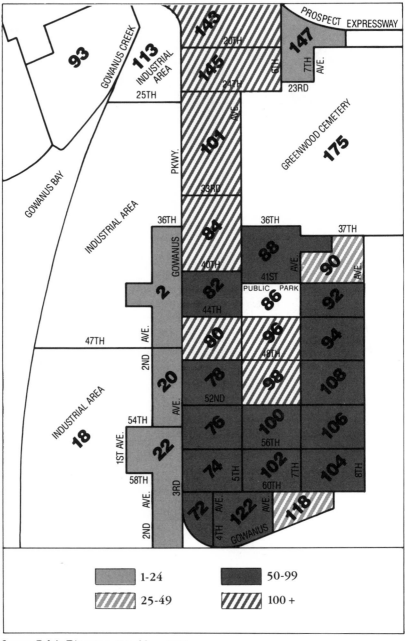

*Source:* Cole's Directory, Brooklyn, 1987.

**Map C–11**
**Irish Names; Telephone Listings, 1981.**

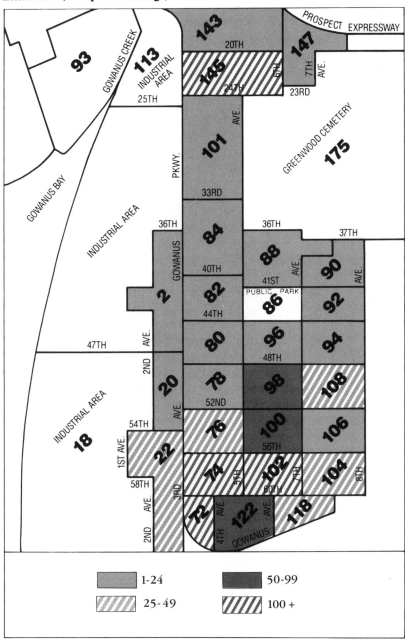

Legend: 1-24, 25-49, 50-99, 100+

*Source:* Cole's Directory, Brooklyn, 1981.

**Map C–12**
**Irish Names; Telephone Listings, 1987.**

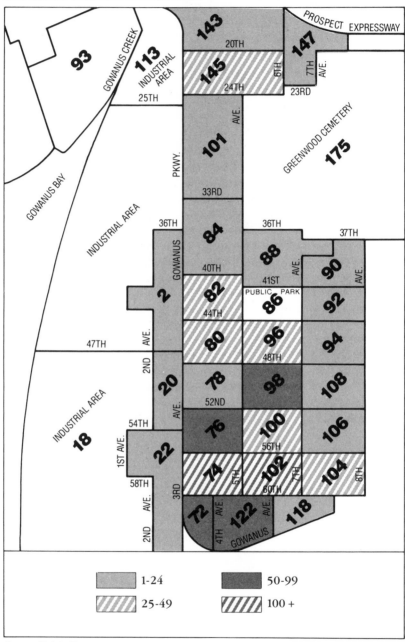

Source: Cole's Directory, Brooklyn, 1987.

**Map C-13**
**Scandinavian Names; Telephone Listings, 1981.**

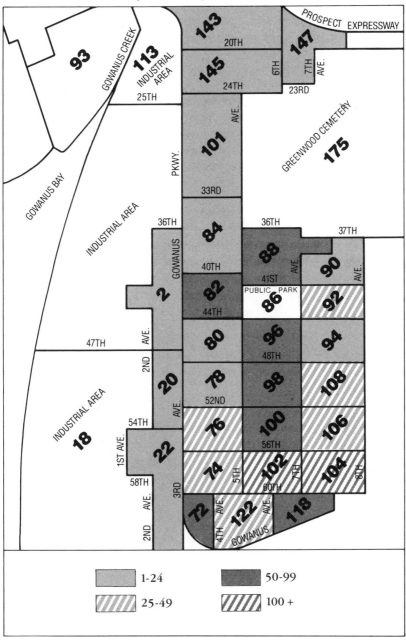

| | 1-24 | | 50-99 |
| --- | --- | --- | --- |
| | 25-49 | | 100 + |

*Source:* Cole's Directory, Brooklyn, 1981.

**Map C–14**
**Scandinavian Names; Telephone Listings, 1987.**

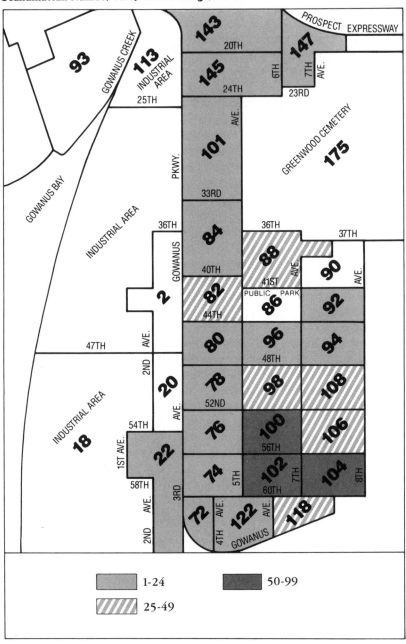

*Source:* Cole's Directory, Brooklyn, 1987.

**Map C–15**
**Greek Names; Telephone Listings, 1981.**

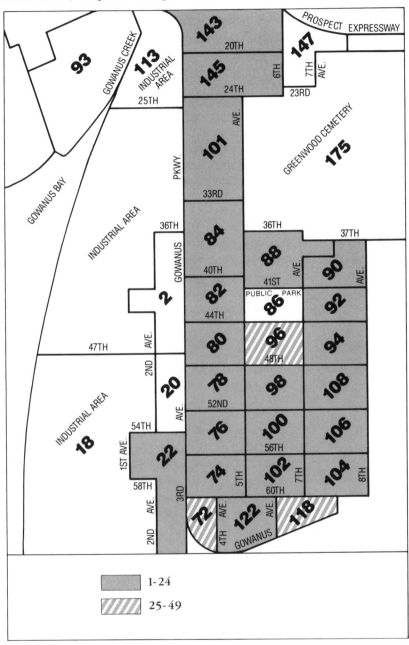

Source: Cole's Directory, Brooklyn, 1981.

**Map C–16**
**Greek Names; Telephone Listings, 1987.**

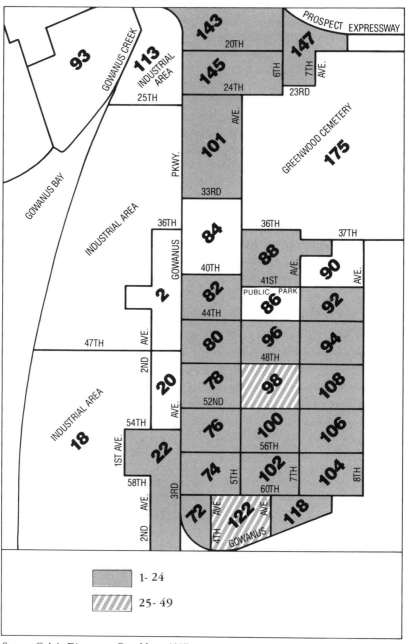

1- 24

25- 49

*Source:* Cole's Directory, Brooklyn, 1987.

**Map C–17**
**Polish Names; Telephone Listings, 1981.**

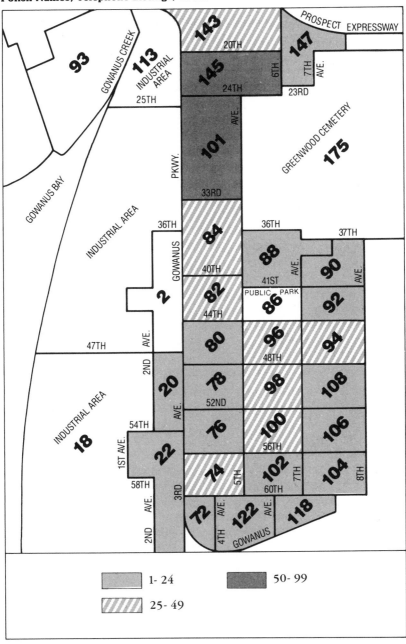

Legend:
- 1- 24
- 25- 49
- 50- 99

*Source:* Cole's Directory, Brooklyn, 1981.

**Map C-18**
**Polish Names; Telephone Listings, 1987.**

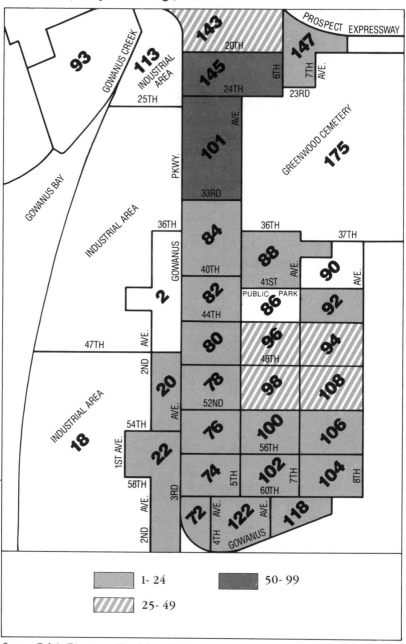

*Source:* Cole's Directory, Brooklyn, 1987.

**Map C–19**
**Other European Names; Telephone Listings, 1981.**

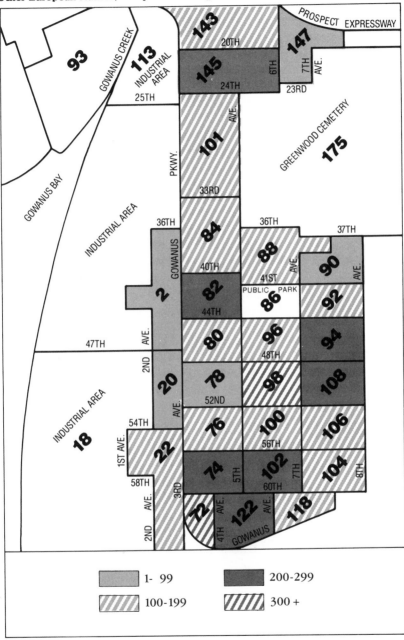

| | 1- 99 | | 200-299 |
|---|---|---|---|
| | 100-199 | | 300 + |

*Source:* Cole's Directory, Brooklyn, 1981.

**Map C–20**
**Other European Names; Telephone Listings, 1987.**

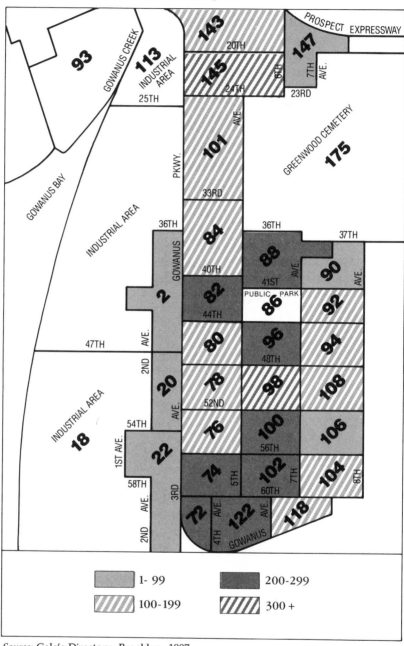

Source: Cole's Directory, Brooklyn, 1987.

**Map C–21**
**Asian, Italian, Hispanic, and Other European Names; Telephone Listings, 1981.**

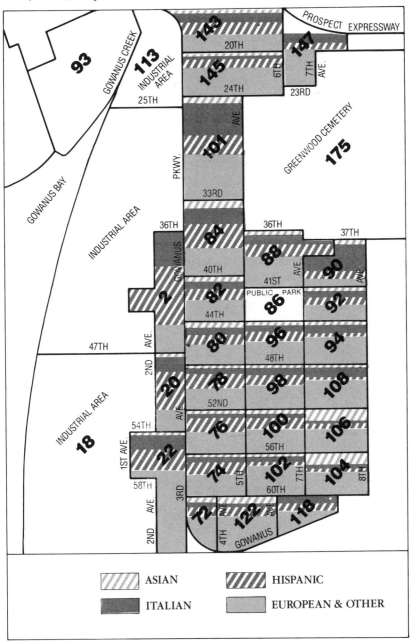

*Source:* Cole's Directory, Brooklyn, 1981.

**Map C–22**

**Asian, Italian, Hispanic, and Other European Names; Telephone Listings, 1987.**

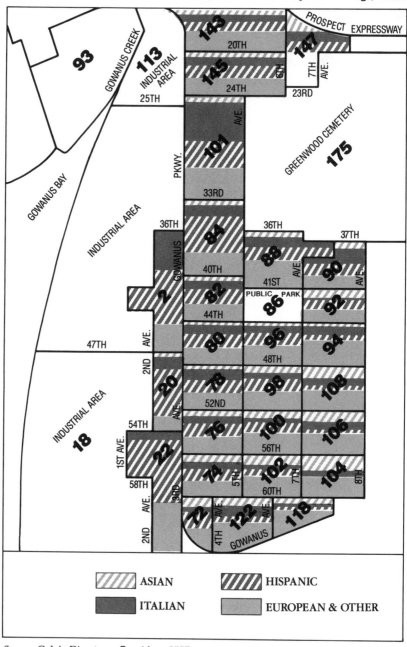

| ASIAN | HISPANIC |
| ITALIAN | EUROPEAN & OTHER |

*Source:* Cole's Directory, Brooklyn, 1987.

# APPENDIX **D**

## Individual Contacts

*Note: The titles of the contacts are as of the time of the interviews.*

**George Adams**
Chief Executive Officer
Lutheran Medical Center
Brooklyn, New York

**Jack Barouh**
Executive Director
Sunset Park Redevelopment
  Committee
Brooklyn, New York

**Elizabeth Bogen**
Director
Office of Immigrant Affairs
Department of City Planning
New York, New York

**Ira Brophy**
Supervisor of Modernization
  and Renting
Brooklyn Army Terminal
Brooklyn, New York

**Dr. William Casey**
Superintendent
Community School District 15
360 Smith Street
Brooklyn, New York

**David Chen**
Deputy Executive Director
Chinatown Planning Council
New York, New York

**Fee Sheung Chin**
Long-time resident of Sunset
  Park's Chinese community
Brooklyn, New York

**Joseph Derwin**
Associate Director
Forecasting
New York Telephone Company
Sixth Avenue at 42nd Street
New York, New York

**Jonathan Erlitz**
Executive Director
Fifth Avenue Merchants
  Association (FAMA)
Brooklyn, New York

**Sheldon Fialkoff**
Deputy Director
Department of Planning
Metropolitan Transportation
  Authority
New York, New York

**Peter Fu**
Director, Brooklyn Office
Chinese-American Planning
  Council, Inc.
Brooklyn, New York

**Alfred M. Fuerst**
Economist and Planner
Office of Information Services
Department of City Planning
New York, New York

**Noel Fuestel**
Local Realtor and
President of Sunset Park Resto-
  ration Committee
Brooklyn, New York

**Sister Geraldine**
Center for Family Life in Sunset
  Park
Brooklyn, New York

**Margaret Guarino**
Vice-President
New York City Public
  Development Corporation
New York, New York

**Dr. Richard Guttenberg**
Director, Student Information
  Office
Office of Educational
  Assessment
Board of Education
Brooklyn, New York

**Reverend Douglas Heilman**
Discipleship
Brooklyn, New York

**Rosalie Hoffman**
Brooklyn Planning Office Staff
Brooklyn, New York

**Marvin Jacobs**
Principal Planner
Board of Education
Brooklyn, New York

**Gregory Johnson**
Director of Planning
Metropolitan Transportation
  Authority
New York, New York

**Al Katz**
Board of Education
Brooklyn, New York

**Robert Kelsey**
Director
Neighborhood Preservation
  Program
Brooklyn, New York

**Sharon B. Levine**
Manager
Citibank, Sunset Park Branch
Brooklyn, New York

**Wilfredo Lugo**
Former Executive Director
Sunset Park Redevelopment
  Committee
Brooklyn, New York

**Frank J. Macchiarola**
Professor of Political Science
Columbia University
New York, New York

**Reverend Peter Mahoney**
Coordinator of Planning
Office of Planning
Catholic Charities
Brooklyn, New York

**Paul Mak**
Director, Eighth Avenue
  Merchants Association and
Assistant Director, Council of
  Neighborhood Organization,
  Brooklyn, New York
Brooklyn, New York

**Inspector Michael Markman**
Police Bias Unit
New York, New York

**Evelyn Mann**
Director, Population Division
City Planning Commission
New York, New York

**Sister Mary Paul, DSW**
Director of Clinical Services
Center for Family Life in Sunset
  Park
Brooklyn, New York

**Dominick Massa**
President
Southwest Brooklyn Industrial
  Development Corporation
Brooklyn, New York

**Sgt. Andrew McGoey**
Sunset Park Community Patrol
  (C-POP)
72nd Precinct
Brooklyn, New York

**Joseph Montalto**
Chairman
Community Board 7
Brooklyn, New York

**Mel Nelson**
Planner
Board of Education
Brooklyn, New York

**Eddie C. Quan**
Manager, Fillmore Real Estate
  Ltd.
Brooklyn, New York

**Marvin Roth**
Head of Human Resources
  Division
City Planning Commission
New York, New York

**Anita Rothovius**
Editor-in-Chief
Finnish Newspaper Company
Brooklyn, New York

**Ann Ryan**
Senior Vice-President
Lutheran Medical Center
Brooklyn, New York

**Dr. Joseph Salvo**
Deputy Director
Population Division
City Planning Commission
New York, New York

**Fritz Sanchez**
Director
Sunset Park Neighborhood
 Stabilization Program
City of New York Commission
 on Human Rights
Brooklyn, New York

**Luis Silva**
Assistant Manager
Citibank, Sunset Park Branch
Brooklyn, New York

**Mel Sokal**
Director
Sunset Park Neighborhood Pres-
 ervation Program
Brooklyn, New York

**James Sparano**
Proprietor
Parish Realty Company
Brooklyn, New York

**Brandon Stewart**
Executive Director
Southwest Brooklyn Industrial
 Development Corporation
Brooklyn, New York

**Morris Sweet**
Urban Planner
Brooklyn Planning Office Staff
Brooklyn, New York

**Dr. Judith Torres**
Manager, Bilingual Education
 Evaluation Unit
Office of Educational Assess-
 ment
Board of Education
Brooklyn, New York

**Frank Vardy**
Senior Demographer
Population Division
City Planning Commission
New York, New York

**Alice Walsh**
Former Head
Sunset Park Restoration
 Committee

**Robert J. Walsh**
Director of Community
 Relations
Lutheran Medical Center
Brooklyn, New York

**Charles Wang**
Executive Director
Chinatown Planning Council
New York, New York

**Wilbur Wood**
Head of Brooklyn Office
City Planning Department
Brooklyn, New York

**Kathryn Wylde**
Senior Vice-President
New York City Partnership
New York, New York

# APPENDIX E

## Ethnic Business
## in Sunset Park

**Roger Waldinger**
*Department of Sociology*
*City College and Graduate School*
*City University of New York*

Research on ethnic enterprise emerged in the United States as part of an attempt to explain the historical differences in business activity between blacks and other ethnic groups. In *Beyond the Melting Pot,* Glazer and Moynihan argued that "the small shopkeeper, small manufacturer, or small entrepreneur of any kind played such an important role in the rise of immigrant groups in America that its absence from the Negro community warrants at least some discussion."[146] Glazer and Moynihan offered some brief, possible explanations, but the first extended treatment came with the publication of Ivan Light's now classic *Ethnic Enterprise in America* (1972). Light's was an ingenious comparison of blacks, not with Jews, Italians, or Irish, but with immigrants—Japanese, Chinese, West Indians—whose racial characteristics made them equally distinctive: the argument developed an imaginative variant of the Weber thesis, showing that it was ethnic solidarism, not individualism, that gave these immigrants an "elective affinity" with the requirements of small business.

As we approach the nineties, it is apparent that ethnic business is no longer a matter of strictly historical interest. Recent developments—the renewal of mass immigration to the United States, the

---

146. Nathan Glazer and Daniel P. Moynihan, *Beyond the Melting Pot* (Cambridge: MIT Press, 1963), p. 30.

**249**

growing importance of small business to the U.S. economy, the evident entrepreneurial success of some recent immigrant groups, the persistently low self-employment rates among native blacks—have made the study of ethnic business a lively field. One can now count numerous empirical studies—of which the recent reports on Korean entrepreneurs in New York, Los Angeles, and Chicago; on the Cuban business enclave in Miami; on immigrant restaurateurs and garment-factory owners in New York—are just a small sample.[147] And as researchers have documented the ability of particular ethnic groups to exploit small business niches in an economy dominated by larger, more sophisticated concerns, they have kicked off a wave of fertile theorizing about ethnic business. The various theoretical schema elaborated thus far—Ivan Light's notion of class and ethnic resources, Edna Bonacich's concept of the middleman minority, Alejandro Portes's argument about the formation of "ethnic enclaves"—have filtered deeply into the literature and have become part of the conceptual vocabulary that scholars use to think about problems of race and ethnicity.[148]

While the field of ethnic enterprise is flush with research, all this activity has generated considerable controversy over the sources of ethnic entrepreneurial success. In a sense, three distinctive approaches to this question have now crystallized: one that emphasizes the characteristics that immigrants bring with them and make them predisposed to do well in business; a second that emphasizes the

---

147. See, for example, Illsoo Kim, *The New Urban Immigrants: The Korean Community in New York* (Princeton: Princeton University Press, 1981); Kwang Chung Kim and Won Moo Hurh, "The Formation and Maintenance of Korean Small Business in the Chicago Area," unpublished manuscript, Department of Sociology and Anthropology, Western Illinois University, 1984; Ivan Light, "Asian Enterprise in America: Chinese, Japanese, and Koreans in Small Business," in Scott Cummings (ed.), *Self-help in Urban America: Patterns of Minority Business Enterprise* (Port Washington, N.Y.: Kennikat, 1980) [on Koreans in Los Angeles]; Alejandro Portes and Robert Bach, *Latin Journey: Cuban and Mexican Immigrants in the United States* (Berkeley: University of California Press, 1985); Thomas Bailey, *Immigrants and Natives: Contrasts and Competition* (Boulder, Col.: Westview, 1987) [on immigrant business in the restaurant and construction industries in New York]; and Roger Waldinger, *Through the Eye of the Needle: Immigrants and Enterprise in New York's Garment Trades* (New York: New York University Press, 1986).
148. For the concept of the "ethnic enclave," see Portes and Bach, op. cit.; Edna Bonacich elaborates an argument about the characteristics of middleman minorities in her article, "A Theory of Middleman Minorities," *American Sociological Review*, Vol. 37, 1973, pp. 583–594; Ivan Light distinguishes between class and ethnic resources in his article, "Immigrant and Ethnic Business in North America," *Ethnic and Racial Studies*, Vol. 7, 1984, 196–216.

importance of opportunity structures as a condition of business success; and a third that points to the interaction between predisposing characteristics and the opportunities that newcomers encounter. Since the various approaches have already been treated at some length elsewhere, I will only sketch out the different frameworks in outline form.[149]

The predisposing factor approach suggests that immigrants or particular groups of immigrants do well because of a propensity toward business: perhaps because they are more hardworking, disciplined, and risk-oriented than others; perhaps because close kin and community ties give them access to resources (low-interest capital, cheap labor, trusting customers) that others cannot acquire so easily; perhaps because they are interested in making a quick dollar and returning home quickly, and therefore are willing to work harder and take more risks than natives; or perhaps because they begin with material resources (capital, prior business experience, transferable skills) that provide an edge in starting out on one's own.

The problem with any of these arguments, as those of us who have emphasized the importance of opportunity structures know, is that they take for granted what needs to be explained. To do well in business may indeed require a propensity toward entrepreneurship, but propensities will not propel a group into business if the niche for small businesses is small or nonexistent or if ownership opportunities are hotly contested by natives. Opportunity-structure arguments emphasize the following: (A) opportunities for ethnic entrepreneurs are patterned and are mainly found in industries where entry is easy but the risks of failure are severe; (B) the potential for immigrant business development is greatest when there are vacant business places to which immigrants can succeed. Such vacancies might arise for either or both of the following reasons. First, the low status, low rewards, or high opportunity costs of running a small business might deter would-be native entrepreneurs. Second, changes in neighborhood ethnic composition might reduce the pool of local native entrepre-

---

149. Since I have discussed these various approaches at some length elsewhere, I will take the liberty of dispensing with references. The reader interested in a more detailed review of the literature on ethnic enterprise might want to consult Chapter 2 in my book, *Through the Eye of the Needle*. I have offered a somewhat different treatment in "Immigrant Enterprise: A Critique and Reformulation," *Theory and Society*, Vol. 15, 1986. My article on "Ethnic Business and Occupational Mobility in Advanced Societies" (*Sociology*, Vol. 19, 4, 1985), co-authored with Robin Ward and Howard Aldrich, provides still a different overview, with considerable emphasis on European material.

neurs; given a naturally high rate of failure among all small businesses, vacancies arise into which immigrant business people can step.

The third major approach focuses on the interaction between immigrants' characteristics and the opportunities that they encounter. Here again, there are several strands of argumentation. Thus, one might acknowledge that immigrants have a propensity toward business, but contend that the propensity is not imported but rather reactive or situational; business is not a way of life, but rather immigrants' best way of making a living when life provides few alternatives. Similarly, one might emphasize the importance of kin and community attachments—especially in securing and training skilled labor—but then point out that these informal resources are particularly valuable in resolving the organizational strains inherent in a small business environment.

In this Appendix, I report on an attempt to replicate and test one of the strongest statements of the opportunity-structure approach thus far: the "Three City Study" of 580 white and East Asian businesses in Britain, conducted by Howard Aldrich, David McEvoy, and their colleagues. The results of their study, which involved both cross-sectional analysis based on a survey conducted in 1978, and longitudinal analysis based on follow-up visits made in 1980, 1982, and 1984, can be summarized in the following generalizations:

1. Asians and whites were essentially similar in socioeconomic characteristics and access to informal, organizational resources.

2. The proportion of Asian shop owners in an area was most strongly associated with the proportion of Asians in the area.

3. Changes in the business population were correlated with changes in an area's residential population: as an area shifted from white to Asian, the proportion of storekeepers who were Asian also increased.

4. Asian and white businesses were essentially similar in survival rates.

5. The proportion of sites occupied by profit-oriented shops declined from 1978 to 1984 as shops were left vacant or converted to non-business uses.[150]

---

150. Howard Aldrich, David McEvoy, and their colleagues, John Cater and Trevor Jones, have published numerous reports on "The Three City Study." Perhaps the most detailed, and the one to which my study is most closely addressed, is "From Periphery

Finding that Asians did not possess characteristics that gave them special advantages in business, the "Three City Study" also concluded that the prospects for Asian business development were poor:

. . . the Asian shopkeeper has exchanged the status of second-class worker for that of second-class proprietor and the visible gloss of self-employment simply acts to conceal the continuing presence of racial disadvantage. The growth of self-employment has generally functioned to absorb surplus labor rather than to increase the economic status of Asians and should thus be seen as a process of involution rather than as a genuine case of development.[151]

This conclusion was in line with the results of Aldrich and Reiss's earlier study of small businesses in American ghetto areas, where they found that the low incomes of minority populations and the decline of central-city economies meant a weak market for the types of local goods that minority or ethnic entrepreneurs typically provide.[152]

## STUDY AREA AND PROCEDURE

I generally followed the design of the "The Three City Study." In this case, however, my comparison groups were whites, Hispanic immigrants, and Korean immigrants. My study focused on the area traditionally defined as Sunset Park, Brooklyn, with modifications to make the boundaries of the study area coincide with census tract boundaries. The study comprised 23 contiguous census tracts where com-

to Peripheral: The South Asian Petite Bourgeoisie in England," pp. 1–32 in Ida Harper Simpson and Richard Simpson (eds.), *Research in the Sociology of Work*, Vol. 2 (Greenwich, Conn.: JAI Press, 1983). Other references include Aldrich et al., "Ethnic Residential Concentration and the Protected Market Hypothesis," *Social Forces*, Vol. 63:4, 1985; the same authors, "Ethnic Advantage and Minority Business Development," in R. Ward and R. Jenkins (eds.), *Ethnic Communities in Business* (Cambridge: Cambridge University Press, 1984), pp. 189–211.

151. Howard Aldrich et al., "Business Development and Self-Segregation: Asian Enterprise in Three British Cities," in Ceri Peach et al. (eds.), *Ethnic Segregation in Cities* (London: Croom Helm, 1981), p. 183.

152. See Howard Aldrich, "Ecological Succession in Racially Changing Neighborhoods: A Review of the Literature," *Urban Affairs Quarterly*, Vol. 10, 1975, pp. 327–348; and Aldrich and A. J. Reiss, Jr., "Continuities in the Study of Ecological Succession: Changes in the Race Composition of Neighborhoods and Their Businesses," *American Journal of Sociology*, Vol. 81, 1976, pp. 846–866.

**TABLE E-1**
**Study Area Ethnic Composition: Store Owners, 1987**

|  | Number | Percent |
|---|---|---|
| White | 317 | 38.5 |
| Hispanic | 293 | 35.6 |
| Asian | 127 | 15.4 |
| Arab | 34 | 4.1 |
| Not identified | 50 | 6.1 |
| Total | 823 | 100.0 |

Source: Census of businesses in Sunset Park, 1986.

mercial activity was to be found. With the aid of several students, I undertook a complete ethnic census of all commercial businesses, establishing the ethnic and national identity of store owners through brief queries of proprietors, managers, or employees. The census came up with a list of 823 stores. Owners were categorized into five broad ethnic categories: whites, Hispanics, Asians, Arabs, and blacks: the distribution of stores among these categories is shown in Table E-1. In addition to identifying the ethnicity of the business owners, we also attempted to identify their nationality and succeeded in obtaining national origins data for 89 percent of the businesses counted in the census. Over 46 different countries were represented among the small business owners in the study area. As Table E-2 shows, the ten largest national origin groups were (in order): Puerto Ricans, white Americans, Dominicans, Chinese, foreign-born Jews, Italians, Koreans, Greeks, Cubans, and Irish.

**TABLE E-2**
**National Origins of Store Owners: 10 Largest Groups**

|  | Number | Percent |
|---|---|---|
| Puerto Rican | 116 | 14.1 |
| White American | 109 | 13.2 |
| Dominican | 99 | 12.1 |
| Chinese | 70 | 8.5 |
| Jewish, foreign-born | 58 | 7.0 |
| Italian | 56 | 6.8 |
| Korean | 35 | 4.3 |
| Greek | 29 | 3.5 |
| Cuban | 17 | 2.1 |
| Irish | 13 | 1.6 |

Source: Census of businesses in Sunset Park, 1986.

We selected 30 stores each from whites, Hispanics, and Koreans enumerated by the business census. Interviews were conducted in the summer of 1986 with the ethnicity of interviewers matched to that of the shopkeepers in most cases. A total of 80 interviews out of the target of 90 were completed, yielding a sample of 22 white-owned stores, 31 Hispanic-owned stores, and 27 Korean-owned stores. [One more Hispanic interview was conducted than planned due to a classification error in the white sample.] The interview formats were adapted from the questionnaire used in the "Three City Study" (graciously furnished by the authors). Though I added an additional battery of questions focusing on social networks and value orientations, this report discusses only findings that are directly comparable to those analyzed in the "Three City Study." It should be noted that there is no longitudinal component to this study; therefore, results reported in this paper speak only to the cross-sectional analysis of the "Three City Study."

## PREDISPOSING FACTORS: ASSESSMENT

As suggested in the brief sketch of conceptual approaches, much of the work on ethnic enterprise has emphasized those factors that predispose immigrants toward business success. Some of the qualities most often mentioned are particularly intractable to study: values, which figure so prominently in cultural arguments, are notoriously elusive. Other factors can be considered to be predisposing only in a very loose sense: if immigrants turn to business out of frustration with their lack of opportunities, what is involved is not so much a preexisting propensity, but a reactive preference. Our focus is on three contentions common to predisposing factors arguments: the contention that sojourning propels immigrants into business; the contention that immigrants are more reliant than natives on informal ethnic resources; the contention that occupational closure leads immigrants to get ahead through business.

### Circumstances of Migration

Whether newcomers arrive as temporary migrants or as permanent settlers—what Robin Ward has called the "circumstances of migration"—is generally seen as a crucial condition of mobility and integration into the host society.[153] But just how do the circumstances of migration influence business outcomes? The literature suggests two possibilities. One argument, offered by Edna Bonacich, contends that immigrants who move as "sojourners" with a clear intention of returning home will opt for business over employment as the better way of rapidly accumulating a portable investment capital.[154] An alternative is suggested by Michael Piore's argument, developed in his book *Birds of Passage*, that migrants provide a satisfactory work force for dead-end jobs in industrial society as long as they maintain the expectation of return.[155] By implication, those same low-level jobs will be unacceptable to permanent settlers, whose ambitions extend to the positions occupied by natives and the rewards obtained from those jobs. Consequently, blocked mobility will impinge more severely on settlers than on their counterparts among the birds of passage.

These two alternative arguments specify an interaction between the circumstances of migration and immigrants' motivation, and that type of linkage cannot really be explored with the data at hand. However, we can document the circumstances under which the Hispanic and Korean store owners whom we interviewed migrated to the United States; the data pertaining to their migration and settlement experiences are displayed in Table E–3. The findings show that settlement orientations and experiences differ among the two groups, though both tend toward permanence rather than sojourning. The Koreans all report having moved to the United States with the intention of settling and evince no interest in returning to Korea. By contrast, a majority of the Hispanic owners report having arrived in New York as temporary immigrants; a substantial proportion still entertain the hope of going home; and ties to their home countries are maintained by the prevalence of return travel home. Evidence of commitment to settlement is indicated by response to questions about citizenship and citizenship plans. Half of the Korean respondents, but just one-third of the non-Puerto Rican-born Hispanic respondents, were citizens at the time of the survey; though the difference is not statistically significant, the fact that the Hispanics are residents of much longer duration than the Koreans suggests that the difference

---

153. Gerald Mars and Robin Ward, "Ethnic Business Development in Britain: Opportunities and Resources," in Ward and Jenkins, *op. cit.*, p. 12.
154. Edna Bonacich, "A Theory of Middleman Minorities," *American Sociological Review*, Vol. 37, 1973, pp. 583–594.
155. Michael J. Piore, *Birds of Passage* (Cambridge: Cambridge University Press, 1979).

**TABLE E–3**
**Circumstances of Migration: Hispanics and Koreans**

|  | Hispanics | Koreans | Significance |
|---|---|---|---|
| Owned small business prior to migration | 14.3% | 15.4% | N.S. |
|  | (28) | (26) |  |
| Brought money | 3.8 | 25.9 | <.10 |
|  | (26) | (27) |  |
| Made trip home | 89.3 | 48.1 | <.001 |
|  | (28) | (27) |  |
| Planned temporary stay | 54.2 | 0.0 | <.001 |
|  | (24) | (26) |  |
| Now planning to return | 34.5 | 0.0 | <.001 |
|  | (24) | (24) |  |
| American citizen[a] | 33.3 | 50.0 | N.S. |
|  | (18) | (20) |  |
| Not citizen but wishes to be | 50.0 | 100.0 | <.05 |
|  | (12) | (11) |  |

*Source:* Survey of business owners in Sunset Park, 1986.

*Note on significance of differences:* Significance was tested by an analysis of variance on interval variables and chi square on other variables.

[a] Base figures for Hispanics do not include Puerto Ricans.

in citizenship status reflects a basic underlying disparity in settlement orientations. This inference is further buttressed by the finding on citizenship plans; just half of the non-citizen Hispanic residents, but all of the non-citizen Koreans, reported that they wished to become citizens.

## Ethnic Resources

The nature of the immigration process is such that immigrants rely on networks of kin and friends for information and for assistance in finding jobs and homes. If immigrants can then mobilize those networks to raise capital or to obtain trustworthy workers willing to work long hours at lower wages they may gain an edge over native competitors, who are less likely to have similarly strong ties and are more likely to rely on market processes in recruiting labor. Just how well this characterization of native owners fits our sample of white business people is open to question, since virtually all of our owners were "ethnics" and many were immigrants themselves. But since most of the whites were native-born, and the immigrants among them were mainly residents of long-standing duration, we can still

**TABLE E–4**
**Ethnic Resources: Whites, Hispanics, Koreans**

|  | White | Hispanic | Korean | Significance |
|---|---|---|---|---|
| Family members owning shops | 25.0% | 38.5% | 44.4% | N.S. |
|  | (21) | (26) | (27) |  |
| Raised capital through: |  |  |  |  |
| Savings | 85.7 | 69.2 | 100.0 | <.01 |
|  | (21) | (26) | (27) |  |
| Family | 28.6 | 38.5 | 18.5 | N.S. |
|  | (21) | (26) | (27) |  |
| Friends | 14.3 | 26.9 | 11.1 | N.S. |
|  | (21) | (26) | (27) |  |
| Bank loan | 28.6 | 7.7 | 0.0 | <.001 |
|  | (21) | (26) | (27) |  |
| Percent capital raised through: |  |  |  |  |
| Savings | 62.3 | 44.0 | 91.7 | <.001 |
|  | (18) | (25) | (27) |  |
| Family | 14.9 | 25.8 | 5.6 | .05 |
|  | (16) | (25) | (27) |  |
| Married | 80.0 | 85.2 | 92.3 | N.S. |
|  | (20) | (27) | (26) |  |
| Married, with spouse | 37.5 | 52.2 | 80.0 | <.01 |
| in business | (16) | (23) | (24) |  |
| Have children in business | 26.7 | 12.5 | 19.0 | N.S. |
|  | (14) | (16) | (21) |  |
| Average number of employees | 2.9 | 2.2 | 2.5 | N.S. |
|  | (22) | (31) | (27) |  |
| Average number of | 0.7 | 1.0 | 1.3 | <.10 |
| relatives employed | (22) | (31) | (27) |  |

*Source:* Survey of business owners in Sunset Park, 1986.

appropriately hypothesize that strong ties to dense social networks will be less common among the group of white owners than among their immigrant counterparts.

As shown in Table E–4, informal, kin, and ethnic resources are important to all three groups of entrepreneurs. A substantial proportion of entrepreneurs have kinship ties to other owners, with Koreans highest in the proportion related to family members owning shops (the difference, however, is not significant). Though our data do not speak to this question directly, such ties are likely to be useful to small owners to obtain information, assistance and, at the very least, to have exemplars upon whom one can model behavior.

Other studies of immigrant and ethnic entrepreneurs have emphasized the importance of social networks in raising start-up capital. The owners queried in this survey, however, indicated that personal savings were the most important source of start-up funds; interestingly, the Koreans were most likely to raise capital through savings and also generated the highest proportion of capital through this source. Hispanics, by contrast, were the owners most dependent on informal community resources: the lowest in the proportion depending on savings, Hispanics were also quite low in the proportion receiving bank loans.

The impact in differences in informal resources can best be seen when examining staffing patterns among the three groups of firms. Potential access to family labor was greatest among the Koreans, since almost all were married; more importantly, married Korean owners were the most likely to be working alongside their spouses, with twice the proportion of Korean owners as whites reporting that a spouse worked in the business. Though the data on children show a somewhat greater prevalence of owners' children working in white stores, employment patterns underline the disparity in informal resources: Koreans had the highest proportion of kin employed in their shops; by contrast, relatives constituted a significantly lower proportion of employees in white-owned firms.

## Occupational Barriers

Immigrant concentration in business may well be a response to blocked mobility in the labor market. Immigrants are likely to fare less well than natives in gaining access to career jobs. Age is one factor: though immigrants tend to be relatively youthful, they generally arrive at an age past the time when most natives begin their careers. The newcomer who starts out in his mid-thirties is less likely to find entry-level jobs than the native who begins a career shortly after the age of 21; and, given his age, and the family responsibilities likely to go with it, the immigrant is unlikely to look favorably on the lower wages that go along with learning a new job. Similarly, the current cohort of immigrants is well-educated, certainly by historical standards. Yet immigrants may find that the schooling obtained abroad does not go far in landing a good job, in part because of language difficulties, in part, because the training required in the states is distinctive, in part because licensing requirements bar entry into the field for which one has trained.

As Table E–5 shows, whites tended to be the oldest among the shopkeepers and Koreans the youngest, though the differences

**TABLE E–5**
**Socioeconomic and Business Characteristics**

|  | White | Hispanic | Korean | Significance |
|---|---|---|---|---|
| Average age | 43.5 | 37.2 | 38.9 | N.S. |
|  | (21) | (27) | (27) |  |
| Years of education | 10.9 | 10.9 | 14.1 | <.001 |
|  | (21) | (28) | (27) |  |
| Father self-employed | 37.1 | 34.5 | 29.2 | N.S. |
|  | (21) | (29) | (24) |  |
| Father blue-collar | 47.6 | 73.1 | 23.8 | <.05 |
|  | (21) | (26) | (21) |  |
| Inherited business | 9.5 | 0.0 | 0.0 | <.05 |
|  | (21) | (26) | (27) |  |
| Self-employed in last job | 42.1 | 12.0 | 3.8 | <.00 |
|  | (19) | (25) | (26) |  |
| Year of immigration | 1968 | 1969 | 1980 | <.001 |
|  | (11) | (25) | (27) |  |
| Years in business | 12.3 | 3.5 | 2.2 | <.001 |
|  | (22) | (31) | (27) |  |
| Age when started business | 30.9 | 33.8 | 35.1 | N.S. |
|  | (21) | (27) | (27) |  |
| Percent with poor or no English | 20.0 | 12.9 | 55.0 | <.001 |
|  | (10) | (31) | (20) |  |

*Source:* Survey of business owners in Sunset Park, 1986.

among the groups were not statistically significant. But as suggested above, the older one is at the time of migration, the more likely is age to be a significant obstacle to mobility. The three groups do differ in the owners' age at the time the businesses were founded, with the Koreans the oldest of all, though again, the differences were not statistically significant. More importantly, a comparison of the Koreans and the Hispanics shows that the former are recent immigrants who opened their businesses shortly after arrival in the United States, whereas the Hispanics are immigrants of much longer standing who nonetheless just preceded the Koreans in their entrance into business. Further evidence of blocked mobility is the fact that the Koreans are the highest in educational attainment and yet poorest in language ability. The Koreans report more schooling than either of the other two groups, who are roughly comparable in educational attainment; just under half of the Koreans had a college education whereas just two of the 22 whites interviewed and three of the 31 Hispanics had gone to college.

Virtually all owners were self-made men and women; only two of the white owners had inherited their businesses from their parents. In spite of the absence of business heirs in our sample, a substantial minority of the owners had come from families with entrepreneurial traditions. Though the differences were not statistically significant, whites were the most likely, and Koreans the least likely, to have had a father who had run a business of his own. The three groups of owners also differed in their careers: a substantial minority of the whites had been self-employed in their prior jobs, whereas virtually all the Koreans had previously worked for someone else. What these disparities suggest is that entrepreneurial cultures may vary considerably among the three groups of owners. Whereas petty entrepreneurship may be a way of life for the whites and Hispanics, it is simply a way of making a living for the Koreans who pursue small business for lack of better opportunities.

Although Koreans are unable to translate their high educational attainments into professional careers, their schooling is a source of relevant business skills. Moreover, Koreans have access to other class resources, in addition to the ethnic resources reviewed above. Almost 30 percent of the Koreans, as opposed to barely 4 percent of the Hispanics, said that they brought money with them upon migrating to the United States. Further, strong evidence of the Koreans' greater access to capital is suggested by the data on sources of capital: all of the Koreans reported relying on savings to generate their start-up funds (a significantly higher proportion than among the other groups), and savings also accounted for a significantly higher proportion of the capital with which their businesses began. One possibility is that Koreans reported money raised through rotating credit associations (Kye) as savings; however, our attempts to probe this question indicated that Kye membership was relatively low and seemed to have a more important social, than financial, component.

## OPPORTUNITY STRUCTURES: ASSESSMENT

To get started, the would-be immigrant capitalist needs access to ownership opportunities; these opportunities, as noted earlier, are most likely to arise when the supply of native owners runs short. That supply might diminish because the rewards of small business are simply too meager and the opportunity costs too great to attract new entrepreneurs. Alternatively, changes in the ethnic composition of residential areas might dry up the pool of native owners, with newcomers providing the replacements instead.

There is some evidence that occupational succession has occurred independently of changes in the study area's residential composition. Relative to their 1980 share of the population, whites were slightly underrepresented among the ranks of local store owners. More importantly, the whites whom we found running shops contained a much higher proportion of the foreign-born than did the area's white population. Although native-born whites made up 31 percent of the study area's population in 1980, they comprised just 13 percent of the owners identified by our census. Foreign-born whites were similarly overrepresented among the owners whom we interviewed. Eleven of the 21 white owners for whom we have data on social origins were foreign-born. And 7 of the 10 native-born owners were the children of immigrants, underlining the linkage between immigration and recruitment into petty proprietorship. Furthermore, the data on business longevity, shown in Table E-4, tell us that white businesses are generally long-established entities.

However, the "Three City Study" mainly emphasizes the consequences of changes in a neighborhood's social ecology for newcomers' business opportunities: the central finding was that the larger a group's share of an area's population, the larger was its share of the area's stores. To see whether this finding held in the Sunset Park area as well, I attempted to conduct a regression analysis of the relationship between each group's 1980 share of the population at the census tract level, and its share of stores in the tract at the time of our survey. Since there were so few Koreans resident in the area as of 1980 there was virtually no variance in their population shares, so I opted to use the percent Asian in 1980 instead as the predictor of business shares for the Koreans.

The results of the regression analysis are presented in Table E-6. The findings show two broadly different patterns of relationship between population concentration and business ownership patterns. For white and Hispanic stores, the relationship between business ownership and population concentration is very strong: population composition explains more than half of the variance in business shares for whites and close to 70 percent of the variance in business shares for Hispanics. For both groups, each 1 percent increase in population concentration produces an increase of roughly 0.7 percent in business shares. One important difference between white and Hispanic business is that the intercept for Hispanics is negative, suggest-

**TABLE E-6**
**Regression of Ethnic Business Share on Ethnic Population Share:**
**23 Census Tracts**

| Group | a | b | b* | r-square |
|---|---|---|---|---|
| Whites | .141 | .690$^a$ | .725 | .520$^a$ |
| Hispanics | −.030 | .758$^a$ | .835 | .694$^a$ |
| Koreans | .086 | −.297 | −.289 | .07$^a$ |

Sources: "Ethnic business share" (dependent variable): Census of businesses in Sunset Park, 1986. "Ethnic population share" (independent variable): 1980 Census of Population, ST4, special tabulation prepared by New York City Department of City Planning (ethnic categories are mutually exclusive).

Note: a = Intercept. b = Unstandardized regression coefficient. b* = Standardized regression coefficient.
* Probability <.01.

ing that Hispanic businesses are much more tightly confined than are white concerns to those tracts where co-ethnic customers are to be found. In contrast to the white or Hispanic cases, there is no ecological relationship between Sunset Park's Korean shopkeepers and a local ethnic customer base. Population concentrations predict little of the variance in Korean business shares. Moreover, the coefficient for ethnic population concentrations has the wrong sign: since Asians have moved into the more heavily white tracts in the southeast part of the area, we can infer from this finding that Koreans are principally located in tracts with Hispanic concentrations.

## Market Orientation

Segmentation in customer markets is one possible consequence of population concentration. If business owners in any particular neighborhood tend to come from the ethnic group that dominates the area, then residents may have little choice but to shop at the stores owned by their co-ethnics. A niche for immigrant merchants might arise for another reason, namely because immigrant customers might have a preference for patronizing their co-ethnics. Often an immigrant community has a special set of needs and preferences that are best served, and sometimes can only be served, by those who share those needs and know them intimately, namely, the members of the immigrant community itself. Immigrants also have special problems that are caused by the strains of settlement and assimilation and are aggravated by their distance from the institutionalized mechanisms of service delivery; consequently, the business of specializing in the

**TABLE E–7**
**Customer Composition: Merchants' Reports**

|  | White | Hispanic | Korean | Significance |
|---|---|---|---|---|
| Percent white | 27.1 | 22.8 | 12.1 | N.S. |
| Percent Hispanic | 49.5 | 71.1 | 79.2 | <.001 |
| Percent Asian | 9.0 | 1.3 | 2.3 | <.05 |
| Why more than 50% white customers? | | | | |
| Neighborhood | 80.0 | 100.0 | 100.0 | N.S. |
| Why less than 50% white customers? | | | | |
| Neighborhood | 75.0 | 88.5 | 100.0 | <.10 |

*Source:* Survey of business owners in Sunset Park, 1986.

problems of immigrant adjustment is another avenue of ethnic economic activity. By the same token native businesses are likely to be hampered in servicing such ethnic markets: natives are less likely to know about immigrants' tastes and buying preferences; natives are not likely to offer the degree of trust wanted in services of a confidential nature; and natives may simply opt out of servicing an immigrant market for simple reasons of disdain.

To test for the protected-market hypothesis, we examined the ethnic composition of the customers served by white, Hispanic, and Korean owners. We asked our respondents to estimate the ethnic makeup of their clientele and then tell us what factors seemed to account for their customer mix.

As shown in Table E–7, the survey results provide very limited support for the notion that ethnic owners depend on co-ethnic patronage to provide them with a protected market. Only Hispanics appeared to find the great bulk of their patronage among co-ethnic customers. Whites reported the highest level of white patronage, but nonetheless mainly catered to a Hispanic clientele. In contrast to both whites and Hispanics, Koreans had no co-ethnics and few Asians as customers, reporting instead that they did most of their business with Hispanics, the dominant local population.

## Explaining Market Orientations

What accounts for the patterns of customer segmentation noted above? To explore this question we followed two approaches. First, we queried owners (in an open-ended way) about their own explanations for customer composition. Next, we used regression analysis to test the effect of population composition on clientele mix. Shopkeepers whose customers were less than/more than 50 percent white were asked why the proportion of customers was so low/high. As in the "Three City Study" responses clearly fell into the categories of "neighborhood composition" or "special products/services" (linguistic facility/difficulty was grouped under the latter), as noted in Table E–7.

Among the very small minority of merchants with mainly white trade, four-fifths of the whites and all of the Hispanics and Koreans said that "neighborhood composition" was the most important influence on their customer mix. As to the great majority of merchants whose customers were mainly non-white, neighborhood composition was the factor most often invoked to explain customer composition. Interestingly, 100 percent of the Koreans attributed customer composition to neighborhood factors, indicating that no special effort was made to cater to the special ethnic tastes of local shoppers.

## Ecological Analysis of Customer Composition

Shopkeepers mainly attribute their customer mix to the influence of neighborhood composition. Following the procedure used in the "Three City Study," I used regression analysis to test whether residential concentration has created de facto protected markets for ethnic owners.

For the regression analysis I used the business sites as units of analysis, making for a total of 80 cases. I ran separate regression equations for each of the three groups. The dependent variable was the proportion of customers reported as white/Hispanic/Korean. The independent variables were (a) the proportion of white/Hispanic/Asian residents in the census tract in which the business was located; and (b) the owner's ethnicity.

The regression equations are shown in Table E–8. As with the regressions of business share, population composition proves a strong predictor of customer composition for both whites and Hispanics, though not surprisingly, the impact of population concentrations and the variance explained by the equation are higher for the Hispanics. Ethnicity of owner, however, has virtually no effect on customer composition, corroborating owners' assessment that neighborhood composition is the principal influence on the ethnicity of their clientele. The findings for Koreans also bear out the owners' reports of who shops in their stores and why, but in this case the data show that an ecological relationship does not apply.

**TABLE E-8**
**Regression Analysis of Customer Composition**

*Whites*

Dependent variable: Proportion of customers white
Independent variable: Proportion of tract white
Owner's ethnicity (white = 1, nonwhite = 0)

| Constant Term | Percent of White Residents in Tract | Owner's Ethnicity | Adjusted r-Square |
|---|---|---|---|
| .038 | .616$^c$ | .039 | .201$^c$ |
| | (.453) | (.064) | |

*Hispanics*

Dependent variable: Proportion of customers Hispanic
Independent variable: Proportion of tract Hispanic
Owner's ethnicity (Hispanic = 1, non-Hispanic = 0)

| Constant Term | Percent of Hispanic Residents in Tract | Owner's Ethnicity | Adjusted r-Square |
|---|---|---|---|
| −.017 | .726$^b$ | −.018 | .271$^c$ |
| | (.544) | (−.029) | |

*Koreans*

Dependent variable: Proportion of customers Asian
Independent variable: Proportion of tract Asian
Owner's ethnicity (Korean = 1, non-Korean = 0)

| Constant Term | Percent of Asian Residents in Tract | Owner's Ethnicity | Adjusted r-Square |
|---|---|---|---|
| .034 | .201$^a$ | −.022 | −.015 |
| | (.064) | (−.096) | |

*Source:* See Table E-5.
*Note:* Figures in parentheses denote standardized regression coefficients.
$^a$ Significance at .10 level.
$^b$ Significance at .01 level.
$^c$ Significance at .001 level.

# SACRIFICE FOR WHAT?
# ETHNICITY AND COMPETITIVE ECONOMIC BEHAVIOR

Small business is no longer a declining economic sector; the proportion of Americans who are self-employed has been rising gradually over the past ten years. Still, going into business on one's own is not for the weak or fainthearted: the risks of failure remain substantial, and those businesses that survive often depend on their owners' willingness to work long and hard. Indeed, the demanding conditions of running a small business are often quite sufficient to deter native whites from entering the retail field, as is apparently the case in our study area (Table E–9).

The store owners whom we interviewed all put in long hours. Owners in all three groups kept their shops open more than ten hours a day; virtually none enjoyed the luxury of a two-day weekend

**TABLE E–9**
**Ethnicity and Competitive Economic Behavior**

|  | White | Hispanic | Korean | Significance |
|---|---|---|---|---|
| Days open | 6.0 | 6.5 | 6.4 | <.10 |
|  | (22) | (30) | (27) |  |
| Hours open daily | 10.5 | 11.7 | 10.7 | N.S. |
|  | (22) | (29) | (26) |  |
| Open Sunday | 28.6 | 58.1 | 42.3 | N.S. |
|  | (21) | (31) | (26) |  |
| Total hours open | 64.1 | 75.6 | 68.0 | N.S. |
|  | (22) | (28) | (26) |  |
| Belong to co-op | 4.5 | 3.3 | 0.0 | N.S. |
|  | (22) | (30) | (23) |  |
| With savings | 35.0 | 32.0 | 70.4 | <.01 |
|  | (20) | (25) | (27) |  |
| Want kids to go | 6.7 | 25.0 | 0.0 | <.05 |
| into business | (15) | (12) | (23) |  |
| Weekly sales | $3759 | $3489 | $4562 | N.S. |
|  | (20) | (25) | (26) |  |
| Meet competitors | 9.5 | 3.6 | 0.0 | N.S. |
|  | (21) | (28) | (27) |  |
| Made profit last year | 63.2 | 84.2 | 70.8 | N.S. |
|  | (19) | (19) | (24) |  |
| Expect profit this year | 75.0 | 88.5 | 90.0 | N.S. |
|  | (20) | (26) | (20) |  |

*Source:* Survey of business owners in Sunset Park, 1986.

rest from work; and many did business on Sunday as well. Indeed, work effort was one major characteristic common to all three groups; although the Koreans and Hispanics kept their shops open longer than whites each day, none of the other indicators of effort produced any statistically significant differences among the owners. Our data also suggest that individual effort is the key factor in store owners' strategies, despite much of the emphasis often ascribed to collective group resources: relatively few reported meeting with other owners to discuss ways of controlling competition, and few belong to buying co-ops that might result in lower wholesale prices.

To what extent owners' prodigious efforts produced success is difficult to determine. One attempt to probe this issue—a question about whether owners succeeded in saving money from the business—showed that a substantial minority of owners in at least each group answered "yes." A considerable majority of owners also said that they expected to make a profit that year; and majorities of those in business for at least one year also claimed to have made a profit in the preceding year. Still, owning a store is not so attractive that the owners we surveyed would want their own children to go into the business: in all three cases, only a minority of the respondents with children said that they would like their children to go into the business when they grow up.

Interestingly, of our outcome measures only two produced significant differences: the proportion reporting savings, and the proportion reporting that they wanted their children to enter the business. A significantly higher proportion of Koreans than either whites or Hispanics reported that they saved money. Since reported profitability does not diverge among the three groups, it is not quite clear how to interpret the finding on savings: nonetheless, the facts that the Koreans report a higher customer volume and higher weekly sales lend credence to these self-reports of high savings. Despite these intimations of greater business success, Koreans were the least enthusiastic about their children succeeding them in business: not one of the owners interviewed wanted his children to take over the business.

## CONCLUSION

We set out to test, in a tentative way (given our small sample), the central findings of the "Three City Study," most notably the conclusion that structural factors of occupational and ecological succession do best in accounting for immigrant groups' share of business positions. Our results suggest that the opportunity structure approach is correct, but only partly so; moreover, its very strongest claims do not stand up, at least not in this case.

One way to summarize our findings is that there are two ways into small business. Ecological succession appears to be the pattern characteristic of whites and Hispanics. For these two groups the association between population composition and ethnic shop ownership is strong: differences in a group's share of the population at the tract level explain between 50 to 70 percent of the variance in shares of businesses. Though ecological variables, however, do less well in accounting for differences in customer composition, they are still quite strongly related to client mix. By contrast, the Koreans have carved a small, but not insignificant, business niche without any tie to a local market of co-ethnics. The Koreans do virtually no business with a Korean clientele; they sell principally to Hispanics and have not as yet benefited from the build-up of Asians in the southeast part of the study area.

Our findings also suggest that there are opportunities for occupational succession, independent of succession at the residential level. White businesses, as we have noted, are long-established; there are few new white business owners; and the white owners are disproportionately foreign-born or children of the foreign-born. The findings of our study are also consistent with the patterns observed by other studies: white participation in business ownership in the retail sector is declining, both absolutely and relative to white population share. Moreover, the decline in white immigration to New York is likely to reduce the number of whites seeking a living in petty proprietorship, since it is precisely foreign-born whites who are most overrepresented among the ranks of the self-employed.

The argument that the small-retailer market areas are so constraining as to select populations with similar characteristics also receives only partial support from our study. On the one hand, the similarities between Hispanic and white owners on virtually every count—socioeconomic characteristics, informal resources, the operating characteristics of their business—are very striking. Other findings—Hispanic owners' much greater reliance on co-ethnics as customers and the strong association between Hispanic population and business shares—also suggest that what is involved here is a simple course of succession driven by changes in local residential patterns. On the other hand, the Koreans differ markedly from both whites and Hispanics. The Koreans bring a distinct set of background characteristics to the running of a business and they have considerably more access to informal, social resources. The evidence from our survey is consistent with the findings of our business census, which shows that Koreans own far more stores than would be expected on the basis of their population in the area alone. And the Sunset Park pattern also jibes with data for Korean business participation at the City-wide level, with Koreans self-employed at more than three times the rate for all others.

A final point concerns the importance of the ethnic small business niche. "The Three City" study argued that there were severe market constraints on England's petite bourgeoisie and that there was ample reason to be skeptical about small business as a ladder for Asian upward mobility. If this study provides any guide for what is happening in other immigrant communities, a more optimistic view would not be misplaced. In contrast to Asians in Britain or, for that matter, the blacks and Puerto Ricans who preceded them, the immigrants who have moved to New York over the past two decades have found a vibrant economy in which their skills have been in demand. That small businesses in Sunset Park are thriving tells us that the incomes of resident immigrants are sufficient to generate considerable local demand. And the prospect of continued opportunities for occupational succession should give immigrants additional chances to serve clients outside their own communities.

Where do these conclusions lead? Apart from the obvious point—that a larger study in more locales is needed to buttress our cited results—a number of implications arise. One is obvious: that an adequate explanation of differences in business success will be multivariate. Immigrants will not go into business unless there are opportunities, but we will need to flesh out differences in characteristics and resources in order to account for groups' differing success in exploiting the existing small business niche. Moreover, it is unlikely that any single characteristic will be crucial in determining a group's business participation rate: for example, our evidence on Koreans points to the importance of both class and ethnic resources. Researchers would also do well by looking closer at the interaction between groups' characteristics and the mix of opportunities and constraints that they encounter. We can locate the source of Koreans' business drive in the mismatch between their skills and the opportunities that they encounter for salaried employed—not in any special feeling or affinity for business. Moreover, the circumstances of Koreans' migration seem to make the consequences of blocked mobility more severely felt. By contrast, such a mismatch is not characteristic of the

Hispanics; hence, their recruitment into business takes the form of a more or less natural succession into vacant places.

The contrast between Koreans and Hispanics also suggests that different patterns of ethnic business development might arise. As Portes and Manning have earlier argued, ethnic entrepreneurs will sometimes be organized in an enclave economy—where they are spatially concentrated and service co-ethnic demand—but in other instances will be organized as a "middleman minority," reliant on co-ethnics for informal resources, but spatially scattered and dependent on customers outside the group.[156] Our study suggests the conditions under which these two different types of ethnic economies will arise. For the enclave, what is needed, at the very least, are numbers and some degree of residential concentration. Ethnic resources are less important in these spatial concentrations; moreover, entrepreneurs active in the enclave may not have to out-compete native business owners, precisely because ecological succession leads natives to filter out of the area. By contrast, middleman minorities will tend to be groups that lack the population base needed for an enclave economy and who scatter across space where market opportunities exist, regardless of the ethnicity of resident customers. Success as a middleman minority will be enhanced by higher than average skills, ethnic resources, and drive. However, servicing nonethnic clients means competing with natives and that probably involves working harder to get business; hence, middleman minorities' firms may have the distinctive operating characteristics we have seen in this study.

---

156. Alejandro Portes and Robert Manning, "The Immigrant Enclave: Theory and Empirical Examples," in Susan Olzak and Joane Nagel (eds.), *Competitive Ethnic Relations* (Orlando, Fla.: Academic Press, 1986), pp. 47–69.

# Index

Asian immigrants—*Continued*
settlement patterns of, 69, 184,
184*n*; and small business, 150–
151, 152, 252–254; in Sunset Park,
84, 122, 132, 133, 134, 137, 145–
146, 170, 182–184, 190–191
Astoria, 64, 68, 136
Auction House, 162
authority, regard for, 8, 25, 95
auto chop shops, 46

**B**

Bach, Robert, 250*n*
Bailey, Thomas, 250*n*
Baltimore, 187
Banco Popular, 107
Bangladesh, 31
banks, 37, 107; Chinese, 38, 150–
151, 155–156
Barbados, 31
Bath Beach, 119*n*
Bay Ridge, 66, 68, 72, 75, 80*n*, 85,
86, 89, 103–104, 123, 127, 128,
129, 131, 135, 136, 149, 152, 174,
183*n*
beauty parlors, 39
Bedford-Stuyvesant, 63, 115, 119,
143, 167*n*, 184
behavioral poverty, 8–9, 95
Belmont, 119
Bensonhurst, 47, 63, 75, 119
Bethelship Norwegian Methodist
Church, 84
Bethlehem Steel Shipyard, 76, 102
*Beyond the Melting Pot* (Glazer and
Moynihan), 249
bigotry, 47–48, 66
*Birds of Passage* (Piore), 256
birth records, 132*n*, 137, 143, 145,
147–149, **148**, 181, 197
blackout of 1977, 109
blacks, 8, 48, 96, 184, 189*n*; African,
32; births, 149; boycotts of Koreans, 47; and country of origin,
33; distribution of, 1980, 118–119;
Hispanic, 33; in labor force, 34,
35; native-born, 24, 25, 33, 34, 35,
63, 149; new, 34, 143; and small

business, 249, 250, 254; in Sunset
Park, 149
Blaine, James, 96–97
block associations, 171
BMT, 80, 161
B'nai Israel, 82
Boggs, Vernon M., Jr, 32*n*
Bogen, Elizabeth, 27*n*, 36, **41**, 41*n*,
46*n*, 138*n*
Bonacich, Edna, 250, 250*n*, 256, 256*n*
Borjas, George, 37*n*
Borough Park, 75, 81, 97*n*, 123, 128,
167*n*, 183*n*
Boston, 51, 59, 187
Bouvier, Leon F., 21*n*, 32*n*
"bricks and mortar programs," 7
Brighton Beach, 62, 63, 68, 75
Breuckelen, 75
Bronx, 41, 63, 66, 119
Brooklyn, 41, 65; ethnic mix in, 30,
69; housing market, 48, 52, 55,
57, 58; New Immigrants and,
141–146; population decline, 89;
redevelopment plan for, 177–178,
177*n*; retail stores, 62, 63. *See also*
specific neighborhoods
Brooklyn Army Terminal (BAT), 76,
87, 88–89, 152*n*, 158, 159–160,
159*n*, 162
Brooklyn Bridge, 76
*Brooklyn Daily Eagle*, 197
Brooklyn Heights, 72, 79, 120, 131,
157, 169, 187, 188
Brooklyn Meat Distribution
Cooperative, 108, 160*n*
Brooklyn Rapid Transit System, 80
*Brooklyn Real Estate Register*, 132*n*,
153–154, 198, 203–206, 203*n*
Brooklyn Union Gas, 107
Brown, Claude, 95*n*
brownstones, 109, 109*n*, 116, 127,
129–130, 169, 171
Brownsville, 56, 66, 99*n*, 119, 168
Buddhists, 32
Buffalo, 41, 68
building management, 100–101
Bush, Irving T., 76, 162
Bush Terminal, 76, 87, 89, 108, 153,
160
Bushwick, 57, 68, 72, 115

**C**
California, 24, 25
Cambodians, 30, 146
Canarsie, 75
Cantonese speakers, 31
capital, small business, 261
Capone, Al, 78n
Caribbean immigrants, 1, 20, 21, 24, 33, 95n, 116, 184; employment rates, 34; employment type, 42; number of, 30–31, 143, 181; and small business, 39
Carnegie, Andrew, 121n
Carroll Gardens, 73, 79, 169, 186, 190
cash grants, 46
Cater, John, 252n
Catholic Charities, 194n
Catholics, 82; Hispanic, 93; schools, 93, 141, **142**
Census Bureau, 156n; as data source, 193, 195, 201; and ethnic classification errors, 26–27; and internal migration, 26; 1980 census, 27, 31, 32, 34, 113–121, 114n, **115**, 116n, 132n, 133, 134–135, 193, **207–217**
Central Americans, 21, 24, 30, 31, 117; employment of women, 42; home ownership, 155; settlement patterns of, 68; and small business, 39, 152; in Sunset Park, 137, 145, 147, 182
Charlotte Street project, 99n
chain migrations, 30, 179, 183
Chicago, 68
children, 95, 117, 164; of New Immigrants, 120
Chinatown, 38, 40, 66, 66n, 67, 153
Chinese, 5, 24, 36; ancestry, vs. country of birth, 31; census classifications and, 26; distribution of, 118, **217**, 219–220, 222, **225**, **226**; and entrepreneurship, 37–38; and ethnic frictions, 47, 67, 67n; and garment industry, 40, 153, 183; gathering data on, 194–195; and home ownership, 155–156, 204; 1980 census, 118; number of, 31; and politics, 170;

professionals, 42; in real estate, 153, 155, 205; regional origins of new, 31; in schools, 138–140, 139n; settlement patterns of, 66–67, 66n; and small businesses, 150–151, 152, 158, 183, 254; in Sunset Park, 116, 132, 133, 134, 135, 136, 144n, 145–146, 150–151, 153–154, 155, 171, 182–184, 183n, **217**
Chinese-American Planning Council, 47, 183
*Chinese Experience in America, The* (Tsai), 67
Christian Front, 81, 174
Christ United Methodist Church, 84
church(es): authority, waning, 25; and early development of Sunset Park, 81–85, 87; and Hispanics, 93, 97
circular migrants, 3, 92, 95, 95n
circumstances of migration factor, 255–257
Citibank, 107
citizenship, 256–257
City University of New York, 44–45
*Clamor at the Gates* (Glazer), 37n
Cleveland, 41
Clinton Hill, 73
Cobble Hill, 72
co-ethnic, 133; enterprises, 37; real estate purchases, 155–156
*Cole's Directory*, 17, 132, 132n, 133, 133n, 135, 138, 149, 154, 156, 189n, 198–203, 198n, 219
Colgate-Palmolive-Peet, 76
Colombians, 145
Commission on the Year 2000, 50, 52, 53, 107n, 176–177, 185, 187
community: action, 108; leaders, 15, 137; organizations, 101–113 role of, 59–60, 170–171; values, 8–10
community development: Block Grants, 110–111; corporations, 59, 113
Community District 7, 73, **112**, 126, 128, 128n, 203; Board, 163, 166, 171, 198
Community Preservation Corporation (CPA), 167n